QLab 3 Show Control

Projects for Live Performances & Installations

Jeromy Hopgood

Focal Press
Taylor & Francis Group

NEW YORK AND LONDON

First published 2014 by Focal Press
70 Blanchard Road, Suite 402, Burlington, MA 01803

and by Focal Press
2 Park Square, Milton Park, Abingdon, Oxon OX14 4RN

Focal Press is an imprint of the Taylor & Francis Group, an informa business

© 2014 Taylor & Francis

Notices
Knowledge and best practice in this field are constantly changing. As new research and experience broaden our understanding, changes in research methods, professional practices, or medical treatment may become necessary.

Practitioners and researchers must always rely on their own experience and knowledge in evaluating and using any information, methods, compounds, or experiments described herein. In using such information or methods they should be mindful of their own safety and the safety of others, including parties for whom they have a professional responsibility.

Product or corporate names may be trademarks or registered trademarks, and are used only for identification and explanation without intent to infringe.

Library of Congress Cataloging in Publication Data
Hopgood, Jeromy.
  QLab 3 show control : projects for live performances & installations / Jeromy Hopgood.—
  1st edition.
    pages cm
  ISBN 978-0-415-85757-4 (pbk.)—ISBN 978-0-203-79726-6 (ebook)
1. QLab. 2. Theaters—Stage-setting and scenery. 3. Performing arts—Technological innovations.
4. Multimedia systems. I. Title.
  PN2091.S8H66 2013
  006.7—dc23   2013032998

ISBN: 978-0-415-85757-4 (pbk)
ISBN: 978-0-203-79726-6 (ebk)

Typeset in ITC Stone Sans
Project Managed and Typeset by: diacriTech

MIX
Paper from
responsible sources
FSC® C014174
www.fsc.org

Printed and bound in the United States of America by Sheridan Books, Inc. (a Sheridan Group Company).

Bound to Create

You are a creator.

Whatever your form of expression — photography, filmmaking, animation, games, audio, media communication, web design, or theatre — you simply want to create without limitation. Bound by nothing except your own creativity and determination.

Focal Press can help.

For over 75 years Focal has published books that support your creative goals. Our founder, Andor Kraszna-Krausz, established Focal in 1938 so you could have access to leading-edge expert knowledge, techniques, and tools that allow you to create without constraint. We strive to create exceptional, engaging, and practical content that helps you master your passion.

Focal Press and you.

Bound to create.

Focal
Taylor & Fr

Contents

Contents

Contents

Contents

Contents

Contents

Contents

Contents

Contents

Contents

Contents

Contents

Acknowledgments

As with any project of this size, there are a number of people without whose help the idea would never have become a reality. Working in the theatre makes one ever cognizant of the sheer power of collaboration. Those who survive long in most of the areas of the entertainment design and technology industry realize the importance of acknowledging all the people who helped them along the way on a project. So, here goes my laundry list of people who helped turn this labor of love into a possibility.

Many thanks to John Holloway for the inspiration to ever get off my tail and write something in the first place. Check out his fantastic *Illustrated Theatre Production Guide*, also by Focal Press (soon in its Third Edition). Stacey Walker, my acquisitions editor, listened to my ideas and brought so many more positive contributions to the project. Meagan White, my editorial project manager, answered every question thrown her way with poise.

There are a number of people who answered questions, explained things that I didn't understand, and generally kept the boat on the right course: David Stoughton of Hamilton College; John Dalziel of Ripon College; Michael J. Riha of the University of Arkansas; and Jake Pinholster of Arizona State University. To Chris Ashworth and the entire Figure 53 family, thanks for answering my countless emails and serving as technical editors of this book. Many thanks are also due to the amazing community of peers at the Figure 53 Discussion List who answered so many questions and requests over the years and without whose support this text would not have happened.

It has been a pleasure to serve as a professor at Eastern Michigan University over the past 6 years. Thanks are due to my colleagues and students for their input and especially to EMU for awarding me a Faculty Research Fellowship to complete my research and writing.

Finally, the two people to whom I always owe the greatest amount of gratitude (for this or any project) are my wife and daughter. Thanks to Katie and Kira for their understanding of the countless hours I spent huddled over my laptop at the Arborland Starbucks. Now that it's all done, let's go to the beach!

Introduction

The entertainment industry is an ever-expanding combination of several different areas (scenery, costumes, lighting, sound, integrated media, automation, etc.). All of these areas work together for the sole purpose of creating new and interesting ways to tell stories and entertain our audiences. As technologies for all these separate areas expand, though, it becomes increasingly important to find ways of unifying control of these areas while keeping the flexibility for each area to function as a unique component of the whole. This need is the driving force behind programs like QLab, which allow for the integration of several different production systems into one centralized control interface.

ENTERTAINMENT CONTROL SYSTEMS

In the early days, it was simple enough to have a board operator for each area and a stage manager calling "go." As technology advanced, increasingly complex electronic devices became commonplace in live performance scenarios. For today's entertainment industry, a show might incorporate dozens of different production specialties, such as lighting, sound, rigging, automated scenery, projections/media, pyrotechnics, or many more. For each of these different areas there might be one or more different **entertainment control systems**, or the combination of elements required to control one element of the production design.

One show might have several entertainment control systems, such as a lighting system, sound system, fog system, or automated machinery system. Each of these systems include the entertainment equipment, necessary cabling (or wireless interfaces) for control signals, and some type of control mechanism. Almost all performances include, at minimum, systems for lighting and sound, though many may include video, automated scenery, or special effects (such as fog, haze, and pyrotechnics).

WHAT IS SHOW CONTROL?

Show control is an often-misused term, but a simple concept to understand. **Show control** is simply a method of linking together multiple entertainment control systems into one master system. Typically speaking, show control is categorized as one of two types: software operating on either a Mac or a PC platform; or stand-alone systems developed in a proprietary fashion by manufacturers. For either method, the concept remains the same – multiple control systems are linked together for the purpose of unifying (and simplifying) their control.

QLAB: A VERSATILE CONTROL SYSTEM

It is worth mentioning that one of the greatest benefits of QLab is its ability to function as *both* an entertainment control system and a show control system. Used in its most basic applications, QLab functions as an excellent method of sound or video playback. In fact, one of its biggest selling points is that anyone can download the basic version of QLab (for free) and use it for any stereo sound project without having to commit to the Pro Version. This is a perfect example of using it as a sound control system. Given the need, though, one can download (or rent) QLab Pro and configure the software to control a wide array of entertainment controllers, such as lighting, sound, special effects, or more. Once you connect QLab to your system and use it to communicate with your other controllers, it has gone from the realm of entertainment control system and become a show control system.

SHOW CONTROL: HISTORICAL BACKGROUND

As with so many of the advancements in the emerging technologies in the entertainment industry following World War 2, the Walt Disney Company (in particular the Disney Land theme park) pioneered methods in show control. There exist hundreds, if not thousands, of book on the history of Walt Disney and his entertainment company. For our purposes, we will focus specifically on a relatively short window of time in the company and specifically look at the creation and advancement of one of Disney's signature attractions – the Audio Animatronic (a trademarked term owned by the Walt Disney Company).

In 1963, The Enchanted Tiki Room became the first Disney attraction to use Audio Animatronic figures that combined movement and audio. The attraction was originally intended to be a restaurant featuring Audio Animatronic birds that entertained the guests while they ate and drank. Eventually, it adapted into a roughly 20-minute stage show featuring a cast of human performers alongside dozens of Animatronic singing birds, plants, and Polynesian masks. To create the movements, programmers used a cumbersome harness system worn by a controller. This device allowed them to record thousands of discrete movements to a magnetic film/tape. These films were played on reel-to-reel-type machines that triggered different series of the film in the desired order. The machines worked in tandem; one playing, then allowing another to take over the signal while the first rewound to a predetermined location and began playing all over again. The signal from these films was both audio recording and control signals sent to the Animatronic devices on the show floor. When the tape sent a signal through the system, it would close an electric circuit thereby triggering a solenoid that opened a pneumatic valve, allowing air to flow through the system and trigger a movement of the Audio Animatronic figure. While this system is mechanically simple, imagine the amount of time and effort necessary to orchestrate a 20-minute show!

Jump forward a few years and advances in computer systems enabled the Imagineers to control these Animatronic devices in ways never before possible. With the developments in computer technology, computer disks and computerized control stations replaced the old harness and tape method. Now, programmers could sit at a workstation and program the movements, saving them to a computer disk. This allowed for more complex movements and the ability to add, delete, or edit control sequences to the show. This new system, called Digital Animation Control System or DACS, became the standard method of controlling all Disney Audio Animatronic Attractions for years to come. In fact, the system is still in use today, but now controls audio, video, and special effects in addition to the traditional Animatronics. Today's DACS system functions as an elaborate method of show control, synchronizing not only events within one show, but combining together multiple events in different shows across the theme park. In fact, all DACS systems across the Magic Kingdom in Disney World are controlled from a single location in the park. Quite a leap from the days of harnesses and magnetic film!

SHOW CONTROL TODAY

Like all other areas of computer technology, show control is a rapidly changing field in which there are a number of competitors on the market. In the world of show control systems, the products can typically be separated into two distinct areas: software packages that run on personal computers (either Mac or PC); or dedicated hardware created for the specific purpose of running a show.

Typically speaking, the theatre and live performance industry tends to favor software packages, whereas venues such as museums, casinos, theme parks, and retail establishments tend to favor a dedicated hardware (though you may well find examples on both sides of the fence using the opposite method described above – or integrating both kinds into a hybrid system). Both types of solutions ultimately provide the same function of controlling multiple entertainment devices within a system. If there is a benefit of one type over another, it could be the versatility of the software system. Since dedicated hardware systems tend to be built for the specific purpose of controlling one specific show, it can be an expensive and time-consuming process to go about equipping multiple shows in this fashion. On the other hand, with software control systems, the software remains the same for each installation. To set up multiple shows, the user simply goes about the process of writing cues and setting up a communication system between control devices. In addition to the comparative ease of using software to control multiple shows, there is also the financial consideration. Dedicated systems tend to be much more expensive than their software counterparts in both purchase and maintenance. It is likely for this reason we see so many small professional theatres and live performance venues favoring the software method to meet their show control needs.

SOFTWARE SOLUTIONS FOR SHOW CONTROL

Like many other types of software, show control software can be divided into two categories: PC- and Macintosh-based. Like any software package, you will find die-hard fans that insist on the dominance of one over another. In the world of show control, I find that the question tends to be "what are the needs of your project?" QLab might not always be the best choice for your particular project, but I find that for my needs it fits the bill more often than not.

QLAB BY FIGURE 53

QLab's origins are in the theatre. In October 2005, Chris Ashworth (founder of Figure 53 and creator of the QLab software) received an email from a friend's newly formed theatre company with a project for which they needed a Mac-based program that could play back multiple audio files simultaneously. Within 2 month's time, the first version of QLab was born. This early version, like subsequent ones, was built on Apple's Core Audio framework to allow for low latency audio playback accurate to a thousandth of a second. A foundation on the Apple system is one reason why QLab has always been a Mac-only program, since it was built from the ground on Apple technology. This first version contained basic functions like audio playback, auto continue, a Go button, and a Cue Inspector with file information and volume controls.

Figure 53 released QLab beta in December 2005 in a way that would come to epitomize their model of utilizing user input. Ashworth wrote a post on the theatre-sound listserv, asking sound designers to download the software and try it out in their own work. The request was for those with a strong background in sound design to put the software through the paces and give feedback to determine how the program should evolve to help the end-users. This attitude has defined the Figure 53 model of building their software on customer feedback and feature requests. Each new release of QLab has strongly relied on the feedback from a loyal network of users and added features based on their responses.

By September 2006, QLab version 1.0.0 released with both a free and Pro edition. Unlike its earliest iterations, Version 1 contained many Show Control features that would come to define the versatility of the software. Enhanced features included MIDI control, video and still animation functions, and 16 channels of audio output. This improved software package quickly began popping up in small professional theatres, auto shows, high schools, regional theatres, museums and more. Within a year of its introduction, QLab made both Broadway and West End debuts in the Broadway revival of *Grease* and the London revival of *In Celebration*.

In January 2009, QLab Version 2.0 released, featuring what amounted to a total visual makeover of the user interface and the introduction of many new control features, such as a visual waveform editor (allowing users to draw fade curves), camera cues, vamping, video animation, scripting cues, and use of MIDI Time Code. In addition, it expanded the amount of audio outputs to 48 channels. Likely, the greatest user-friendly change in Version 2 was combining all the control screens into one centralized user interface. In Version 1, there were a number of floating screens that had the tendency to get hidden behind one another and clutter up your workspace. By combining them all together, this made for one unified, sleek, workspace.

The year 2013 marked the release of Version 3, the most current version of the software featuring a number of advances that should prove to establish it as an industry standard for years to come. The user interface was again totally revamped for a sleek, streamlined look in blacks and grays. In addition to the functions in previous versions, QLab 3 added a number of advances in audio, video, control, and workflow. The changes in QLab 3 make for a robust show control solution that enables users to become less dependent on external hardware and equipment. In the coming chapters, we will explore QLab 3 together, focusing on how to best integrate the show control software into your entertainment control system.

Preface

As a theatre educator and a freelance designer, every year I encounter a wide range of artists in the entertainment industry. I am a people person who loves to get to know those with whom I work (a trait common to many of us in this industry). If you spend enough time talking to people and listening to their experiences, certain patterns start to appear. One such pattern I noticed early in my teaching career was the complaint that, while there exist countless texts for most mainstream software titles, these books are nonexistent for most of the applications used in live performance. For many of these applications, technicians must learn on the job or through self-guided experimentation. As an educator, this always made me feel that someone should be writing these books – both for the students in the classroom and for the technicians in the field. Somehow, after all these years, books of this nature remain a rarity.

As a designer, I am always looking for new technologies that increase productivity and improve my product. In 2006, I became aware of a new program on the market that changed the way I worked on sound and projections. What was more, this software was free. Likely, you have guessed by now that the software in question was QLab. This robust show control software enabled me to work in a Macintosh environment (something relatively unheard of for show control) and featured an easy-to-understand user interface. Perhaps most important to me was that Figure 53, the makers of QLab, truly understood customer service. I quickly introduced the free version of QLab into my classroom and started training my students in its use. In addition to the classroom, I implemented a QLab control system in our two theatres at Eastern Michigan University. The software was a huge jump from the old Compact Disc/MINI Disc system it replaced, and again, the students raved! It was around this point, though, when my students began asking where they could find a book on QLab so that they could learn more. They always seemed surprised to find there was not one on the market. In 2012, as I began to hear rumors of the forthcoming third edition of QLab, I decided to write this text.

WHO SHOULD USE THIS BOOK?

When I set out to write this text, it occurred to me that there are two groups of people who could most benefit from such a book: students and teachers. To me, students are not only young people enrolled in a class. No doubt, this group makes up a large percentage of the people who will read this book, but I am also referring to a group of people who are life-long learners and interested in educating themselves about new and exciting trends. This group might include professional stagehands, technicians, community theatre enthusiasts, technical directors, trade show/event designers, museum/installation designers, or more. Show Control has crept into a wide array of applications from theatre to live music, museums, trade shows, performance art, Halloween entertainment, casinos, and retail. With such a wide array of fields represented, it only stands to reason that the end users would be as varied and eclectic!

The second subset of users for this text, teachers, are a group I strongly associate with (as I am one myself). I remember how quickly the excitement faded after getting my first teaching job when I realized I would be the one who had the ultimate responsibility of creating lesson plans and projects for hundreds of eager undergraduates. When perusing many of the textbooks for my classes, it occurred to me that most of the books were not written with the instructor in mind. It was for this reason that by my second semester of teaching, I transitioned to handouts and projects of my own creation in favor of working strictly from a textbook. Books should be useful to both instructor and student!

It is with this in mind that I set out to write a practical book that would function as both an instructional manual with hands-on projects and a useful quick reference guide. The book is intended to primarily serve novice and intermediate users alike, with the hope that even expert users might find some insight in its pages, as well. A key component of the book is in readers utilizing the supplementary materials housed on the companion website. Whether you are using this as part of a formal classroom experience or in your own home, the structure of the book allows for the reader to learn at his or her own pace and tackle QLab projects on an individual basis. By downloading the lesson packets from the companion website, my hope is that the learning experience will be enriched by working along from home at your own pace on the same projects shown in the book. In my experience, learning by doing is always the most effective way to ensure retention.

Audio Systems

Before one can truly understand the applications of a program like QLab, it is first necessary to understand the basics of sound systems and how they function. For most designers or technicians in the entertainment industry, sound systems fall into three basic categories: recording systems, reinforcement systems, and playback systems.

Recording systems tend to consist of a Digital Audio Workstation (DAW), a computer running sound-editing software in conjunction with audio interface hardware. This audio interface allows the user to convert the analog signal from a microphone into a digital signal for editing in the audio software. With the decrease in cost of computers and the proliferation of mass-market software such as Apple's Garage Band, most anyone can experiment on their own DAW. Recording systems allow designers to create the audio that will be played back in live performance later.

Typically speaking, a recording system will have a computer running (at minimum) one sound-editing program. Many designers utilize multiple programs for their varying strengths. Common applications for this are Apple's Logic or Avid's Pro Tools. Pro Tools or Pro Tools Express comes bundled with a consumer-grade series of digital audio interfaces that allow users to input audio via a number of different connector types. In addition to analog outputs for speakers, there are also headphone outputs for monitoring purposes. This type of setup is shown in detail in Figure 1.1.

A **reinforcement system** exists to take live sound and amplify it for live performance. The traditional reinforcement system utilizes microphones to pick up live audio and send it through signal processors [like an audio mixer, equalization (EQ), effects processors, etc.], then through amplifiers, and finally out to speakers. Figure 1.2 illustrates this type of setup. Until QLab 3, the software had no integrated reinforcement controls. With the addition of the Mic Cue in Version 3, though, QLab can now be truly seen as a reinforcement system, as well. QLab Mic cues can control up to 24 input signals, activating a microphone, setting levels, assigning Audio Unit (AU) effects (such as reverb, EQ, distortion, etc.), and more.

Figure 1.1
Recording system.

A TYPICAL RECORDING SYSTEM

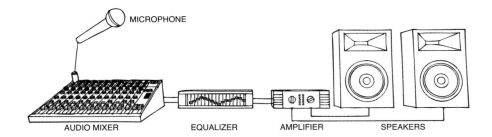

Figure 1.2
Reinforcement
system.

MICROPHONE

AUDIO MIXER   EQUALIZER   AMPLIFIER   SPEAKERS

Playback systems are a combination of equipment necessary to play back pre-recorded audio in a live performance situation. In the past, the audio source files were saved on everything from reel-to-reel, compact discs (CDs), mini-discs, or microcomputers. Today, almost all live performance venues use some type of computer running a software system to play back audio files. Like the reinforcement system, the audio signal might be sent out through an audio mixer and signal processors before being routed through amplifiers before ultimately outputting through the speakers. Depending on the budget and needs of your installation, QLab 3 can function almost totally independently of traditional audio equipment like audio mixers, EQs, and other signal processors. Of course, each setup has its own specific needs and rarely are any two systems exactly alike.

As a rule of thumb, each playback system likely has a computer that outputs audio through either a standard 1/8" headphone cable or a digital audio interface. The system outputting through the 1/8" headphone jack will often be a basic stereo system, with audio signal split into left and right channels (no matter the number of speakers it routes into). The digital audio interface allows QLab to split the audio signal into independent signals to be sent to individual speakers in the system (allowing for directional sound). To find examples of differing types of playback systems, reference the end of this chapter.

1.1 Reinforcement/Playback System Components

The world of audio can seem a bit intimidating to the beginner with the vast amount of equipment and terminology. Although audio equipment is not the main focus of this book, there are some basic terms with which one must be familiar in order to understand how to set up a sound system. The following list details typical reinforcement/playback system components and their functions:

1. **Microphone:** A transducer that turns audio waves (sound) into electrical signal. This signal is low voltage and not powerful enough to activate a speaker on its own, so it is necessary to send the signal through other hardware components. Typically speaking, there are two types of microphones most used in live performance situations: a dynamic microphone and a condenser microphone.
    - A **dynamic microphone** utilizes a small moveable induction coil attached to a diaphragm. The coil, positioned in the magnetic field of a stationary magnet, moves when sound waves strike the diaphragm. This movement creates small electrical impulses. These impulses are the signal that will be later translated through a speaker into sound. Dynamic microphones are sturdy, resistant to moisture, and require no external power source to operate. These attributes make the dynamic microphone a common choice for live performances, particularly in the club environment.
    - A **condenser microphone** utilizes the same diaphragm concept as the dynamic mic, but instead of the induction coil uses small stationary metal plates and another series of magnets attached to the diaphragm. As the diaphragm moves, the change in proximity of the magnets to the plates creates small electrical impulses that become the audio signal. Condensers are typically much more expensive than dynamic mics, but also have a wider frequency response range – meaning they can capture a wider range of sounds and tend to be more sensitive to volume. Unlike the dynamic microphone, though, a condenser mic requires external power in order to power the microphone. This is typically supplied from the audio mixer in the form of "phantom power" or a small 48-V power supply sent from the mixer to the mic.

2. **Input Source:** As previously stated, the input source can be any of a variety of different devices. Professional CD or mini-disc players were once a common component for their ability to allow the user to cue a CD track to a certain time for playback. Although these still remain in some playback systems,

computers have largely replaced them for their ability to run playback software like QLab, which far surpasses the function of a CD.

3. **Mixing Console:** Hardware used to combine multiple audio signals and allow the user to create a mix of these signals to output in different ways. The console (sometimes called an audio mixer or sound board) routes signals, sets volume levels, and affects the qualities of the audio signal. Most consoles receive a variety of different signals in a live performance: audio signals from the playback computer, vocals from singers, multiple channels of audio from different instruments in the band, boundary microphones on the stage, shotgun mics above the stage, and more. There will typically be a minimum of one channel per audio signal dedicated on the audio console, although in some cases you might see two channels "ganged" together for one audio source.

4. **Signal Processors:** Devices that affect the quality or timbre of the audio signal. Most typical would be EQ, audio filters, reverb, delay, and dynamic processing. Some mixing consoles have built-in signal processors, whereas some signal processors are stand-alone devices. In addition to dedicated signal processing units, computers also have the capability of running a plug-in program to affect the quality of an audio signal. In the Mac architecture, these plug-ins are referred to as AUs. With the emergence of QLab 3, AUs can be used for live performance inside of your playback system.

5. **Amplifier:** A device that increases the signal from the microphone or computer to power a speaker. Amplifiers must be plugged into an external power source in order to amplify the audio signal.

6. **Speaker:** A transducer that changes the electrical signal from the audio source into audio waves (sound). Speakers come in many different varieties related to what frequency of sound they best produce. *Subwoofers*, for instance, produce the lowest frequency of the audio spectrum (typically below 100 Hz), whereas *tweeters* produce the highest sounds within the spectrum. In addition, some speakers will have built-in amplifiers in the speaker cabinet. These "self-powered" speakers work well for on-location events and have slightly bulkier cabinets, due to the additional hardware enclosed. One disadvantage to these speakers is the need to be plugged in to a power source near where the speaker will be positioned.

1.2 Understanding Basic Signal Flow: Input/Output

With the potential of having so many different components in one audio system, it can easily confuse the beginner (and has led many an expert to scratch their heads). One concept essential to setting up any type of a sound system is signal flow, or how the audio gets from its source to the speakers and what happens to it along the way. Think of audio as a flow of water that travels along a series of pipes (audio cables) and through several different faucets (mixers, amps, etc.) along the way to its final destination of the speaker.

For most audio devices, there is both an input that allows the audio signal in and an output that allows for the signal to be passed on to another device down the chain. The most basic sound system would include a microphone, an audio playback device, a mixer, an amplifier, and a speaker. When adding QLab into the mix, there is another layer of routing to consider within the software itself. The following section breaks down the basics of signal flow and details a few different possibilities for configuring your own QLab playback system.

1.3 Reinforcement/Playback Systems

Figure 1.3 presents a traditional reinforcement/playback system. In this elementary system, the microphone receives a signal from the human voice and outputs it into an input channel of the mixer. For this example, we will assume that the singer is performing to a pre-recorded song playing back from a CD player. This song travels as an audio signal from the CD player into another of the mixer's input channels. The mixer will be used to set the volume levels of each channel in order to make a nice balanced mix and output in two channels (left and right) into the amplifier. In turn, the amplifier will output the left signal through its Channel A and the right signal through Channel B. Each of these channels will feed into the input of a speaker and give us stereo sound.

Looking to a slightly more advanced system, let's say that your venue needed more than two speakers. Let's also assume that these speakers need to have a slightly different timbre in their playback. Using the same configuration as before, one could simply add two more output channels to have a total of four speakers. In order to achieve a slightly different timbre for the front of house speakers and the rear speakers, one would need to add an equalizer to the signal flow between the mixer and amplifiers (see Figure 1.4).

Figure 1.3
A traditional reinforcement/ playback system.

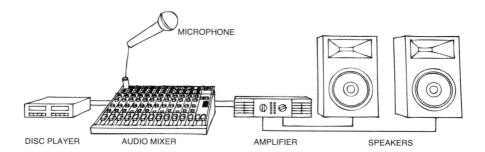

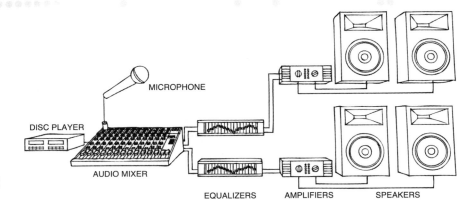

Figure 1.4
A multispeaker
system with signal
processing.

MICROPHONE

DISC PLAYER

AUDIO MIXER

EQUALIZERS   AMPLIFIERS   SPEAKERS

1.4 The QLab Playback System

In each of the previous examples, the audio playback device was a CD player. This setup is perfectly serviceable for examples like the one above where a song plays from beginning to end and stops or pauses before the next use. For the following examples, we will examine how adding QLab as the playback device changes the way that one must think of signal flow.

Outside of the realm of the hardware, QLab has its own software signal flow to consider. The signal begins with the **Audio File** saved onto the computer's hard drive. This file is played back in QLab by using an **Audio Cue** that targets the audio file for playback. Each Audio Cue has an **audio output patch** associated with it that assigns the audio file to a specific audio device. As a default, QLab will use your computer's built-in audio card for output, but you can plug-in up to eight different external audio interfaces and output to any of those. Along the way, QLab can assign an AU to any Audio Cue and change the quality of the sound, emulating a traditional equalizer, delay, compressor/limiter, reverb, or more. In this way, QLab allows the user to decrease the amount of external hardware necessary to achieve signal processing. Finally, the faders inside QLab allow you to assign how much of the audio signal will go to which output on the audio device. This feature allows QLab to behave exactly like a traditional audio mixer, allowing the user to manipulate audio signals and route them to multiple audio devices. All of these functions above can now be managed through the use of a QLab computer and an audio interface alone. In short, QLab 3 has removed the need for thousands of dollars of audio equipment!

Once the signal outputs from the computer, it operates in much the same fashion as the traditional playback system by travelling through a mixer, signal processors, amplifiers, and speakers. Depending on the needs of your particular installation, the mixer and signal processors could be eliminated and handled exclusively through QLab, leaving only the requisite amplifiers and speakers.

1.5 Audio Devices

If your budget does not allow for an external audio interface, there must be some type of a device used in order to send the signal to the amplifiers. In this case, one would most often output from the computer using the 1/8" headphone jack into an audio mixer and from the mixer directly into the amplifiers. One consideration for these types of rigs is that most computer headphone jack outputs are unbalanced audio lines and very prone to picking up additional noise along the audio line. If outputting directly from your computer's 1/8" jack, always use a **Direct Input (DI)** box to change the signal from unbalanced to balanced. Basically, a DI isolates the input signal from the output signal in order to reduce unwanted noise while still passing the audio signal through.

1.6 System Configurations

The following examples illustrate different system configuration possibilities. There are a number of different systems one could set up, and only the designer truly knows which system is best for the job.

Basic Stereo Playback System

The playback system shown in Figure 1.5 is one of the most basic configurations one can accomplish. The computer running QLab is the input source, supplying audio files for playback and allowing the designer to manipulate the file in a number of ways such as choosing start and/or end time, changing the tempo of the original recording, adding fades, looping the file, and more. In this configuration, the audio outputs through the computer's built-in sound card via the 1/8" stereo headphone jack. This stereo signal passes into the DI box and outputs from the two separate output channels (left and right channels) assuring a balanced signal from each channel. From here, the two signals pass into the amplifier, which increases the electrical impulse to a level high enough to activate the speakers. A basic amplifier will typically have two input

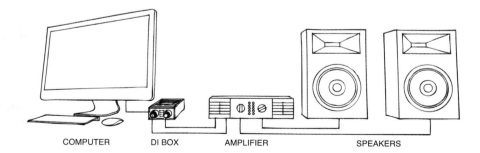

Figure 1.5 Basic stereo playback system with QLab, DI, amplifier, and two speakers.

COMPUTER   DI BOX   AMPLIFIER   SPEAKERS

and output channels (A and B). In this case, the right channel of the audio signal is routed to Channel A with the left channel in the amplifier's Channel B. This setup means that the playback will have the appropriate directional sound as the original recording.

It is worth noting that the industry practice of color-coding right and left channels suggests that the right channel be red with the left channel being white. This convention makes it easier to track stereo signal flow and guarantee accurate stereo reproduction. Many a designer has accidentally reversed to cabling only to find that the right channel plays from the left speaker and vice versa!

Intermediate Stereo Playback System and Multiple Speakers

The system shown in Figure 1.6 adds a bit more flexibility from the first. Like the first example, QLab will be outputting from the 1/8" stereo headphone jack. Because of this, QLab can only use two channels of control (right and left). Unlike the first example, though, the signal passes from the DI box into an audio mixer. With a little creative patching, the sound designer would be able to route this signal to multiple speakers controlled via the audio mixer if the project called for such control. It would not be automated within QLab, but this method is a functional solution when your budget doesn't allow for purchasing an audio interface. From the audio mixer, the signal flow would remain the same as before, travelling from the mixer into the amplifiers then speakers.

Intermediate Multichannel Playback System with External Signal Processing

In the previous systems, the use of stereo output is a definite limitation of QLab's capabilities. QLab has the ability to output its audio feed to up to

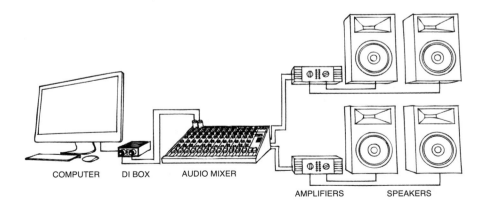

Figure 1.6
Intermediate stereo system with QLab, DI, mixer, amplifier, and four speakers.

COMPUTER   DI BOX   AUDIO MIXER

AMPLIFIERS   SPEAKERS

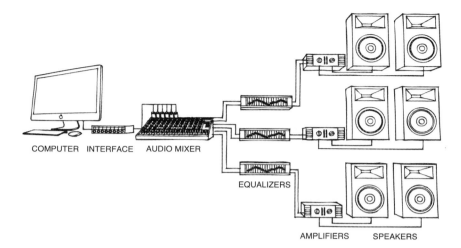

Figure 1.7
Intermediate multichannel system with QLab, Firewire audio interface, audio mixer, EQ, amplifiers, and six speakers.

COMPUTER   INTERFACE   AUDIO MIXER

EQUALIZERS

AMPLIFIERS   SPEAKERS

48 independent channels. This means that, by plugging in an audio interface, your audio could be routed to any one of 48 separate speakers (providing the device has 48 outputs). There are a number of different types of audio interfaces available from peripheral component interconnect devices built-in to your computer system (typically called a sound card) to external audio interfaces connected via USB, Firewire, or, most recently, Thunderbolt. Most mainstream external interfaces come equipped with anywhere from 4 to 12 analog outputs. The system shown in Figure 1.7 above utilizes such an external device connected via Firewire, sending out audio signals to six different speakers. In this example, the six outputs from the audio interface go into an audio mixer that allows the designer to apply different effects on the separate channels, such as reverb, high-pass filtering, and compression. The mixer then outputs the audio signal to three different EQs, allowing for equalizing of each signal. From the EQs, the signal passes through three separate amplifiers and then out into the six speakers. In this system, the use of the mixer and EQ gives a higher level of control to the designer with regards to signal processing.

Advanced Multichannel Playback System with QLab Signal Processing

The final system (Figure 1.8) utilizes many of the new functions of QLab 3 in order to eliminate some of the additional external hardware. Like the system above, the computer outputs to an external audio interface that outputs the audio signal through six independent channels. In this example, though, using the built-in audio effects capabilities of QLab negates the use of an audio mixer and equalizers. By assigning AUs to individual cues or assigning global effects busses, the designer can achieve EQ, reverb, compression, filtering, and more

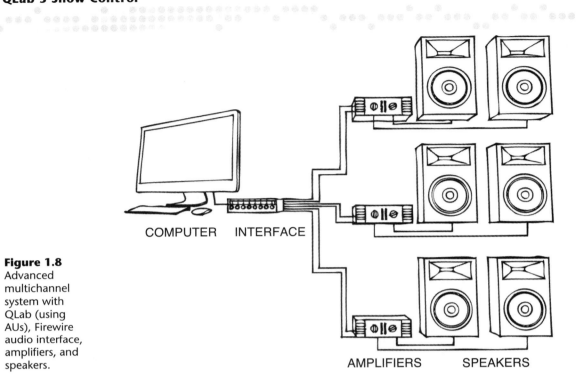

Figure 1.8
Advanced
multichannel
system with
QLab (using
AUs), Firewire
audio interface,
amplifiers, and
speakers.

COMPUTER   INTERFACE

AMPLIFIERS   SPEAKERS

without investing in expensive hardware. Perhaps more importantly, this setup allows a great amount of flexibility for no additional cost. All of the signal processing can be added, eliminated, or balanced at the click of a button *within* QLab rather than having to physically change settings on hardware. For the playback system in my university, we have now relegated the mixer to use in musicals only and almost eliminated physical signal processing altogether.

As you can see, there are a number of different systems to choose from and each has its pros and cons. It has been my experience that the versatility of QLab is its strongest feature. How I use it is exactly that; how I use it. As you spend some time getting to know the software, you will likely find other configurations that work best for your individual needs. That's the fun of designing – each design has unique needs and offers up different challenges from the last!

Installation and Preferences

Now that we have covered the basics of sound systems and understand a bit more about different sound system configurations, the next logical step is looking to QLab itself and addressing how one sets up the software to interact with the sound system. For those who have used QLab 1 or 2 in the past, it might come as a bit of a surprise to see how much the software visibly changed between Versions 2 and 3. Rest assured, though, all of the same functions remain in the newest version – you just might access them in a different fashion now. We will work from the assumption that this is your first time to use QLab 3 and start from the beginning.

2.1 QLab 3 Specifications

One of the first thing that most people will notice is that QLab 3 requires the Apple OS 10.8 (or later) operating system – more commonly referred to as Mountain Lion. Many of the new functions in Version 3 are dependent on the architecture of this operating system, such as 64-bit integration. Since it is a 64-bit application, the software is now capable of taking full advantage of the total amount of RAM on your computer, a major advantage over the 32-bit coding of past versions. Speaking of RAM, the rule of thumb is, when working with audio and video playback, always equip your system with enough to exceed your current needs. This is particularly true today, as the manufacturing techniques are changing for some Apple computers to make it more difficult (and in some cases impossible) to upgrade the factory-installed RAM on your own.

Actual minimum system specifications for QLab are difficult to assess, since your use of the software will dictate the amount of "horsepower" necessary to run the application. The chart below lists some rules of thumb that will be useful in configuring hardware for different uses. As always, there are a number of configurations that would work for any given situation. The recommendations made below are my choices for a baseline model that will remain useful for the longest window of time before requiring upgrade.

RECOMMENDED SYSTEM REQUIREMENTS

Sound Playback/Reinforcement
Suitable models: MacBook Air, MacBook Pro, Mac Mini, Mac Mini with OSX Server, iMac, Mac Pro
Mac OS 10.8 (Mountain Lion) or later
2.5 GHz dual-core Intel core processor
4 GB RAM (for basic sound playback)
8 GB RAM (for more complex cueing needs – i.e. numerous simultaneous cues)
256 GB storage (budget allowing, flash memory is preferable to traditional hard drives in both speed and durability)

Video Playback
Suitable models: MacBook Pro Mini, Mac Mini with OSX Server, iMac, Mac Pro
Mac OS 10.8 (Mountain Lion) or later
2.3 GHz quad-core Intel core processor
Intel Graphics 4000 (for basic video playback – one video output)
ATI Radeon HD 5870 (for advanced HD video output – multiple video outputs)
8 GB RAM (for basic video playback)
32 GB RAM (for more complex cueing needs – i.e. numerous simultaneous cues)
1 TB storage (budget allowing, flash memory is preferable to traditional hard drives in both speed and durability)

2.2 Understanding QLab Licensing

As mentioned earlier in the book, one of the biggest reasons for QLab's popularity over the years is Figure 53's commitment to having a free version of QLab available for basic audio playback. This remains true for QLab 3, where the free version allows for saving workspaces for playback with stereo output (two channel maximum), unlimited cue numbers, group cues, and fade cues. In other words, for most basic sound designs that only need stereo output, you could get by with downloading the free version and installing it on an unlimited number of computers! In addition, Version 3 offers some free video features, as well. This free software has been particularly successful for students and small professional theatres that cannot afford a large audio system, but want to have computerized audio playback.

For anything other than basic audio playback, though, one should look to the different licenses available for QLab. As mentioned earlier, customer service has always been a benchmark of the QLab name. Nowhere is this truer than in their pricing and options for professional licensing. Understanding that no two installations are alike, Figure 53 has broken down the QLab software into separate licensing packages so that the customer who only needs professional audio capabilities doesn't have to pay for an entire system of functions they will never use. QLab 3 has even expanded on this model, by adding different pro-tiers of both audio and video functions. Licensing is split into five different packages: Basic Audio, Pro Audio, Basic Video, Pro Video, and Pro Bundle (a combination of all licenses).

The names of each license describe the types of cues included, each one opening up a higher range of function to the software package. Basic Audio offers eight channels of audio input/output with eight channels of audio per file. Pro Audio allows for up to 48 channels of audio output, with 24 input channels and channels of audio per file. In addition, Pro Audio integrates audio effects via AU plug-ins and allows for Timecode cues. With the Video licensing, Basic Video features less of the versatility of the Pro version (lacking unlimited multiscreen surfaces, edge blending, keystone correction, making and shutters, video effects, Syphon input/output, and Timecode cues). Unlike QLab 2, musical instrument digital interface (MIDI) cues no longer have their own license. Instead, they are integrated into both Pro Audio and Pro Video licenses, with the ability to send MIDI messages, MIDI Show Control/Open Sound Control cues, play back MIDI files, and more.

Offering up these different packages is only the first step, though. In addition, they offer a substantial discount for academic licensing (students, teachers, and institutions). For those in the professional sector who find a need for the software in limited runs, there is also the ability to rent at a modest price (currently $3/$5/$7 per day, depending on selected tier). Rentals give the full capability of the pro license for a predetermined amount of time programmed directly into the license. When you reach the end of your time period, the license will revert to Free. For a comparison of the features in each different licensing package, visit the QLab website at **figure53.com qlab/buy**

2.3 Installing the Software

Like many applications today, the QLab software is only accessible via download through their business website: Figure53.com. Whether you will be using the free or the Pro version of QLab, the first step will be downloading the software from their website. There is only one program to download – the free version is the same platform as the Pro. Adding a license simply unlocks additional features. Some of the Pro features can also be tested in the free version.

When you click on the download icon, the software will begin to download as a ZIP archive. Depending on how you have your computer set up, it will likely appear in your Downloads folder as a program icon called QLab. Drag the icon from your Downloads folder onto your desktop or into your Applications folder. Once you have done so, you are set up and ready to go!

2.4 Adding a License

Provided you are interested in using the advanced applications in the Pro version of QLab (many of which will be required for the projects throughout the book), you will then need to visit the Figure 53 website again to download your license. As mentioned earlier in this chapter, there are a number of licensing options depending on your needs. Whether you go with a license purchase or a rental, both types of licensing are available for purchase through the QLab website. For purchase, you simply select which license package you prefer and pay through their secure server. For the rental, you indicate the type of license, starting date, and the number of days required for your purposes. For both methods, you will receive an e-mail that includes both your receipt and the license for installation. Installing the license is as simple as dragging the installation file from the e-mail onto the QLab icon.

When you start up the software, you will be asked to authorize the license. You must be online in order to do this, or you will have to go through an offline authorization process that gives you a code to send to Figure 53 via e-mail from another computer. Once you have done so, they will send back an authorization file that you will need to then install onto the computer. If you do not do so within a set period of time, the license will revert to basic functions until authorization occurs.

To make certain that your license was correctly installed, simply open up the QLab software and click the word **QLab** in the Menu bar at the top of the screen. In the drop-down menu, click on **Manage Licenses**. This will open an interface that shows you the licenses installed on your computer (Figure 2.1). It will indicate the type of license bundle, license terms, name of licensee, and end date (should it be a rental).

Figure 2.1
QLab licensing window.

In addition to the license, it will show a button labeled "deauthorize and delete this license." This button is important to remember should you be installing the software on multiple computers. Standard licensing allows that you can install the software onto one programming computer, one playback computer, and one backup computer (for a total of three authorized installations). As a professional designer, one might install the software onto a number of different computers. Should you forget to deauthorize, though, you will lose one of your potential licenses (there is no way to deauthorize other than through QLab on the authorized machine).

2.5 Organization

No matter how you plan on using QLab, you will quickly discover that having an established organizational method will make the process of programming, trouble-shooting, and playback much easier. Unless you are creating your cue list from the ground up on the computer to be used for playback (and, really, even then), it is important to create a logical file storage method and remain consistent across each computer you use. In order to aid in this, I always create a show folder to be saved onto the desktop of my computer. I will typically name this folder for the show or project that I am working on. Depending on the number and/or type of files associated with the project, I might add a number of sub-folders inside of the master show folder.

Let's look at a hypothetical show featuring music, still imagery, and videos. For this show, called *The Distant Thunder*, I create a master folder on my desktop called (you guessed it) "Distant Thunder." Within this folder, I create three sub-folders called "Music," "Stills," and "Videos." This will help me organize the project as I go along and save a lot of time during the process of creating a cue list, since everything will be in a logical location. I typically try to take it one step further and make sure that I name (or re-name) any files associated with the project as something very descriptive.

For example, that distant thunder we were talking about before; in this project, let's assume that there will be numerous different sound cues of thunder. For each of the thunder cues, I might make certain that they are numbered chronologically (i.e. Thunder1.wav, Thunder2.wav, and so on), so that when the time comes to program, I don't spend all my time listening to them to decide what order they should be placed in for playback. It could be as simple as this, or as complex as naming one "John_is_shot_and_dies_painfully.wav." Ultimately, this system should be unique to you and your thought process, as it is ultimately intended to exist only for your benefit or those working on the project.

One thing to consider is that once a show is saved on one computer, it will be looking for the same paths on another computer for playback. In other words, if you created your show folder on the desktop of one computer, then moved it to the Downloads folder of another computer, your cue list would not function properly (since all of the file paths would have been listed as Desktop not Downloads). Likewise, over time your show folder might become cluttered with deleted files, unused choices, or multiple takes. If you are transporting this over to another computer for playback, you likely will not want to bring along those unused files. Since QLab 2, there has been a useful function called **Bundle Workspace** that aids in both of these problems.

Once you are finished with your project and ready to transfer the Workspace from one computer to another, simply click **File** button on the Menu bar and select the **Bundle Workspace** option in the drop-down menu. This function creates a brand new folder for your workspace and a copy of all the files reference within it. All cues in your cue list(s) will then be updated and saved with the new media files in the bundled folder. This can then easily be transferred to the new computer for playback. I strongly recommend always saving these to the desktop, as it is the easiest logical location to drop the file for other computers.

2.6 Physical Connection

Chapter 1 details the many different types of configurations one might use for QLab sound systems. Keep in mind that, for any type of system you will have to set up a physical connection between the computer and the speakers. For those with a computer having internal speakers, you will only be able to listen to your files in stereo. It is important to always listen to your files in a fashion that most closely approximates the conditions of your project. Whether the file is used for a museum installation, a theatre piece, or a rock and roll show, you cannot trust the sound made by onboard speakers or even headphones to replicate the actual sounds heard once in the space. If possible, it's nice to work with the same physical connections, amplifiers, and speakers. Most of us cannot afford this luxury, though, so make certain that you have factored in time to be in the space with the equipment beforehand so everyone else on the project doesn't have to wait for you to set levels on the fly.

As a reminder, the basic methods of connecting your computer to a sound system will be either through an 1/8" headphone jack (stereo) or through an audio interface via USB/Firewire/Thunderbolt/PCI connectors. If using the 1/8"connector method, make sure to use some type of Direct Input to balance the signal (see Chapter 1, Section 1.5 for details).

2.7 Workspace Settings

To this point, we have mostly discussed hardware and the physical attributes of sound systems. One final area to look at before jumping headfirst into programming, though, is how to establish software preferences for how QLab will behave once you begin to use it. The following section details how to do just that by using workspace settings. It is always important to look at workspace setting *before* starting a project, as there are several functions that, when enabled, will make your programming much easier! Keep in mind, though, that you may well find yourself returning to the workspace settings to make adjustments.

To access the workspace settings, click on the gear-shaped icon in the lower right-hand corner of the program window (see Figure 2.2). Once you click on the icon, the program's interface will flip to reveal a new window entitled Settings for: Untitled Workspace 1. The page is separated into two columns: the left column contains the menu for selecting various preference settings; and the right column features content changes for each menu item clicked on the left. It is important to note that, once established, settings will remain in place for all future files added to your workspace. In the section below, we will go through each of the settings possibilities to get you ready to start working with sound in QLab. We skip some of the settings tabs in this section, as they are not related to sound control. Go ahead and open up your workspace settings to reference while reading along.

General

The General settings (Figure 2.3) are just that – settings related to the general function of your QLab workspace. These are basic functions that generally allow you to control the visual appearance of cue lists, control playback positions, or save you from the legwork of cue numbering. Most of these are self-explanatory.

- The first checkbox allows you to fire a trigger when the workspace is first opened. This could be particularly useful if you want to automate the GO command for a certain cue number at the opening of the document.
- The second area is what is sometimes referred to as Double GO Protection. The default minimum time set between GO (firing a cue) is set as 0.0 seconds. In some situations (provided you don't have rapid-fire cues), you might want to set a slight buffer of 0.5 seconds to defuse any accidental "double-clicks" from the operator. The second checkbox in this area can typically be ignored,

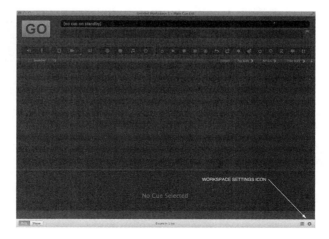

Figure 2.2
Workspace settings icon.

unless you know that you will be using an X-Keys programmable keyboard device (or any other hardware that does not produce a "key-up" event). If you intend to use this type of peripheral device, simply deactivate the "key-up" checkbox and you will be ready to go.

- The third setting controls the increments of auto-numbering. When checked, you can establish a numbering increment for new cues. The default is 1, meaning that each cue inserted will progress chronologically by adding 1 to the previous number. Sometimes, it is wise to leave a numeric buffer between inserted cues.
- The general preferences also allow you to control the behavior of the play-back position in QLab. The playback position is an indicator that shows what cue is selected for playback once the operator hits GO. By default, the playback position changes to any cue you might click (for instance to edit the settings in a subsequent cue). If you deselect this checkbox, though, you can keep the playback position independent of any cue you select.
- The fifth general setting allows for setting the panic duration. In QLab 3, when you press ESC, the panic command will begin; fading out cue play-back over default duration so as to not abruptly stop (particularly useful in live settings). This setting allows you to change the time from the default of 1.5 seconds to any duration.
- Finally, the last of the general preferences simply allows you to change the size of cue rows from small, to medium, or large.

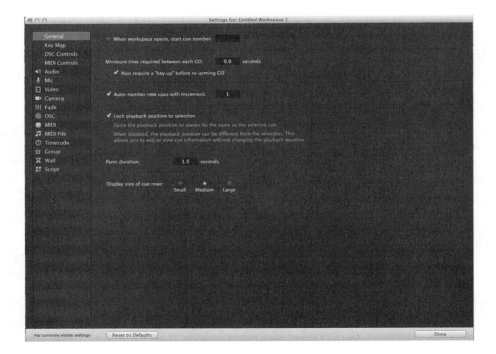

Figure 2.3
General settings window.

Figure 2.4
Key map window.

Key Map

One of the most versatile of QLab's functions is the ability to program **Hotkeys**, or a pre-programmed key on your keyboard used for triggering certain control functions. In the hotkey interface, it shows the factory settings programmed into QLab for these controls (Figure 2.4). For instance, the standard button used for firing GO is the computer's space bar. You can reassign any of the play-back controls to any key on the keyboard (alphanumeric, space bar, or control + alphanumeric). In addition, the ESC button is pre-programmed to panic all (meaning fade out any cue playing over a brief timespan) or to immediately Hard Stop All if you double-tap the escape button.

OSC Controls and MIDI Controls

Open sound control (OSC) and musical instrument digital interface (MIDI) are two protocols used for communicating with a wide range of electronic devices. Since the use of OSC, MSC, and MIDI is covered in depth later, it is best to simply say these two tabs establish how QLab communicates over an OSC network or by using MIDI protocol. Essentially, all of these functions exist to allow for QLab to communicate with, control, or be controlled by OSC or MIDI devices (or other instances of QLab running on networked computers).

Audio: Signal Flow

QLab Software Signal Flow

In order to better understand the following settings, it might be wise to first discuss in detail the idea of QLab software signal flow. I use the term software signal flow because, as QLab is a program, there is no true signal flow in the traditional sense. Instead, the audio signal is routed through many different software patches and

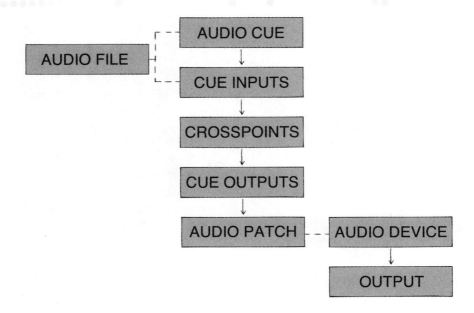

Figure 2.5
QLab software
signal flow.

control functions before outputting to the audio device. Figure 2.5 illustrates the key concepts of QLab's signal flow. Refer back to it often for the following description.

Audio Cue

The Audio Cue is heart of the QLab audio playback system. The Audio Cue targets an audio file for playback and allows a number of control functions like time and looping, volume levels, output patch control, trim, audio effects, and more.

Audio File

The audio file is a digital recording of an audio signal saved onto the computer's hard drive. This file is targeted by the Audio Cue for playback but not, strictly speaking, a component of QLab. The nature of the audio file, be it mono, stereo, or multichannel audio, affects how QLab utilizes it within the Audio Cue. The number of channels in the audio file equate to the number of inputs for the Audio Cue.

Inputs

Each channel of the targeted audio file is translated as an input for the Audio Cue. Typically speaking, most audio files are either mono (one channel) or stereo (two channels). This means that, unless you are dealing with a multichannel audio file, most Audio Cues will have only one or two inputs. It is worth noting that, even though most files only utilize two input channels, QLab allows for up to 24.

Crosspoints

Crosspoints can be thought of as a way of routing the audio signal from an input into a Cue Output. Each input channel aligns with a row of crosspoints to its right. The input sends the signal down the row to each of the 48 crosspoints. In audio engineering terms, this is referred to as **bussing**. Although the bus, or signal path, sends the audio signal to each of the crosspoints, it is up to the programmer to "activate" the crosspoint. By doing so, the programmer assigns the amount of audio signal to enter the crosspoint and thereby travel into one of the 48 cue outputs.

Levels Faders (Cue Outputs)

Each cue, be it Audio or Mic, has the potential of outputting 48 channels of cue output into one of eight audio patches. The levels faders within an Audio Cue control the amount of the audio signal transmitted into the audio patch.

Audio Patch

The audio patch is another layer of abstraction between the audio file and its ultimate destination of the speakers. Essentially, QLab allows for connecting your computer to one or multiple audio devices at once (up to eight audio patches, in total). The patch is the software link between QLab and the audio device or devices.

Audio Device Output Routing

The final layer to the signal flow within QLab is the Device Routing. By selecting the Edit Patch function within QLab, you can open an interface that then allows you to route the audio signal from the Audio Cue into the desired output channels of the audio device. For this step, the Audio Cue Output from above is now the audio device's input. By using the crosspoints matrix of the Device Routing window, you then route the cue output into one or more level faders for device outputs. Following this, the device outputs the audio signal into the remaining components of your sound system (mixer, signal processing, amplifiers, and speakers).

Audio: Settings

This settings tab controls all of the audio patches, volume limits, and default levels for new Audio Cues added to your workspace (see Figure 2.6). In addition, it allows for the editing of external audio devices, routing signals, and audio bussing. The control structure can seem a bit intimidating at first, but once you understand a few key concepts, you can begin navigating the system with ease.

When first looking at the screen, you will notice that it is divided into three distinct areas: Audio Patches in the upper left, Volume Limits in the upper right,

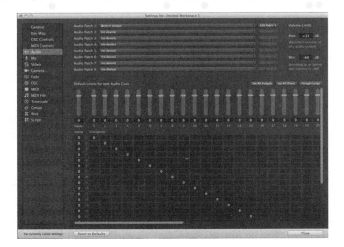

Figure 2.6
Audio settings
window.

and default levels in the lower half of the screen. It is this last area that we will
focus on first.

Default Levels for New Audio Cues

The default levels control panel (Figure 2.7) is the starting point for setting up
how QLab deals with signal flow for Audio Cues. Not only does this panel allow
for the creation of default volume levels, but it also is the method for establishing the path that the audio signal follows on its way to the audio device.

The Matrix Mixer

The **Matrix Mixer** is an important concept in QLab that will be used in multiple
applications, so it is essential for your success to understand how it functions. In
short, the matrix mixer is a combination of controls that allow for signal routing
and volume control. This interface in its whole might take some getting used
to for the beginner, as the graphic interface changes somewhat for its use in
different scenarios. The following section breaks down the Matrix Mixer interface and its use. Refer to "Audio: Signal Flow" section to see how many of the
following components fit within the larger picture of the software signal flow.

Inputs

The column on the lower left-hand side of the screen, numbered 1–24, represents the cue inputs. As discussed earlier, each Audio Cue has the potential of up
to 24 audio inputs. In a standard audio file, there will likely be one or two inputs
only. For a multichannel audio file, you could have multiple input channels. Each
input corresponds to the crosspoints row directly to its right, listed 1–48.

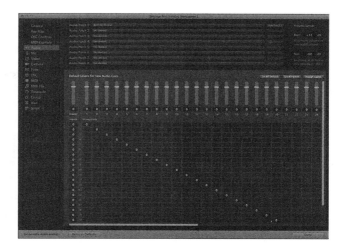

Figure 2.7
Default levels for
new Audio Cues.

Crosspoints

Crosspoints are a method of assigning an input signal to a Cue Output. The collection of all of the crosspoints is referred to as the **crosspoints matrix**. As mentioned earlier, each audio input is bussed to every crosspoint to its right, though they can be set to mute. In a two-speaker stereo configuration, input 1 would be assigned to crosspoint 1 in its row. Input 2 would then be assigned to the crosspoint 2 in its row. Each of these faders is connected to the cue output listed at the top of its column.

Cue Outputs

Each Audio Cue has up to 48 possible cue outputs, as represented by the levels faders at the top of the columns. Each column, 1–48, receives any audio signal that is turned on in the crosspoints matrix beneath it. Each cue output can thereby receive an audio signal from any of the 24 audio inputs.

By default, input 1 is assigned to cue output 1. This is repeated for each subsequent channel, with input 2 connected to cue output 2, and so on. This typically means that the left channel of audio is in fader 1 and fader 2 controls the right. For a multispeaker system, though, it is common to re-assign the signal so that input one busses into multiple crosspoints, allowing for the audio signal from channel one to be passed into multiple speakers.

Setting Levels Faders

The sliders at the top of the window are referred to as the levels faders. These levels faders control the amount of audio signal that goes through the cue outputs and into the audio patch. This slider is a graphic representation of classic faders on a soundboard.

In audio, the term **UNITY** is an important concept to understand. On a traditional soundboard, there is a point roughly 2/3 of the way up the slider that will be labeled as +0 dB or UNITY. Essentially, this means that you are neither adding to nor taking away from the original audio signal. This is why the faders always default to this position in QLab.

Another key concept that can be confusing to the beginner is that 0 **does not** mean no volume. To take the volume all the way to silence, pull the slider down to the bottom and notice that it now has no text in the box below it. This means there will be no audio signal passing through the channel – or that it is MUTED. A quick key that can help you in setting levels is option + click on the slider. This will toggle between MUTE and UNITY.

Master Fader

You will note that there is a **master fader** on the left of the screen (positioned above the inputs column), in addition to the sub-faders in a row to the right. The master fader controls the mix of all outputs, relative to their original levels. In other words, the master controls the overall volume output of the combined group of faders, allowing for the increase or decrease of all cue outputs from one fader.

Pro-Tip ▽

A goal of any audio project is to create a balanced sound mix, with the appropriate amount of audio coming out of each speaker. Frequently, different amplifiers (even those of the same make and model) will output at differing volume levels. Outputting an audio file with the same output levels on each channel will, in this situation, lead to an unbalanced mix – where some speakers output at louder levels than others. To eliminate this problem, it is best to set up default levels for each of your outputs, so that each speaker outputs at an ideal volume (even if this means that it needs to receive more or less of an input).

The simplest way to set default levels would be to go into QLab and play a mono audio file. Go to the "Device & Levels" tab of your Audio Cue and set each of your output sliders to MUTE. Slowly bring them up until you get your desired mix. Once you have done this, write down the levels and go back into the Audio Settings and set the sliders to match those in your notes. This will guarantee that each Audio Cue you add to your workspace will begin at the appropriate preset audio levels. If you find a need to change the individual cue, you can do so within the "Device & Levels" tab for the Audio Cue in question.

Keep in mind, you will need to have a different type of mix for each space and show you work on. Sometimes, it is preferable to have all speakers outputting at the same volume. At other times, it might be advantageous to have the house front speakers at a louder level. The designer must determine the needs for each given project.

Default, Silent, and Gangs

Another set of tools for the default Audio Cue levels are set all default, set all silent, and assign gangs. The first two need little explanation. **Set all default** returns each input to 0 dB and sets the crosspoints matrix to one-to-one. **Set all silent** toggles each input and crosspoint to – infinity, thereby muting all output. The final tool, **assign gangs**, allows you to pair faders or even crosspoints together into groups, so that any action taken by one will affect the ones linked together. For instance, once you have set your default levels for Audio Cues, you might want to gang together all of your stereo pairs so that the front of house speakers are paired together and will either increase or decrease together. This may not work for all installations, but many times it will save you lots of work to do so, if possible.

Audio Patches

Once you have set the default levels for new Audio Cues and assigned the signal routing, the next step is to look at the audio patch. An audio patch is the digital path that an audio file takes between an Audio Cue and the audio device. There are eight audio patches, which can each be assigned to a different audio device (either your internal sound card or external audio devices). Any Audio Cue can be assigned to output to one of the eight different patches, meaning that you can have separate sounds running to up to eight different devices. A friendly reminder, though – if you want to output to this many devices at once, you will definitely want to maximize RAM, bus speed, and hardware drive speed.

All available audio patches are shown at the top of the Audio Settings tab. The default setting for Audio Patch 1 should be "Built-In Output." This is your computer's built-in sound card and speakers. If you want to use an external audio device, click on the arrow at the end of the Built-In Output button and select your device in the drop-down menu (see Figure 2.8). If going with an

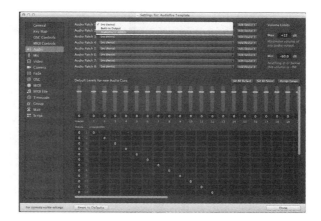

Figure 2.8
Assigning an audio patch.

audio device, you will need to understand the process of assigning Device Routing for your audio device. These controls are found by clicking on the "Edit Patch" button to the right of the chosen audio patch.

Edit Patch: Device Routing

Upon clicking the Edit Patch 1 button, a window will appear showing three tabs. The Cue Outputs and Device Outputs tabs are used almost exclusively for adding global audio effects. As such, we will examine these in later chapters. For now, click on the Device Routing tab located in the center of the screen (Figure 2.9).

The second tab of the Edit Patch 1 window is called Device Routing. This allows for routing your audio to the output of the audio device. Built-In Output will only be stereo (meaning there will be only two channels of output – one for left and one for right). The window is similar to the Matrix Mixer in default levels for new Audio Cues, although it functions slightly differently.

In the case of the Device Routing, some of the terms are a bit different. First, look to the left of the screen in the Matrix Mixer. You will notice that there are 48 inputs, rather than the 24 seen in the default audio levels earlier. This is because **the Cue Outputs serve as inputs for the Audio Device Routing**. The column to the left of the screen labeled **inputs** corresponds to each of the 48 cue outputs from an Audio Cue and indicates how much of the audio signal will be transmitted into the crosspoints matrix to the right. Again, if the input level is set to 0 (which is the default), then this means that channel one of the crosspoints will receive the full signal strength of the audio signal. If necessary, you could decrease the amount of signal so that one or more of your crosspoints received a diminished signal. To set the level on this, simply click the box to highlight the number 0, then slide your mouse down to decrease volume or up to increase (noting that 0 dB is the maximum amount).

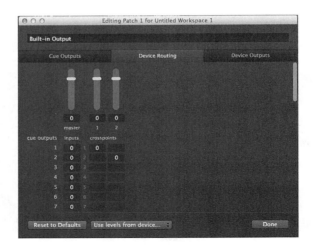

Figure 2.9
Device routing tab.

Crosspoints

Using the crosspoints matrix, you will select a device output (or outputs) for each of the inputs and assign the level of signal from 0 dB UNITY all the way down to –60 dB. The most common configuration would be to assign input 1 to output 1, input 2 to channel 2, and so on. In this configuration, each Audio Cue's level fader corresponds directly to the same number of device output. Since the intention for this example is to create a basic stereo output, then input 1 will be routed into output 1 at 0 dB and input 2 into output 2 at 0 dB (see Figure 2.9). In this configuration, Fader 1 will control the left channel and Fader 2 will control the right channel. Chapter 3 deals with the process of setting up a more complex multichannel sound system.

Volume Limits

After setting default levels and editing your audio patch, there is one final function of the Audio Settings window. This important control feature is the ability to establish volume limits – a useful tool when considering the differences between equipment and spaces. This feature is located in the upper right corner of the Audio Settings window (see Figure 2.10).

The MAX limit is a simple concept – allowing the user to set a peak level for volume output. This function is best suited to protect equipment and hearing. Before the cueing process begins, it is best to go into the space for your project and test the extreme limits of volume. Start with a good rock song and slowly raise the MASTER slider until the volume reaches an uncomfortable level. This is your MAX volume setting. This simple step can save your equipment from being damaged by an inadvertent volume spike.

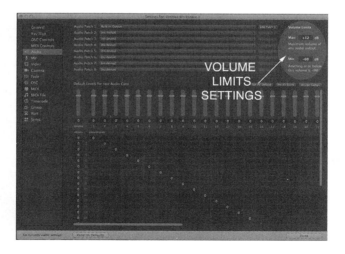

Figure 2.10
Volume limits.

On the other end of the spectrum, it is important to tell QLab what level is perceived as silence in your system. If QLab thinks –60 dB (the default MIN level) is silent, but your system is silent at –45 dB, then all of your fade-outs will sound too abrupt, as they will reach silence faster than expected. To eliminate this, use the same song as above and slowly pull down the MASTER fader until you cannot hear any volume output. Note the –dB level setting at which you cannot hear sound from your speakers. This number is your MIN volume output. This simple step will save you a lot of time during tech if you take a few minutes up front to set volume limits.

Mic

The next workspace setting deals with Mic Cues, a new feature added to Version 3 that truly add a level of versatility to the software that did not exist before. Now QLab can function both as a sound playback system and as a sound reinforcement system. In order to take advantage of the Mic Cue, though, you will have to have an external audio device with inputs for microphones and outputs to send the resulting microphone signal. Due to clocking inconsistencies between separate devices, **Mic Cues must always use the same device for input and output**. It is also worth noting that the audio device used for Mic Cues should ideally have phantom power capability so that you use condenser microphones that require the 48 V power signal to operate. Figure 53 has an exhaustive user-created list of audio devices that have been tested in the QLab environment at wiki.Figure53.com.

Essentially, a Mic Cue allows you to insert into your cue list a command that activates the input (or inputs) of an external audio device and/or mutes them. Through the Mic Patch settings, you can route the audio input signal produced by the microphone out through any of the device's outputs.

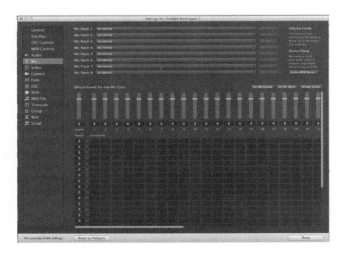

Figure 2.11
Mic settings
window.

The settings tab for Mic Cues as seen in Figure 2.11 mirrors that of Audio Cues, without a volume limits control (as the max and min volumes are the same as those set in the Audio Cue settings). There are eight Mic Patches that allow you to edit the device in the same fashion as an Audio Cue. Likewise, there is the ability to set default levels for new Mic Cues and the ability to gang. These settings will be addressed in detail in Chapter 7, Mic Cues.

Fade

Fade Cues control how Audio Cues either fade in or fade out volume. The Fade Cue is an essential part to every sound project in QLab, as such special attention should be paid to the fade settings to ensure consistency and ease in programming. Figure 2.12 shows the fade settings window.

The fade settings fall into two basic categories: (1) fade length and (2) fade shape. At the top of the window, you will see that the default fade time is set to 5 seconds. This is a nice time for a medium paced fade. Although you may find yourself going considerably shorter or longer for individual fades, 5 seconds is generally a good starting point. The shortest fade duration possible is 0 seconds, which represents an instantaneous change in levels.

The second aspect to address is the fade curve shape. As a default, the "S-Curve" appears in the curve shape dialog. You could also choose to create your own custom fade curve, should you so desire. When looking at the graph, there are two basic components – time and volume. The "x-plane" shows time in seconds, whereas the "y-plane" shows volume in dB, with the bottom being – infinity and the top being 0 dB. Looking at the settings panels, the graph on the left indicates curves for fade-ins, whereas the graph on the right indicates fade-outs. The S-curve is a nice starting point for most fades, as it is a subtle fade. If you find a need to change the fade curve for an individual fade in your workspace, you can do so in the EDIT window for that particular Fade Cue.

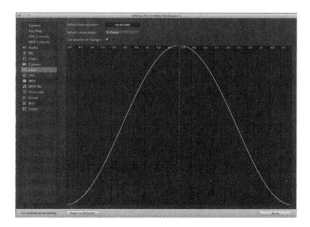

Figure 2.12
Fade settings window.

Group

Group Cue settings (Figure 2.13) establish the default mode for how new Group Cues behave when inserted into your Workspace. **Group Cues** allow you to combine multiple cues into one common folder for playback in your cue list. There are four different modes for how the cues inside a group (referred to as **children**) fire. Use of different modes is covered in depth in Chapter 9. For now, I would recommend leaving the mode set to "start first child and enter into group" as this is the most common use of the Group Cue.

Wait

The final audio-related setting is for the Wait Cue (Figure 2.14). The wait settings allow you to establish the default duration for a Wait Cue. A **Wait Cue** does what one might expect – inserting a pause into playback for a predetermined amount of time. This cue is one created for flexible programming in QLab. Each cue has the ability to add either a **Pre-Wait** or a **Post-Wait** adding a predetermined amount of time either before playback or after. QLab also allows for the use of a Wait Cue in this same way, to insert fixed pauses in your playback. Whichever method you choose to employ is a matter of personal preference.

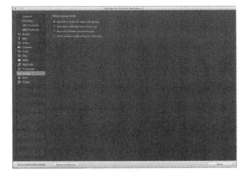

Figure 2.13
Group settings window.

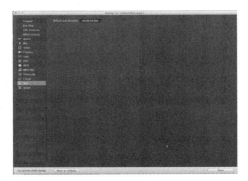

Figure 2.14
Wait settings window.

Setting Up QLab with Your Sound System

As we learned earlier, QLab's default setting is stereo output unless connected to an external audio device. For basic sound systems, this could be all that you need for functional sound playback. In many situations, though, it is necessary to create **directional sound**, sending your audio signal to speakers positioned around your audience so the audio has a realistic feel originating from the correct location. Nothing kills the credibility of a sound design like having music from an onstage record player ring out through the house speakers. We all know that the sound should originate from the object that creates the sound. Luckily, with QLab, an audio device with multiple outputs and a few speakers, you can make directional sound with ease.

3.1 Multichannel Sound Systems

A **multichannel sound system** is a type of sound system that incorporates multiple speakers for sound playback, each with its own control channel thereby allowing for the maximum flexibility of volume and panning. This concept is often confused with surround sound, because of its similarity. It is important to note that the concepts we are discussing, though similar, are not the same as the surround sound found in your local movie theatre. Surround sound mixing is a complex process of assigning direction within the DAW (digital audio workstation). The multichannel method used in this chapter can be a stereo signal routed to individual speakers within QLab or a multichannel WAV file with each channel pre-assigned to an individual speaker. Also, it is important to note that for the purposes of this chapter, we will discuss multichannel sound systems specifically for the live theatre environment. Although we will focus on theatre, these principles are applicable for any type of project from outdoor venues to found spaces or trade-show floors.

For the purposes of discussing multichannel sound systems, we will use a basic system layout that is common to many theatres (see Figure 3.1). In this system, there are eight individually controlled speakers – three are stereo pairs, with the

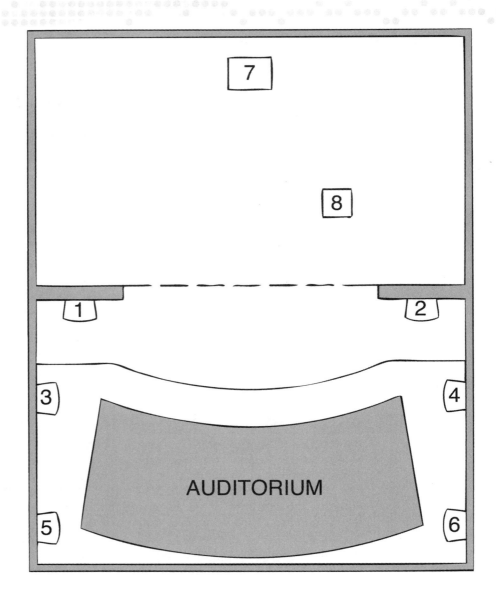

Figure 3.1
A multichannel
sound system
installation.

last two being used on their own. As you can see in Figure 3.1, speakers 1 and 2 are the stereo pairs (meaning speaker one gets the left channel and two gets the right channel) located on the proscenium. Speakers 3 and 4 are stereo pairs located in the front sides of the auditorium. Speakers 5 and 6 are stereo pairs located in the rear sides of the auditorium. Speaker 7 is a subwoofer located on the stage – in this case in the rear of the stage, pointed toward the back wall of the theatre to diffuse the sound. Finally, speaker 8 is located inside of a prop used onstage during the show – that pesky record player we mentioned earlier.

All audio files being used are stereo, but we will configure QLab to send those two channels to any of the eight independently controlled speakers to create directional sound.

3.2 External Audio Devices

As mentioned in earlier sections, an internal audio card or an external audio device is necessary to output audio from QLab to your sound system. Like most computer hardware, there are a number of different brands and models of audio interfaces that one can choose from, but they all perform the same basic function – to serve as an input/output device (I/O). This equipment allows you to input from an analog signal like a microphone or take a digital signal from USB/Firewire/PCI cable and send the signal out through different output channels.

For the purposes of better understanding how such a device works, let's examine a common interface used for theatrical applications: the Echo Audiofire 12 (Figure 3.2). Echo is a California-based company that has specialized in computer audio solutions for over 30 years. The Audiofire 12 is an IEEE-1394a (commonly referred to as Firewire 400) interface. In terms of I/O channels for the price range, the Audiofire packs quite a punch. In addition to signals received from the Firewire, there are 12 balanced ¼" TRS analog I/O channels with MIDI I/O, digital syncing via word clock, and 24 bit 192 kHz sample rate. One of the best features is that, with two Firewire ports, you can daisy chain two units together to achieve 24 channels of I/O.

The strength of the Audiofire unit in combination with QLab is that your sound system automatically becomes capable of both multichannel audio playback and also up to 12 channels of audio reinforcement (microphones plugged in to your system). It is worth noting, though, that since the Audiofire 12 does not have phantom power, microphones would be limited to the dynamic variety. If using condenser mics, either look for a different type of audio interface or use an external phantom power supplier. In the following section, we will look at how to set up QLab to send audio through the appropriate channels for our eight-channel theatre configuration.

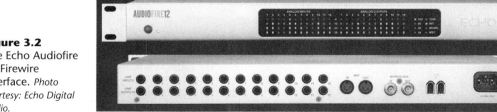

Figure 3.2
The Echo Audiofire 12 Firewire interface. *Photo courtesy: Echo Digital Audio.*

3.3 Setting Up QLab with an Audio Device

Now that we understand the basics of how an audio interface works, the next logical step is to see how to set up QLab to "talk" to the interface in question. There are a few steps to go through in order to make it work correctly, but once you have done so, programming for your multichannel sound system in QLab becomes a snap.

As mentioned in the beginning of this chapter, we will use the Audiofire 12 for all of the following examples and set up QLab to send out eight channels of audio to the eight independent speakers in our multichannel system. Since many of you won't have the Audiofire device, I have included a number of photographs in this section to make it easier to follow no matter what type of device you have at home.

If you are working with the free version of QLab and/or only using your computer's built-in output, you will only be able to see two output channels in QLab. This is because your basic computer sound card only has stereo output. You can, however, use the free version of QLab with an external audio device and experiment with these settings – just remember that you will be limited to only two channels of output while using the free version.

3.4 Audio Patches

In Chapter 2, we examined the basics of the audio patch within Settings. For the following sections, we will explore the application of these concepts and set up our own multichannel sound system with QLab. The following project breaks down how to configure the Audio Settings in order to have cue output one communicating with speaker one, and so on.

Project 3.1 ▼

> **Multichannel Audio Output**
>
> *Step One:*
> With QLab turned off, plug in your external audio device (follow the instructions provided by your manufacturer for order of operations).
>
> *Step Two:*
> Open a new QLab workspace and save it. I've called mine Audiofire Template, with the idea that I will be using this same configuration for other projects in the future.

Step Three:

Click on the Gear symbol in the bottom right corner to open up your Settings window. First, select the Audio Settings window. Your audio patch 1 will likely be assigned to either "no device" or "built-in output." Click on the arrows at the end of this button and change audio patch 1 to be assigned to your external audio device. In my case, it reads "Audiofire 12." See Figure 3.3 for a screenshot of this step.

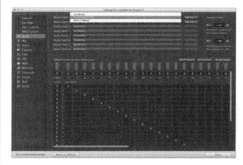

Figure 3.3
Assigning an audio patch.

Step Four:

The next step is to set up the signal routing directly from the Audio Cue into the audio patch. To do this, look in the Default Levels for new Audio Cues panel at the bottom of the window.

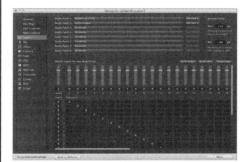

Figure 3.4
Default levels settings.

In Figure 3.4, you can see that the default setting for signals is a one-to-one routing, meaning input 1 from the audio file goes to crosspoint 1, which is routed to the output channel 1 levels fader of the device. The zeroes line up diagonally, descending from the upper left corner down to the lower right. This setup would be ideal for a multichannel audio file with 24 different channels, each dedicated to an individual speaker. In our case, though, we only have a two-channel signal (stereo) to route out to eight different speakers.

(Continued)

For this reason, we will only be using inputs 1 and 2. Channel 1 will typically be the left audio signal, with channel 2 functioning as the right.

Step Five:

Our goal is to set up the routing so that the cue output number (the levels faders at the top of the screen) corresponds to the appropriate speaker number, as seen back in Figure 3.1. In this illustration, we can see that speakers 1, 3, and 5 are located on the house left, whereas speakers 2, 4, and 6 are on the house right. As such, house-left speakers should receive the left channel of the Audio Cue and house-right speakers receive the right channel. Speakers 7 and 8 will receive both channels. Understanding this, *input 1 should be routed into crosspoints 1, 3, 5, 7, and 8, and input 2 routed into crosspoints 2, 4, 6, 7, and 8* (see Figure 3.5).

Figure 3.5
The crosspoints matrix.

The next step in the signal flow is to edit the audio patch. Since we assigned the Audiofire 12 to Audio Patch 1, it is this patch we will be editing. Look in the Audio Patch portion of the Settings screen and click on the button at the end of the row labeled "Edit Patch 1." This will open up an interface for routing signals and setting the volume levels for your device (Figure 3.6). Click on the center tab, labeled "Device Routing."

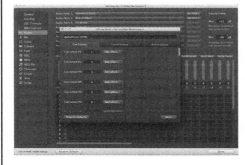

Figure 3.6
Editing patch.

Step Six:

The Device Routing tab will look remarkably similar to the default levels for new Audio Cues (see Figure 3.7). One difference you will note, though, is that there are only 12 sliders at the top of the screen, whereas there were 48 in the Audio Cue default settings. This is because there are only 12 channels of output available on the Audiofire 12. This window will change its appearance depending on the number of outputs available to it. If you only use the Built-In Audio as your device, then there would only be two available outputs.

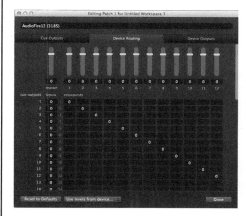

Figure 3.7
Device routing tab.

Another difference is in the input channels. Although the Audio Cue settings had only 24 inputs possible, there are 48 for the device routing. This is because the inputs for your audio device correspond to the cue outputs from your Audio Cue settings. In other words, the 48 possible channels of cue outputs directly route in as the inputs for your audio device.

By setting up the crosspoints in step five, each cue output number matches the speaker number for our setup. Since the default device routing is set at one-to-one, you will not have to make any changes to the device routing settings. With these settings, cue output 1 will control speaker 1 and so forth down the line, speakers 1–7.

Step Seven:

One final step that can help with future troubleshooting is the ability to label your cue outputs through the Edit Patch window. Click on the Cue Outputs tab to open the window. These settings are typically used for assigning an Audio Effect to your cue outputs, but can be very useful in that each cue output can be renamed from their original numbering system to an identifier. In the case of our theatre setup, I thought it might be useful to label cue outputs 1–7 by their individual speaker descriptions

(Continued)

QLab 3 Show Control

(see Figure 3.8). I renamed cue output 1 to PRO L (proscenium left), and cue output 2 as PRO R. By giving each speaker its own name and number, this can assist in clearing up any confusion during the cueing or troubleshooting process. Click "Done" when finished and all of your device editing will be saved.

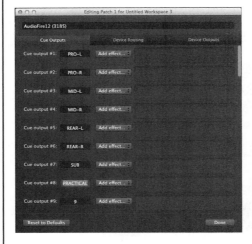

Figure 3.8
Naming cue outputs.

Step Eight:
Save your work! This will now function as a template for your multichannel sound system.

3.5 Audio Device Volume Levels

As a sound designer, you might frequently find yourself working on one type of audio interface for your programming and then going into a performance space with a different type of audio interface altogether. This can lead to some interesting changes to the volume settings for your show, as different audio interfaces will invariably output at different volumes from location to location. If you were unable to change the output levels on the new audio interface, it would mean hours of re-programming to get the show set to the appropriate volume levels. Luckily, QLab addresses these differences between audio devices by allowing for the editing of volume settings of the device in question.

Like setting the Default Levels for new Audio Cues in Chapter 2, this process is simple, but will require some quiet time alone in the theatre to fine-tune the volume settings for that particular location. One might ask why it is necessary

38

to set the volume levels through the device, if there are default level settings for each Audio Cue? The simplest answer is that the purpose of setting the volume output for your audio device should be to make certain that there is an equal amount of audio coming from each speaker in the theatre. In this way, any subsequent level changes can be done within the individual Audio Cue and the balance (or unbalance) occurs through manipulating the Audio Cue in question.

Project 3.2 ▼

Balancing Audio Device Output

For the following project, you really will need to have some level of equipment beyond the basic onboard speakers on your computer. The project will take you through the process of balancing the output for your system, so that all speakers sound appropriate to your desired mix. **Use the saved Workspace from Project 3.1 above for this project.**

Step One:

To make changes to the output settings of any audio device, either open the Settings window and click the Edit Patch button corresponding to your device or click the Edit Device button (a small button with three dots inside it) in the Device & Levels tab of your Audio Cue (see Figure 3.9).

Figure 3.9
Edit device button.

Step Two:

On selecting the Edit Patch window, you will need to select the Device Routing tab. Once you have done so, you will see the same interface used in Section 3.4 earlier to assign routing. Instead of focusing on the crosspoints matrix, though, this time, we will look at the levels faders at the top of the window. These sliders control the output from each physical channel on your audio device. As discussed in Chapter 2, these sliders are a graphic representation of the classic faders on a soundboard. By

(Continued)

default, the master and subsequent output channels will be set to 0 dB or UNITY. As a reminder, this means that the signal coming into the audio device will be output exactly as received. There is the potential, though, to either amplify or decrease the amount of audio signal going out of each channel. It is by adjusting these sliders you overcome any differences in the default speaker volume levels and create a balanced mix in your theatre.

Step Three:
In order to get a balanced mix on the speaker output, first position your-self in the center of auditorium of the theatre so as to get a realistic per-ception of what your audience will be hearing. The process will likely require getting up and moving around some, but the center is a good place to start.

Step Four:
Pull a test song into your workspace as an Audio Cue set to Infinite Loop. Press GO. At this point, go back to the Device Routing tab and pull all but the MASTER volume sliders down to mute. For the following steps, it is best to either (1) set up an ad hoc network between a laptop and your QLab control computer so you can screen-share and control QLab live; (2) use the QLab iPad app to access QLab and control the Settings live; or (3) bring in an assistant to run QLab for you while you give them thumbs up or thumbs down signals from the auditorium for setting levels. In either case, it is essential to actually listen to the changes being made *in real time* rather than running back and forth and trying to remember what it sounded like before.

Step Five:
Slowly bring up your fader for output 1 until the volume reaches a level that is almost uncomfortable, but not too loud. This process is fairly sub-jective. The purpose of setting it louder than the desired playback level for the show comes from the fact that the theatre's acoustics will change when you have an auditorium full of patrons. Each body will serve to absorb and dampen the overall sound, thereby decreasing the volume. This is why it is always a good idea to make your initial settings a bit louder in the programming.

Step Six:
Once you have achieved the desired volume level for channel 1, repeat these steps for each of your auditorium speakers. This can be a time-consuming process, but it is well worth the wait to ensure your design sounds the same from throughout the house. The ultimate mix is the designer's preference. Some designers might prefer the proscenium speakers to be louder than the house speakers in their mix, but I find it

easier to set all of the levels at the same output volume, and then change the standard mix through the default audio levels settings. Like most things in QLab, there are a number of ways to achieve the end goal. The process should ultimately be the one that makes the most sense to the designer and best fits the project.

3.6 Audio Effects and How to Use Them

As discussed in earlier chapters, QLab 3 has the ability to use Audio Units (AUs) to affect the audio signal in some useful ways (i.e. equalization, pitch-bending, hi-pass filtering, reverb, delay, and more). There are three methods of using AUs: either as an individual effect on one Audio Cue; as a global effect send applied to a Cue Output; or as an effect applied to a device output. In this section, we will discuss the last two methods. Utilizing Audio Effects on Audio Cues will be covered in Chapter 5: Audio Cues.

Audio Effects and Cue Outputs

Cue outputs are signals sent out from the Audio Cue. They route directly into one of the eight available audio patches and then into an input of the audio device. As seen in previous sections, these cue outputs typically contain an audio signal. In the case of Audio Effects, though, a cue output can be created for the specific purpose of applying a global effect to your playback.

Applying AUs to a cue output is comparable to the use of an AUX, or EFFECTS RUN, in traditional recording terminology. Typically speaking, an AUX is used to create a sub-group controlled by one fader. This is often referred to as an EFFECTS RUN, since one of the best uses for the AUX is to assign certain effects (like reverb) to a group of signals.

In QLab, assigning an effect to a Cue Output creates a digital path for your sound system that routes your signal down a path with one or more AUs assigned to it. These AUs act as signal processors, changing the sound of the audio signal and exporting this changed signal as a separate channel on your Audio Cue. By raising the level on the Cue Output slider, you can control the amount of the affected signal heard in your mix. The possibilities are nearly limitless on how one might use this in a live theatre environment.

Currently, only AUs that output in mono are available for applying to a Cue Output. Of the Apple AUs, this means that the AU Matrix Reverb cannot be applied to a Cue Output.

Project 3.3 ▼

Creating an Illusion of Distance through Audio Effects

One common effect frequently desired is the need to make an audio recording sound like it is coming from the distance. Certainly, you could just make it softer, but that doesn't really emulate a distant sound. For sounds in the distance, higher frequencies are eliminated and more of the low and mid frequencies persist. To achieve this effect through QLab, we will use a low-pass filter; an AU that allows frequencies lower than the set limit to pass through, whereas anything higher will be eliminated. With QLab 3 Audio Effects capabilities, you can apply effects to Cue Outputs, so that these effects are always at the ready for any cue in your cue list. By doing so, you can add a low-pass filter to any cue by simply raising the assigned Cue Output slider. The following project takes you through the process of setting this up.

Step One:
Download Project 3.3 from the companion website.

Step Two:
The Cue Output assignment is a component of editing your audio patch, so the first step is to click on Edit Patch 1 (or whichever patch you will be using for audio output). Once you have opened this interface, look at the first tab labeled "Cue Outputs" as seen in Figure 3.8 earlier in the chapter.

Step Three:
In order to assign an audio effect to a Cue Output channel, simply click on the button to the right of the Cue Output labeled "Add effect..." By clicking on this button, a drop-down menu opens labeled "Apple." By hovering over the Apple label, you will see a list appear of all of the available AU plug-ins for use (Figure 3.10). Click on the effect labeled "AULowpass." This assigns the low-pass AU plug-in to the selected cue output.

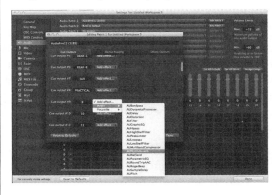

Figure 3.10
Available AU plug-ins.

Step Four:

When you select AULowpass, the control window for this AU will instantly open (see Figure 3.11). This window is not a part of QLab, rather the control window designed by Apple for this AU. This is the same window you would see in any application using the plug-in. You can think of the control window as an external device with knobs and sliders on the front for you to adjust. For now, close this window. We will return to it in a moment.

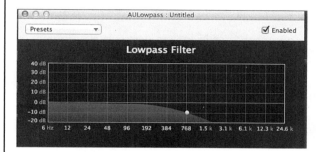

Figure 3.11
AULowpass control interface.

Step Five:

One great feature of the Cue Outputs editing window is the ability to rename a cue output. For this instance, we will look at Cue Output 3, the next available unused cue output in our system (since we are using stereo output). Click on the black box to the right of Cue Output 3 and type in "LO PASS." When you click enter or select an area outside the box, the number 3 will be replaced with the word LO PASS. This will be useful in the cueing phase, as all your sliders will now be labeled with their function. Leave the Settings window and return to Audio Cue 1 in your cue list. Click on the Device & Levels tab of the Inspector Panel of this cue and you will see that the level fader is newly labeled with its purpose (see Figure 3.12).

Figure 3.12
Labeled faders.

Step Six:

Click on the Device Routing tab of the Edit patch 1 window. In the row beside Cue Output 3 (now labeled LO PASS), insert a 0 in each of the two slots.

(Continued)

Step Seven:
The process detailed in steps one–six assigns Cue Output 3 as a low-pass filter effects send, meaning the audio signal will be routed through Cue Output 3 with the effect applied to the signal. One final step must be done in order to enable this function. Currently, the audio effect is applied to Cue Output 3, but there is no input signal routed into the fader. In order to accomplish this, slide the crosspoints up to 0 for both input 1 and input 2 in the column located beneath the newly labeled "LO PASS" fader. This routes the left audio channel (input 1) and the right audio channel (input 2) through Cue Output 3 to apply the low-pass filter effect (Figure 3.13). Now, the fader can be used to increase or decrease the amount of filtered audio signal sent out into the mix.

Figure 3.13
Assigning signal flow.

Step Eight:
Select Audio Cue 1 and press the space bar or GO button in the upper left-hand corner. This file is set on an infinite loop for use in setting up appropriate effects. Select Cue Outputs 1 and 2 and pull them both down to negative infinity (- INF). This will eliminate all audio that is not affected by the low-pass filter.

Step Seven:
To re-open your AULowpass control window, look to the left side of the "Devices & Levels" tab. You will see the Audio Output Patch. Click on the button with three dots and this opens the Edit Device window. By selecting Cue Outputs, you can scroll down the window until you see LO PASS (Cue Output 3). In the row to its right, you will see AULowpass shown. To remove this audio effect, you would simply click the "x." For our purposes, though, click the "Edit" button, which will re-open the control window (see Figure 3.14). With your Audio Cue playing, you will now be able to affect the amount of low-pass filtering in your mix.

Step Nine:
When the AULowpass window first opens, you will notice a grid. The grid represents the frequency and volume of the resulting filter. The yellow dot will be on the right-hand side at 6,900 Hz and 0 dB. If you click on this dot

and slide it to the left, you will notice the sound quality changing. Pull the dot to the left and stop at 555 Hz. Next pull the dot down until it reads -10 dB. This combination should create an effect that sounds like the band is playing in the distance.

Figure 3.14
Editing the audio effect.

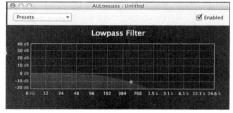

Figure 3.15 Editing the Low-Pass filter settings.

Step Ten:
Once having gone through all of these steps, the low-pass effect will be available for any subsequent Audio Cue added. This process can be replicated for any type of mono-output audio effect desired. Simply add an AU effect to another cue output, rename it, and it will also be available for all cues. It is worth noting that multiple AU effects can be applied to one given cue output. You can combine together a graphic EQ, delay, and hi-pass filter to one cue output, if desired.

3.7 Multichannel Audio File Usage

One final thought to consider once you have set up QLab 3 as the playback component of your Audio System is the use of multichannel audio files. If you have an audio device with more than two channels of output, you can configure your system for directional sound playback through the individual output channels (as seen in Section 3.1). In this type of system, you can either route an individual Audio Cue through the chosen outputs on a cue-by-cue basis or you can create a **multichannel audio file**, a specific type of audio file (typically

WAV) that contains a number of channels imbedded within it. In this case, QLab automatically recognizes the number of channels present in the audio file and assigns them to the respective output channels of your device. Simply put, by using a multichannel audio file, you can create a directional mix at your DAW, rather than spending the time assigning multiple files to outputs within QLab.

As for the creation of these files, there are a number of DAWs on the market that can output multichannel WAV files. Audacity is one such program – downloadable free for Windows, Mac, and Linux available under the GNU General Public License (meaning the software is an open source, free software that can be changed to suit your needs and free to share with others). You can record live audio or edit audio files in Audacity and save as mono, stereo, or multichannel audio formats. In addition to DAWs, there are also programs available that can take individual mono sound files and combine them together into a multichannel audio file. One such program is SoundFilesMerger, which combines multiple audio files and exports them as either AIF or WAV format.

Like any system, there are pros and cons to using multichannel audio files. On the positive side, you can use one file that contains several outputs imbedded within it. This means that one could create complex sound effects with multiple layers, each coming from a different direction, without the need to input multiple different audio files. This makes it much easier to organize. On the other hand, let's say you created a complex car crash sequence in this fashion and everything works perfectly – except for the fact that your director hates the car horn. In this case, you would have to go back to your DAW and redo the entire file to correct that one component. Had you created a Group Cue with each section imbedded as a child within, you could simply replace that one sound effect on the fly and play it back for the director. So, even though programming a Group Cue might be more work up front, it allows for flexibility and has the potential to save time in the tech process. Another consideration might be the computer used for playback. Multichannel audio files use a considerable amount of CPU than running multiple mono or stereo audio files concurrently. If you don't have an abundance of RAM, perhaps the multichannel route is not best for your given situation. As with many of the other QLab features, versatility is the key. What is right in one situation will not be true in another. Knowing that you have the ability to achieve the same goals in multiple ways is a cornerstone of the QLab platform.

Getting to Know QLab Sound Control

Sound control has always been a benchmark of QLab and remains one of the greatest strengths of the QLab 3 system. The following chapters deal with understanding the intricacies of QLab 3 as related to sound control.

4.1 Understanding Cues and the Cue Structure

Cues are the foundation of most traditional control systems for live performance, be it lighting, sound, effects, or projections. In theatre, the time-tested model is assigning specific cue numbers to each type of event to occur during the live performance and then allowing the stage manager to call them out and the operators to hit a go button, thereby triggering the cue. Within QLab, the structure is quite similar in that any QLab file will be composed of multiple cues with varying specific functions combined into a single workspace for playback purposes. Understanding this structure and how cues function within the QLab system is essential to mastering the software.

What Is a Cue?

In the simplest terms, a cue is a QLab command with an assigned function. For instance, an Audio Cue is a command assigned to play back a given audio file. A Fade Cue raises or lowers the volume of an Audio Cue or changes the attributes of other cue types. A MIDI Cue sends a MIDI message, and so forth. Once you insert a cue into your workspace, it automatically becomes part of a cue list. The **Current Cue List** is shown in the middle row of the page, the largest allocation of space in the workspace. In this window, cues are shown in their playback order featuring a wealth of information about the individual cues in the cue list. An individual cue and all of its listed information is referred to as the **Cue Row**.

Visually, each cue row features all the necessary information about the given cue and all its properties. The cue row contains (in order from left to right):

1. **Cue Status:** This is the first column to the left side of the row, listing information like whether the cue is on deck, active (running), broken, or flagged. There are particular icons to indicate each of these different statuses (see Figure 4.1).

   The playback position icon, a large gray arrowhead pointing toward a cue, denotes the playback position of the cue list. This icon indicates which cue in on-deck to be played when the Go button is pressed. It will be always located first in the cue row.

   Once you press Go, the play head will move to the next cue in your cue list, and an active cue icon will appear beside the cue being played back. This icon is a small green arrowhead pointing toward the active cue.

   A red x icon indicates a broken cue, or one with some programming error that disables its playback. Whenever you see this icon, the cue will not be able to perform its intended function until the error is addressed.

   Finally, a cue can be flagged as a visual reminder. Flagging is addressed in detail in Section 4.2. For now, know that flagging a cue will not change its intended behavior.

2. **Cue Type:** Each cue performs a specific function, whether it is audio playback, video, fading, or sending MIDI signals. The second column in the cue row indicates the type of cue by inserting an icon as a graphic representation of the type of cue.

3. **Cue Number:** Each cue will have a unique number to identify it for playback. When a cue is created, QLab uses a chronological numbering system based on your preferences established in the Settings menu. Typically, cues will be numbered by a sequence of 1. You can later change the cue number, but no two cues can have an identical number. Likewise, should you choose to assign letters to your cues, this can be done. Just be aware that there

PLAYBACK POSITION

BROKEN CUE

ACTIVE CUE

FLAGGED CUE

Figure 4.1
Status icons.

is no built-in system for assigning letters, and each cue would have to be named manually or by using scripts.

4. **Cue Name:** The fourth column lists the cue name. Many cues have a default name, such as the name of their target file. If you choose to do so, however, the cue name can be changed to anything. Simply double-click the cue name, type in a new one, and press enter.

5. **Cue Target:** The fifth column indicates the cue target – the file or QLab cue accessed upon playback. A target may be a file (such as an audio file) or another cue in the workspace.

6. **Cue Timing and Duration:** The following three columns entitled Pre-Wait, Action, and Post-Wait all relate to the cue timing and duration. Pre-Wait refers to the amount of time set to insert a wait before the action (i.e. adding a 1-second pause before a scream is heard). The Action column lists the duration of the cue (how long it will play). Finally, the Post-Wait refers to the amount of time set to be inserted as a wait after the action occurs.

7. **Continue Mode:** The final column in the cue row indicates the cue's continue status. Frequently, a number of cues need to be arranged in such a fashion as to have multiple cues fire simultaneously or to have a subsequent cue start the exact moment one ends. To address these needs, QLab allows three options: Do not continue, Auto-continue, and Auto-follow. Do not continue is the default setting, and as such, there is no icon to indicate this setting. Auto-continue (firing both cues simultaneously) is indicated by a down arrow, whereas auto-follow (firing the subsequent cue once the first is completed) uses a down arrow with a circle at the top. These icons are illustrated in Figure 4.2.

Cue Lists

Cue lists are the collection of cues organized together for a purpose. When you click Go, the cue list will play back cues in the order they were programmed from the top of the list to the bottom (unless special cues are inserted to change the playback order). The playback position icon shows which cue is "on-deck" or ready to fire. Once you reach the end of your cue list, hitting Go will perform no action unless the playback position is reset to a cue within the cue list. Any workspace can have one or multiple numbers of cue lists within it.

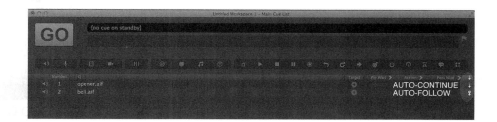

Figure 4.2
Continue mode icons.

Pro-Tip ▼

Time Display Modes

For Pre-Wait, Action, and Post-Wait columns, time information can be displayed in one of two different modes: Time Elapsed or Time Remaining. The default setting for any new cues is Time Elapsed, showing the amount of time that has passed in the cue's playback. The alternate method shows the amount of time remaining, more like a countdown. To toggle between these different modes, simply click on the angled bracket icon beside the Pre-Wait, Action, and Post-Wait headings. You can assign different time display modes for each of the three columns. Personally, I prefer setting Pre-Wait and Post-Wait as Time Remaining and the Action as Time Elapsed, as this makes more sense to me. Whatever method you choose, consistency is recommended, so that you don't confuse your operator.

Cue Sequences

Cue sequences essentially mean the order in which cues progress and how they interact with subsequent cues. As described in the cue properties earlier, each cue has a continue mode. Cues can be set up to have no continue, auto-continue, or auto-follow. For some projects, you could link together every cue in the cue list to play automatically after the first cue is fired. The image frequently used to discuss this concept is a series of dominoes: tipping the first domino will cause all the subsequent dominoes to fall until a stopping point is inserted.

In addition to playback cues, there are also special types of control cues that can manipulate the cue sequence. For instance, a go-to cue could redirect the cue sequence to a cue out of the regular order.

Playback Position

There is only one playback position for a cue list. You can select any cue within your cue list and make that as your playback position. Once a cue sequence has been fired, then the playback position will move to the beginning of the next cue sequence (skipping broken cues).

4.2 The Workspace

Within QLab, each new document you create is called a workspace. A workspace is the collection of cue lists and cues that will be played back for your live performance. Understanding the workspace system is fundamental to mastering QLab. In the following section, refer to Figure 4.3 to identify the various workspace components. The workspace is broken into four separate rows in that each contains subsets of control and information.

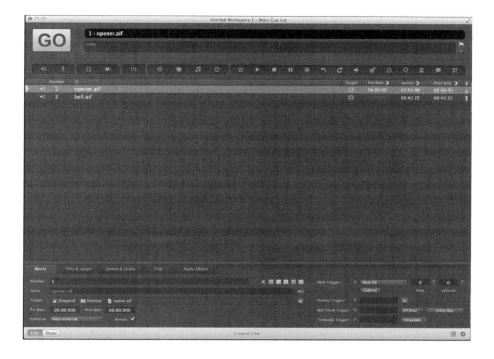

Figure 4.3
The QLab
workspace.

GO/Standby/Notes Panel/Flag

For each workspace, the top row will contain a panel used to both control the cues and view information about them. In the left corner is the GO button. This button, when clicked, triggers any selected cue. In addition to clicking the button with the mouse, the GO button can be activated by clicking the spacebar on your keyboard.

Looking to the right of the GO button will reveal the Standby Window. This window displays the cue selected to play once the GO button is clicked. By default, it will show both the cue number and the name.

Directly beneath the Standby Window is the Notes panel. The function of the Notes panel is to allow for creating a note specific to a cue. Although displayed as a small row in the Edit view, once QLab is placed in Show mode, the window is substantially larger and allows for the programmer to leave notes that might be beneficial or informative for the QLab operator.

Finally, in the lower right-hand corner of the row, there is a flag icon with a checkbox beside it. Clicking this button will flag the selected cue, placing a flag icon in the cue row and also activating a small icon in the bottom right-hand corner of the screen of a triangle with an exclamation point inside. Clicking on this button adds the selected cue to the Broken Cues and Warnings window; a listing of any broken cues or warnings within your workspace. Flagging a cue is a great way to mark a cue that you want to revisit at a later time to correct as the flag does not change anything about the playback of the cue but simply marks it for easy reference.

Toolbar

The second row of the Workspace is a graphic interface called the Toolbar, used for adding cues to your cue list. The Toolbar is visually divided into five different sections: Audio, Video, Fades, MIDI/OSC, and Control Cues. We will delve into the function of these cue types in the following chapters, but the basic use of each category should be relatively self-explanatory.

By clicking on any of the icons in the Toolbar, a cue will be added to your workspace directly after the selected cue. This method essentially leaves the cue as a place keeper until you access the cue and link it to a media file or assign its specific action. In addition, you could also drag new cues into a specific location directly from the Cue Bar.

The Current Cue List

The third row, which takes up the majority of the workspace, is the Current Cue List. Any cue added to your workspace will appear in this cue list. Each cue will be organized in a list fashion, with individual cues on separate rows containing all the pertinent information about the cue (such as cue type, number, file name, target, timing, and cue duration). The organization of all cues into a logical playback order is the foundation of QLab.

Pro-Tip ▼

For those users of QLab 3 who are transitioning from Version 2, two noticeably absent features in the graphic interface are the Toolbox and Load to Time Panel. Though they are not constantly present in Version 3, there are still quick keys that can be used to access these popular tools.

Cue Toolbox
The Toolbox is a hidden interface very similar in function to the Tool Bar. Pressing ⌘K will open the Toolbox in the left-hand side of the Cue List window (Figure 4.4). For beginners, I recommend leaving the Toolbox open while programming for the simple fact that each icon has the cue name typed out beside it. This allows for ease in selecting cues while you are

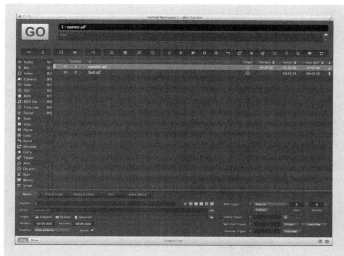

Figure 4.4
The toolbox.

unaccustomed to the icons' meanings. If you are working with a small screen, though, it certainly does eat up a lot of screen space.

Load to Time Panel

Load to Time is a function that enables loading a cue to a particular time, rather than having to play from the beginning. ⌘T will open the panel, replacing the Toolbar (Figure 4.5). There are two methods of loading to a time: either by typing in the desired time on the left side of the panel or by using the scrub bar to slide the circle icon to a particular point in the cue. Once you have the desired time selected, pressing the space bar will play the cue from that selected point. A useful, though little known, function of the Load to Time panel is the ability to input a negative time. By inserting a negative time (i.e. −10), the toolbar will automatically load up your cue or cue sequence to a point that is 10 seconds **from the end** of playback. This comes in handy for those moments where you just need to go to the end of a sequence.

Figure 4.5
The Load to Time panel.

It is worth noting that, until you press the "Done" button on the right-hand corner of the Load to Time panel, it will stay up for all subsequent cues. This means that, for those who preferred the old organizational system, you could simply open the Toolbox and Load to Time panel and leave them open for the duration of your cueing session (though it does cover up the Toolbar).

Inspector Panel

The Inspector Panel, located in the third row, is likely the most used component of the QLab workspace, as it describes every available parameter for the selected cue in the cue list. Depending on the cue type, there will be two to seven different tabs in the Inspector Panel, allowing the programmer to affect every aspect of playback related to the cue. Much of Chapter 5 is dedicated to exploring the function of the Inspector Panel.

Edit/Show

The bottom row of the workspace is noticeably different in appearance, with a light gray background framing in the bottom portion of the program window. In the left-hand portion of this row, there are two buttons: one labeled Edit and the other Show. This marks another new approach to function for QLab 3 over previous versions. In the past, there was only one workspace, and upon completing the programming, the workspace could be locked to ensure that the operator did not accidentally change any aspect of the show. In Version 3, there are actually two different modes dedicated to these different roles. Edit Mode allows the programmer to access all the control functions of any cue, whereas Show Mode only allows for playback and locks out the editing of any cue in the workspace.

Workspace Information

In the middle of the bottom row, there is a short informational section detailing the number of cues and cue lists used in your workspace.

Broken Cues and Warnings Panel

Moving to the right-hand corner of the bottom row, there will be either two or three icons, depending on your programming. The first icon, Broken Cues and Warnings, is only present if your workspace has either broken cues or if the programmer added warning flags, as mentioned earlier. A broken cue is displayed as a red x in the cue row of the affected cue. By clicking on the Broken Cues and Warnings button, a panel will open replacing the Inspector Panel. This panel lists each cue that is broken or flagged and details the warning for the said cue. This is a fast way to look over a cue list and determine what errors need correcting.

Cue Lists and Active Cues Panel

The next icon shown on the bottom right-hand corner is the Cue Lists and Active Cues Panel. By clicking on this button, a sub-panel will open in the right-hand corner of the current cue list (Figure 4.6). This panel performs three functions: to show available cue lists, to show which cues are active (currently playing), and to control the playback state of all active cues.

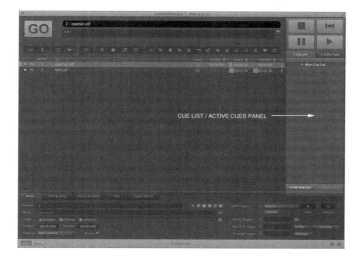

Figure 4.6
The cue list/active
cues panel.

Cue Lists

The programmer has the potential for creating an unlimited number of cue lists for any QLab workspace. This function allows for a thorough organizational structure. Think of using one cue list for pre-show music, one for different acts within a play, intermission, etc. Although this is not necessary, it can reduce the workspace clutter for a particularly large production. In addition to using a cue list for playback purposes, sometimes I will create a cue list as a quick palette from which I copy/paste into my current cue list and then delete it after programming.

In terms of creating cue lists, you can select any cue or number of cues from your current cue list and simply click on the +Add New List button to move them from your current cue list into a new cue list. In addition, once a cue list has been created, you can simply drag cues from your current cue list into the desired cue list. If you want to add the cues to the new cue list without removing them from the current list, simply select the files and copy and paste them into the new cue list. If you need to delete a cue list, select the desired cue list and click on the Delete Cue List button. It should be noted that cue lists are treated as any other cue type in QLab – they are simply a cue that holds other cues within them. By clicking on a cue list, you will notice that a set of options appears in the Inspector Panel called Basics and Sync. These preferences control the basic naming functions as well as allow for the triggering of a cue list through Hotkey, MIDI, Wall Clock, or Timecode.

Cue lists are tied to group cues in a fundamental way. If you have a Group Cue created in your workspace and drag it into the Cue Lists Panel, it will automatically create a cue list. Likewise, dragging a cue list from the Cue Lists Panel into the current cue list will result in creating a Group Cue containing the selected cues.

Active Cues

Clicking on the Active Cues tab opens a panel showing the number of active cues (or cues currently in playback on your cue list). Depending on your workspace state, there will be a varying number displayed on the Active Cues tab. If nothing is currently active, it will read 0 Active Cues, and clicking on it will only show a blank screen. When there are active cues, though, clicking on the tab will reveal a list of active cues and their time elapsed (how long they have been playing) with an x button listed at the end of each row (Figure 4.7). This x represents a panic button that, when activated, will fade the selected cue out over a 5-second duration. This panel can be incredibly useful when using Fade Cues in a cue list. A Fade Cue can mute the volume of an audio cue, but unless it is set to "stop target when done," the audio cue will continue to play, though muted. If you have a series of these cues playing in the background, the CPU usage goes up even though they are muted. Using the Active Cues Panel is a quick way to spot if you have cues playing longer than their desired duration.

Active Cue Control

At the top of the Cue List and Active Cues Panel, you will find four buttons used to control the playback of all active cues. There is Stop All, which stops all cues. The Reset All button stops playback and resets all cues to their original state (i.e. moving the playback position back to the beginning of the cue, etc.). Finally, the Pause All button pauses all currently running cues, whereas the Resume All button resumes playback of all paused cue.

4.3 Adding Cues

New cues are added in one of two ways. The first, mentioned earlier, is to use the Toolbox or Toolbar to insert a cue place keeper and then assign a target and attributes within the cue. The second way is by simply dragging a media file into the cue list. By doing this, the appropriate cue type will be generated, and the target will be pre-established.

Figure 4.7
The active cues panel.

4.4 Setting Targets for Cues

For most cues in the workspace, there will be a target, and no cue can have more than one target. As mentioned earlier, a target is either a media file or another cue within the cue list to be affected by the selected cue. If inserting cues as place keepers, as mentioned earlier, you will eventually need to assign a target for your cue. Like most functions in QLab, there are multiple ways to do this.

For cues that play media files (sound, video, MIDI), the method is different than from cues that affect other cues (fades, control cues). For media playback cues, you can click on the arrow icon in the Target column, and a window will appear in which you select the desired file and click open (see Figure 4.8). If this method seems to be time consuming, another option is to simply drag and drop the desired media file into the cue row. This will automatically target the file. Be careful to actually drop it on the desired cue, though, and not above or below, as this will have the undesired effect of creating a new cue rather than targeting the cue in question.

For setting the target on a cue that affects other cues, you either drag the desired target cue (i.e. Fade cue) onto the receiving cue (the Audio Cue to be faded up or down in volume) or double-click on the target column and use your keyboard to input the cue number of the desired target cue. When attempting to set a target through the drag and drop method, the cue will show you if the targeted file is of a type that can affect. If you drag your cue to another and a blue rectangle appears surrounding the potential target cue, this means that it can be set as the target (see Figure 4.9). If this does not occur, the

Figure 4.8
The open target window.

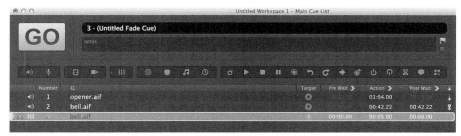

Figure 4.9
The blue rectangle indicates a target-able file type.

cue is not an acceptable type for your cue. Examples for this would be trying to assign a Fade Cue to another Fade Cue. In this case, one Fade Cue cannot target another, so the blue rectangle would not appear.

4.5 Navigation and View Quick Keys

As with most programs, there are a number of quick keys to increase productivity. Some of the most useful shortcuts for navigating your Workspace are listed below.

Shortcut	Description
↓	Select the next cue (when cue list is selected)
↑	Select the previous cue (when cue list is selected)
+	Move to the top of the next cue sequence
-	Move to the top of the last cue sequence
→	Expand the selected Group Cue
←	Collapse the selected Group Cue
>	Expand all Group Cues in the cue list
<	Collapse all Group Cues in the cue list
⌘↓	Select the next cue
⌘↑	Select the previous cue
⌘→	Select the next Inspector tab
⌘←	Select the previous Inspector tab
option-⌘↑	Move the Playback position up
option-⌘↓	Move the Playback position down
⌘I	Open/Hide Inspector panel
⌘K	Open/Hide Tool Box
⌘L	Open/Hide Cue Lists/Active Cues panel
⇧⌘L	Toggle between Cue Lists/Active Cues
⌘B	Toggle Broken Cues and Warnings panel
⌘,	Open Settings

Pro-Tip ▼

Searching the Workspace

One great productivity function in QLab 3 is the ability to search for text within your cue list. Simply click ⌘F, and a search tool will open in the place of the Toolbar. Insert the text you want to search for, and QLab will search through the cue numbers, cue names, file names, and notes to find the text you inputted. It will highlight all the results featuring the text, and then you can use the arrow key controls in the search tool to jump from result to result until you find the desired reference.

4.6 The Tools Menu

In addition to the number of functions available through quick keys or buttons, there are also a number of productivity tools located under the Tools heading in the control window at the top of the screen. These tools can either be activated through the Tools menu, or by selecting the quick key listed below.

Load to Time – ⌘T

Using the command T function toggles the Load to Time Menu with the Toolbar.

Renumber Selected Cues – ⌘R

This tool allows the programmer to select a group of cues and renumber them. Upon pressing command R, a pop-up window will appear asking for the start number and increment of change for subsequent cues.

Delete Number of Selected Cues – ⌘D

Similar to the last tool, this one selects the cue numbers of a selected sequence of cues. The main difference is that, instead of renumbering, this tool simply deletes the cue numbers altogether.

Jump to Cue – ⌘J

This tool allows for quickly moving to a cue within the cue list. Simply click command J and a pop-up window will appear, asking which cue number you would like to jump to.

Copy or Paste Levels – Shift + ⌘C/Shift + ⌘V

Many cues have levels settings that indicate the playback volume of the selected cue. If you wish to copy levels from one cue and apply them to another, you may do so using this tool.

Copy or Paste Integrated Fade Shape – Control + ⌘C/ Control + ⌘V

Like the tool above, this one allows for the copying and pasting, but of integrated fade shapes. An integrated fade is an increase or decrease of volume within an Audio Cue separate from an actual Fade Cue. Using this tool, you can copy and paste an integrated fade shape from one Audio Cue to another.

4.7 The Window Menu

There are two tools not immediately apparent in looking at the workspace, both hidden away in the Window menu at the top of the screen. The first of these tools, the **Audition Window** is a new component in QLab 3 that dramatically changes the way in which you can view your cues while editing (Figure 4.10). To open the audition window, either click Window > Audition window or type ⌘ + shift + A. The purpose of the Audition Window is to allow the editing of cues while they playback. Once opened, the audition window serves as a new destination in which audio and video cues will play back (instead of the normal patch to which it is assigned). The benefit of this is the ability to edit and see your results in real time – especially beneficial for Video Cues.

The second window tool is the **Timecode Window**, a special window that will open to display incoming timecode for your workspace. By clicking Window > Timecode, you will open the window as a moveable screen (Figure 4.11). This window will display the message "waiting…" until the timecode is received; once a transmitted timecode is detected, the counter will begin ticking away. This is particularly useful in situations for which timecode is used as a trigger.

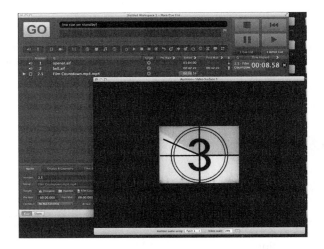

Figure 4.10
The audition window allows for live previewing of cue playback without leaving your workspace.

Figure 4.11
The timecode window.

60

Audio Cues

Audio Cues are the foundation upon which QLab was built. The first versions of the software dealt specifically with audio playback, though soon thereafter incorporated a number of new features. The purpose of an Audio Cue is simple, to play back an audio file. Though the function of it is simple, the complexity with which the Audio Cue can be manipulated is quite impressive. The following chapter delves into the Audio Cue in detail and explores its use and execution.

5.1 Inserting an Audio Cue

Like any other cue, an Audio Cue can be inserted through the Toolbar, Tool Box, or by dragging an audio file directly into the cue list. QLab 3 supports wide range of audio file types including WAV, AIF, MP3, and MP4. Likewise, the audio file can be mono, stereo, or multichannel audio.

5.2 Inspector Panel: Basics

Once an Audio Cue is inserted into your cue list, the Inspector Panel can be used to access a wide range of control functions related to the cue. There are five tabs within the Inspector Panel that house a number of these functions: Basics, Time & Loops, Device & Levels, Trim, and Effects. Each of these tabs contains specific control functions that affect the playback of the given Audio Cue. The first tab, Basics, allows for manipulating the baseline information about the audio cue. The tab is divided into two sections: cue info and triggering (Figure 5.1).

Figure 5.1
The Basics tab
contains cue
information and
triggering options.

Cue Info

Aligned to the left half of the screen, cue basics deals with information related to cue numbering, naming, targeting, and playback. The following list includes all the control parameters.

- Number: Assign a cue number.
- Color: Assign a specific color to the cue row. Each given cue row can have one of five colors. This allows for ease in assigning a visual representation for certain cue types (i.e. red for sound, yellow for projections, green for MIDI,etc.).
- Name: This input allows for the naming of the cue. In addition, beside the name window, there will be an icon that communicates what type of cue it is.
- Target: Assign a specific target file to your cue.
- Pre-Wait/Post-Wait: Assign a pre- or post-wait to the selected cue.
- Continue: Establish the continue status of the cue as do not continue, auto-continue, or auto-follow.
- Armed: This button allows for you to arm the given cue. Arming a cue means that it will perform its assigned action and pre-/post-waits. The default is for a cue to be armed. Should you chose to disarm a cue, it will still perform pre- and post-waits, but not execute the cue action.

Triggering

QLab allows for versatility in control, offering an ability to personalize playback control for different installations. The triggering window allows the programmer to expand the control possibilities from simply pressing a Go button to allowing the versatility of MIDI, hotkey, wall clock, or Timecode triggering.

- **MIDI Trigger:** This button allows for the programmer to control QLab actions through MIDI, using either a MIDI keyboard or an another device that sends MIDI control signals. By selecting this function, you could give total control to a performer who could trigger effects from the stage simultaneously with their musical performance.

Pro-Tip ▼

Assigning a MIDI Trigger

One of the most common functions of using the MIDI triggering is to assign a key on a MIDI keyboard as a trigger for the cue. By clicking on "Note on" in the MIDI Trigger window, this sets the cue to be triggered by a note being pressed on a MIDI keyboard attached to the system. You can input the numeric value for that note in the Note input and assign a velocity to it (meaning the note must be kept with certain intensity in order to trigger the cue) in the Velocity input. One timesaver is clicking the "Capture" button. After doing so, a message will appear reading "waiting for MIDI" beside the capture button. If you press a MIDI key, it will assign the note and velocity to match this action.

Sometimes velocity can be a sensitive issue in assigning triggers, and you may want to avoid assigning a velocity at all. In this case, simply insert the words "any" or "all" in the velocity input. This will make the cue trigger any time that MIDI note is played on the keyboard. You can also enter "greater than" or "less than" amounts for more precise control (i.e. <10 or >10).

- **Hotkey Trigger:** This window allows you to set any key on the keyboard as the trigger for a specific cue. Once assigned, either the spacebar or the assigned hotkey will trigger the action. To set a hotkey, simply click in the input window beside Hotkey Trigger and then click the button you want to assign to the action hotkey. Once you do so, this will automatically place a check in the check box, noting that the hotkey is active. To deactivate, you can uncheck the checkbox. To remove it altogether, simply click on the "x" button to the right of the input window.

Note that, when assigning Hotkeys, there are certain keys already used by the workspace. In this case, a warning message will appear reading, "Hotkey used by workspace." These keys cannot be assigned as the action hotkey unless you first go to the Settings window and remove them from the Key Map. In general, you can use any key or key combination on your keyboard excluding the Command key, as it is reserved for other functions.

- **Wall Clock Trigger:** The wall clock trigger allows you to assign an action at a particular time on the computer's clock. To do so, simply input a time in either 24-hour mode (military time) or standard time (selecting either AM or PM). For instance, if you were creating an installation to play a movie at 6 PM every day, you could simply input 18:00:00 or 06:00:00 with PM selected in the drop-down menu. Once checked, QLab would execute the action at that time every day. Should you need to change the event to only occur on a certain day, simply click on the "Every Day" button and select the desired day(s).

- **Timecode Trigger:** Every cue in a QLab workspace can be triggered by an incoming timecode – either MIDI (MTC) or Linear (SMTPE). The last setting in the triggers portion allows for assigning a timecode for when your cue should fire. Likewise, one could input the real time in seconds for when the cue should fire. For either method, it is essential to make sure your selected cue list is configured to accept incoming timecode.

To do this, open the Cue List panel (⌘L) and select the desired cue list. The Inspector Panel will now feature two tabs: Basics and Sync. Click on the Sync tab and select the checkbox reading "Trigger cues in this list from incoming timecode." Select the appropriate settings (mode, sync source, SMTPE format) to match your timecode (see Figure 5.2). When completed, this will allow your cue list to be triggered from an external timecode.

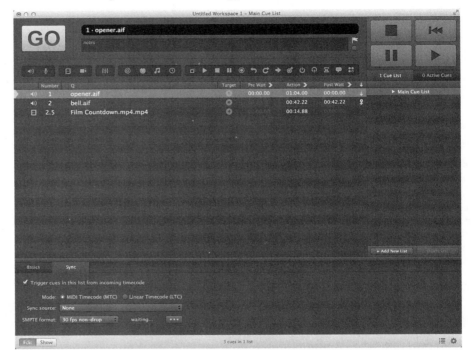

Figure 5.2
The Sync tab for a cue list contains options for triggering the cue list through timecode.

5.3 Inspector Panel: Time & Loops

The Time & Loops panel contains a number of different functions for manipulating the playback of an Audio Cue (see Figure 5.3). In short, these functions

Figure 5.3
The Time & Loops panel.

control start/end time of an Audio Cue, number of times it is played, integrated volume levels (dynamics), and rate of playback (tempo).

The Waveform Display

The waveform display visually takes up the majority of the Time & Loops panel. In fact, all the other control functions in the Time & Loops panel directly affect the waveform; so it is wise to address the waveform display before moving on to the other tools in the Time & Loops panel.

For those unfamiliar with the concept, a waveform is a graph that illustrates the change of amplitude (volume) of a sound over a certain period of time. In an audio waveform, the x-axis (horizontal) represents elapsed time, whereas the y-axis (vertical) represents volume. Waveforms have been an essential component of audio editing software for years. A waveform can give a lot of information to the use without having to even listen to the recording. For instance, look at Figure 5.4 to see the comparison of two waveforms.

The first waveform shows a sound file recorded at a very low level. There are very few peaks that crest above the baseline. Without ever listening to this file, the experienced operator could tell that the levels for this file would need to be boosted. Likewise, looking at the second waveform, one can see that the peaks take up the majority of the window. In this case, the recorded levels were too high making for a "hot" recording. In this case, you would want to diminish the output levels before playing the track and putting undue stress on your speakers.

Looking at the QLab waveform display, you will notice that the elapsed time of an Audio Cue is listed at the top of the display. This in a handy tool for determining exact timing on fades and cuts within the track. One handy function of the waveform display is the ability to modify the Audio Cue's start time or end time. When a new Audio Cue is inserted, the waveform will show a faint yellow line with a downward-pointing arrowhead at the beginning and

Figure 5.4
The two waveforms offer up a lot of information about their audio files.

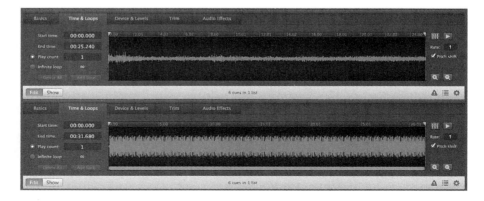

Figure 5.5
Waveform
start/end.

end of the waveform (see Figure 5.5). This indicates the start time and end time of the cue.

All Audio Cues default to the start time and end time of the inserted audio file, though you might find it useful to change this for your playback purposes. One of the best examples of this function comes when importing sound files from compact disc. There might be a brief pause recorded at the beginning of the file, which would cause the Audio Cue to appear late, even if triggered at the appropriate time. By setting the start time at the true start of the audio file, this problem can be averted. To achieve this, simply slide the start icon to the appropriate location on the waveform, and this will become your new start time. This process is quite simple, given the ability to visually see where the audio begins on the waveform. It might take some slight adjustment to get your timing precise, but it is infinitely simpler than the old method of editing the file, burning it to disc, and then trying again. As you might have guessed, the process is identical if you want to change the end time of a cue. Simply slide the end time icon to the desired stopping point in your waveform.

Pro-Tip ▼

The process of changing the start/end time of an Audio Cue (and all other changes made to an Audio Cue within QLab, for that matter) are considered **non-destructive**. Even though the unwanted audio occurring before the start time or after the end time is trimmed away, the data still remain as part of the original audio file. This process is referred to as non-destructive, meaning the original file is not changed in any way but only the manner of its playback.

Waveform Zoom

One of the important control functions of the waveform is the zoom in and zoom out buttons. By clicking on the zoom in button, the waveform is magnified, giving the programmer the ability to view it with more precision. You will note that, as the waveform is magnified, it no longer fits in the window in its entirety. To view the entire timeline of the waveform, simply grab the scrub bar at the bottom of the waveform window and slide it to the right or left. When magnified, you might notice that what seemed like a millisecond of time may be more substantial than originally thought. This is why the zoom controls are essential for accurate editing or trimming, especially if the intention is to create a seamless loopable file.

Pro·Tip ▼

Like many other Macintosh-based programs, QLab incorporates the use of Multi-Touch gestures for many functions. If you have a track pad, either on your laptop or the external Bluetooth variety, you can use Multi-Touch gestures to accomplish the waveform zoom without clicking the magnify or reduce buttons. Simply position your cursor in the waveform display and perform a two-fingered scroll to zoom. Slide two finger up to magnify or two fingers down to reduce. In addition, a mouse scroll-wheel will function in the same fashion.

Preview Cue

The Preview Cue button (shown in Figure 5.3) is a tool that is used for testing the playback of an Audio Cue without having to press the Go button and advance to the next playback position. The preview button, when inactive, displays the standard play icon. Once activated, you will notice it changes to a pause icon, enabling you to pause playback.

Times, Loops, and Slices

To the left third of the Time & Loops panel, there is a column with five rows (Figure 5.6). These five rows control the basic functions of start time, end time, and number of times the Audio Cue might loop. The use of each function is described in the following text.

- **Start Time:** This panel allows the programmer to type in the exact start time of the Audio Cue, down to thousandths of a second. This allows for trimming off unwanted audio at the beginning of a sound file.

Figure 5.6
Control functions:
Time, loops, and
slices.

- **End Time:** This panel offers the same type of control function as start time, except it allows for trimming off any unwanted audio at the end of a file. The input process is the same, and anything after the inputted timecode will not play back (once again, in a non-destructive fashion). This function is particularly useful when you need to have one cue auto-follow another, but the first cue has "dead air" at the end. By manipulating the end time, you can create a seamless auto-follow scenario.
- **Play Count:** The play count establishes the number of times a cue will play back. By default, all cues default to one, meaning that they will play only once. One can easily set the play count to loop two or more times. Note that the action of the cue will increase for each loop cycle, meaning the action of a 1-second audio cue looped four times would become 4 seconds.
- **Infinite Loop:** Sometimes, you will find yourself in a situation in which a cue must be looped endlessly until faded out. To accomplish this, simply click the Infinite Loop button. This function is particularly useful for special effects loops like crickets (something every designer should have in their collection) without actually using a 30-minute audio recording. Special attention must be paid to original audio file, though, to make sure it is truly "loopable." Having even a tenth of a second of silence or difference in the end of the file versus the beginning will draw attention to the loop and destroy the intended effect.
- **Slices:** Slicing is a new function within QLab 3 that allows for the looping of internal sections of an Audio or Video Cue. This simple addition adds multiple layers of flexibility to sound playback, particularly in the tech situation. Frequently, sound designers are called on to create music or effects to play over scenic transitions in a play. One common problem is in the timing of how long it takes for the shift from one scene to another. Often, the sound designer must lengthen a particular piece of music to match the complexity of the scenic shift. In the past, this always meant going back to the DAW to record a new, longer section of music. With slices, though, a designer can feasibly locate a section within the music to repeat, thereby lengthening the music.

To insert a loop into a cue, simply click the location in the waveform to place the end of your slice. Likewise, if you created the file in an audio editing software with markers, those markers will translate into slices automatically when imported to QLab. If you want the first 3 seconds of an Audio Cue to repeat, place your cursor at the 3-second position in the waveform viewer and click the "add Slice" button. Once you have done this, you will notice that a handle appears at the top of the waveform timeline similar to the playback position icon in your cue list. This indicates the end of the slice. To fine-tune the ending position, simply grab the slice position icon in the timeline and slide it to the desired location.

Once a slice is inserted, two numbers will appear at the bottom of the waveform, both reading 1. This indicates the number of times your slice will loop before proceeding to the next slice. Click on the first number and change it to 2. This will create a slice that plays back twice before progressing to the next section in the Audio Cue. Likewise, if you want to make the loop repeat an infinite number of times, simply insert "inf" instead of a number, and the infinity symbol (∞) will replace it.

If you wish to remove a single slice, simply change the number back to 1, and it will function like it is not there. Likewise, you can grab the handle and pull it out of the workspace to delete it. If you wish to delete all the slices, click on the button labeled "Delete All." Be careful about simply trying to delete the number from the slice, though. If you delete the number, an infinity symbol (∞) will replace it, giving you an infinite loop cycle within your cue.

To end an infinite loop cycle, you must use the DeVamp Cue in conjunction with your Audio Cue. Once triggered, a DeVamp Cue tells a cue to stop repeating and progress to the next slice once the next loop cycle has completed. This is addressed in depth in Chapter 8, Control Cues.

One final use of slices is simply to insert visual markers in your waveform that make it easier to identify key spots during tech. If, for instance, there is a spot in the middle of a song where a certain instrument enters and you want to note that location, simply insert a slice and keep the loop number set to 1. There will be no function to the slice, other than serving as a visual marker for your own use at a later time.

Pro-Tip ▼

There is no quick method for the looping of a file that has slices (infinite or otherwise). You will notice that once a slice is inserted, the play count and infinite loop buttons disappear. To create a fixed loop sequence of any file that has slices, the best option is to copy and paste the cue the number of loops desired and set an auto-follow at the end of each cue except the final in the sequence. If you need to create an infinite loop, copy and paste the cue twice with an auto-follow at the end of the cues. As a final step, insert a Play Cue as the third cue in the sequence and target it back up to the first cue of the sequence. This will create an infinite loop. If all the three cues are inserted into a Group Cue, then you can assign a Fade Cue to this group, allowing for the termination of the loop's playback.

Integrated Volume Levels and Tempo

The last two functions of the Time & Loops panel offer further non-destructive editing options for your audio file. The first of these functions allows the programmer to insert volume changes within the audio cue. In musical terms, this is referred to as dynamics. In QLab, it is referred to as the **Integrated Fade**

Envelope. When you click on the "toggle integrated fade envelope" button, a yellow line will appear placed horizontally across the top of your waveform with a circle at the beginning and end of the line (see Figure 5.7). For users familiar with the volume automation in programs such as Apple's Garageband or Logic, the same basic principles apply to the integrated fade envelope. Like the waveform, the fade envelope works in an x-/y-axis fashion; the horizontal line represents elapsed time, whereas the vertical represents the master volume of the selected Audio Cue. The straight line at the top of the waveform represents 0 dB (unity) with no changes to the output of the audio file. The bottom of the waveform window represents -INF dB, or silence. To add integrated fades to the sound cue, just click on the yellow line at the point in the timeline where you want the volume to change. This will insert a control point, represented by a solid yellow dot on the yellow line. You can now pull this control point down and to either the left or the right in order to create a fade curve. By inserting multiple control points, it is possible to create various different fade curve options. The best way to learn how to shape a fade curve is by experimentation.

Controlling Tempo

The final control function of the Time & Loops panel is called **Rate**. This button allows the programmer to change the rate at which the audio file plays back. In essence, this allows for control of the tempo of an audio file. This function is quite useful given its ability to control pitch shift. Traditionally speaking, when an audio file is sped up, the pitch of all notes within the file would also increase or vice versa if slowed down (think of the effect of playing by changing the rpm settings on a record player). Today, most sophisticated audio editing software allows for the increase or decrease in playback speed without this pitch shift occurring. In QLab, by using the check box beneath the Rate button, one can choose whether to have the pitch shift occur or not. This function allows for versatility.

As discussed earlier in this chapter, many plays feature music or sound effects playing over scenic changes. Consider that you need to cover a 15-second scenic shift, but only have 12 seconds of music. By using the rate function, you could simply insert a rate of .8, and what once took 12 seconds to play would now take 15 seconds. Make sure to deselect the pitch shift button, though, otherwise the pitch of your audio recording will be quite different from the original. Always keep in mind that there is a limit to the amount of rate change one can apply without sounding too fake. Depending on the type of

Figure 5.7
Integrated fade envelope.

instrumentation, it might not work at all for some music, but it is a great tool for certain effects.

Project 5.1 ▼

Manipulating Start/End Times

The following project details the process of setting start time and end time of a file, inserting slices, and changing the playback rate.

Step One:
Download Project 5.1 from the companion website.

Step Two:
Cue 1 is an Audio Cue that contains music with "dead air" at the beginning and end of the file. Select Cue 1 and click on the Time & Loops tab in the Inspector Panel. Note the waveform that shows a flat line at the beginning and end of the audio file.

Step Three:
Using the waveform zoom tool, zoom in to look at the beginning of the Audio Cue. You will see that the audio signal does not begin until almost 2 seconds into the recording.

Step Four:
Slide your cursor to the top left corner of the waveform timeline (where it reads 0.00). You will notice a triangular point at the beginning of the timeline pointing down. There should be a yellow line directly beneath its point. When you hover over this icon, your cursor will change into a new icon: a black vertical line with arrows pointing to the right and left. This controls the placement of the Audio Cue's start time. Slide it to the right, stopping just before your audio signal begins in the waveform. You will notice that the area before the yellow line will now turn blue, indicating that it will not be played back as part of the Audio Cue. Releasing the icon will move the start time to this point.

Step Five:
Move to the end of the waveform. There is roughly 5 seconds of silence at the end of this cue. Slide the arrow icon at the end of the waveform back to the end of the audio signal. Again, you will notice the area past the yellow line will be highlighted in blue. Releasing the icon here will move the end time to this point.

Step Six:
Notice that the Start Time and End Time listed to the left of the Time & Loops tab will now list the exact time in the audio file that playback begins and ends.

Project 5.2 ▼

Adding Slices

Step One:
Download Project 5.2 from the companion website.

Step Two:
Select Cue 1 and click the spacebar. This will fire the cue for playback. The music begins with an introductory phrase that is easily repeatable. For this portion of the project, let us assume that we need to add a few more seconds to the length of the Audio Cue. In this case, it can be easily accomplished by adding a slice that will create a loop within the Audio Cue.

Step Three:
Zoom in to the waveform. The first musical phrase is ideal for creating a loop. If you zoom in to around the 6-second mark, you will see the phrase ends around 5.95 seconds. This would be an ideal location to add a slice. To do so, simply click at this point on the waveform to place your marker. A yellow line will appear where you clicked.

Step Four:
Click on the "Add Slice" button on the left corner of the window. This will add a slice at the location marker. You will see a white number 1 at the center of the slice. This indicates the loop count of the slice; the number of times the slice will repeat. Click on the number and change it to 2.

Step Five:
Select the Audio Cue and click the spacebar. You will hear that the slice repeats twice now. Slice placement must be precise or you might hear a slight "hiccup" at the point of repeat where the end of the slice does not correctly align with the beginning. If this occurs, simply go back to the waveform and slide the yellow line at the slice end until it aligns appropriately to accomplish seamless looping.

Project 5.3 ▼

Manipulating Playback Rate

Sometimes you might find that the Audio Cue playback is slightly too short or long. In the past, this meant going back to your DAW to create a new file. With QLab 3, there is now the possibility of changing the playback rate of the Audio Cue to make it either faster or slower. The following steps detail the process of making an audio file play back at a faster tempo.

Step One:
Download Project 5.3 from the companion website.

Step Two:
Select Cue 1 and click the spacebar. This will fire the cue for playback in its unchanged state. In the Time & Loops window, click on the "Rate" panel to the right of the window. It should read 1. This indicates that the file will play back at its recorded rate. Changing this number will make the playback rate either faster or slower. For instance, insert .9 into the rate panel. Click Go again, and you will notice the Audio Cue plays back at a slower rate. By inputting 1.1, the same file will play back faster.

Step Three:
In these instances, above you will notice that the checkbox labeled "pitch shift" was selected. This is why the audio file sounded very different from the original when fired. If you uncheck the checkbox, you will notice that the pitch remains unchanged from the original when played back at a different rate.

Step Four:
By inputting 1.05 and unchecking the pitch shift box, the resulting Audio Cue will be slightly faster than the original but with an unchanged pitch. Notice that the Start Time and End Time remain the same in the Time & Loops window, but the Action Time in the Cue Row will change to match the true playback time of the Audio Cue.

5.4 Inspector Panel: Device & Levels

Chapters 2 and 3 covered in detail the setup involved for setting up and editing audio devices, audio patching, ganging channels, and creating default levels for new cues. As such, you should be familiar with every function in the Device & Levels panel. Figure 5.8 and the following information should serve as a quick refresher.

Figure 5.8
Device & Levels tab.

Audio Output Patch and Edit Device

Note that the Audio Output Patch allows you to assign which audio device you want to use for this particular Audio Cue. The button to the right of this allows for the editing of the Audio Device.

Default Levels

By clicking on this button, you can set the levels to the pre-assigned default levels set in the Settings window.

Set All to Silent

Clicking on this button will mute all channels.

Assign Gangs

Ganging is a function that allows the linking of control of multiple cue outputs or crosspoints. Simply click on the Assign Gangs button and insert either a number or a letter in the open space beneath any slider (in the window where volume levels normally reside). For instance, place an "A" in the space beneath cue output channels 1 and 2, then click the Assign Gangs button again. This will now have paired output channels 1 and 2, making them move in unison. You will also notice that the two channels have a similar color. Additional gangs will have unique colors, as well.

Visible Channels

This window allows for the change in visible channels. If, for instance, you are only using stereo output, there is no reason to see channels 3–48. Instead, type 2 into the Visible Channels window, and only output channels 1 and 2 will remain visible.

Levels and Crosspoint Matrix

This area of the window is identical to the levels settings seen in the Audio Settings earlier in the book. The Master and all audio inputs are shown in the left hand column. The cue outputs are situated to the right of the Master, with the crosspoint matrix shown beneath for assigning an input channel to the appropriate cue output. Once patched, the sliders control volume, and the Master controls the volume of all other outputs.

Had an Audio Effects been assigned to a cue output, as detailed in Chapter 3, the slider (or sliders) for this effect would be listed (if you gave the effect a unique name).

The true ability to establish directional sound resides in the Levels control panel. Referring to the sound system shown in Figure 5.6, let us imagine that you are designing sound for a play in which a gunshot rings out through the auditorium. The purpose of this should be twofold: to startle the audience and direct their attention to the location in which the actor will enter. If the sound rings out through the rear House Right speaker, then you would want to bring the slider up for Channel 6 and mute all the other sliders. Let us assume, then, that during the tech rehearsal period, the director changes the blocking to have the actor now entering from House Left. Obviously, the gunshot cannot still come from House Right, or the effect would only lead to confusion as the audience looks back and the actor enters on the opposite side. To remedy this, simply mute Channel 6, and bring up Channel 5 instead. Now the gunshot will appear to come from the rear House Left position.

5.5 Inspector Panel: Trim

Trim allows for the adjustment of the volume levels of all cues and fades within a given Fade Cue series (Figure 5.9). We will cover this concept in detail in Chapter 7. For now, simply imagine the trim setting as a way to increase or decrease the volume setting of the target Audio Cue, thereby affecting the volume levels of all the subsequent Fade Cues.

5.6 Inspector Panel: Audio Effects

Like other audio effects explored earlier (applying them globally to either a cue output or a device output), the Audio Effects panel allows for assigning an Audio Unit (AU) as an effect. Unlike the global effects, though, the Audio Effects tab will only affect the selected Audio Cue (Figure 5.10). This is particularly useful in a number of situations.

As a sound designer, the sound of a church bell is one that often pops up in productions. Without fail, though, the number of bell peals provided by the designer never seems to be exactly what the director had in mind. For this

Figure 5.9
Trim tab.

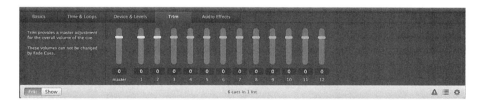

Figure 5.10
Audio effects tab.

example, let us look at a recording of a church bell with three peals. Once in tech, the director decides that two would be more appropriate. The only problem with this scenario is that, in cutting off the last peal, you lose all the reverberation of the bell as it fades out to silence. In this scenario, the Audio Effect would be an ideal choice. The following project will examine how to easily cut this audio file and still maintain the reverberation needed.

Project 5.4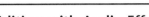

Editing with Audio Effects

The following project details the process of editing the end time of a file while using Audio Effects to disguise the edit.

Step One:
Download Project 5.4 from the companion website.

Step Two:
Play Cue 1. You will notice that it has three bell peals. For this project, we will be changing the end time of the file back so as to cut off the final peal.

Step Three:
Select the Time & Loops tab in the Inspector Panel. In the Waveform Editor, you will see the three distinct peals of the bell. Grab the slider at the end of the waveform and pull it to the left until the yellow line is placed just previous to the third peal.

Step Four:
Play Cue 1 again. You will notice that the sound file ends quite abruptly, without the reverberation of the bell left ringing.

Step Five:
Click on the Audio Effects tab in the Inspector Panel. On the left side of the screen, click the "add effect" button. A drop-down menu will appear. This should display any AUs installed on your computer. In this case, select the Apple button, and then select the AUMatrixReverb button. This will open the control interface for the plug-in.

Step Six:
Click on the "Presets" button in the upper left corner of the AUMatrixReverb control interface. The drop-down menu will reveal several options. Click on the button labeled "Factory." There will be several options that appear in a drop-down menu to the right of the button. Select one of them.

Step Seven:
Go back to the workspace and click go to activate playback of Cue 1. Listen to the effect. Go back to the control interface for the AUMatrixReverb plug-in and change it to a different factory preset. Keep experimenting until you get the right sound.

Mic Cues

Two of the most important functions of any sound system are playback and reinforcement. Historically speaking, QLab has always been particularly strong in the playback area, but noticeably lacking in the ability to add reinforcement to a system. QLab 3 integrated the new Mic Cue to address this deficiency and allow for adding live microphone control, routing, and signal processing effects. The following chapter deals with the use and control of Mic Cues in the QLab workspace.

6.1 Understanding the Mic Cue

At its core, the Mic Cue functions in much the same way as an Audio Cue. It receives an audio signal, outputs the signal through an audio patch, allows for application of audio effects to the signal, and then routes the signal to the patched outputs of an audio device. The main difference between a Mic Cue and an Audio Cue is that, with the Mic Cue, the patch is an audio input and output (I/O) patch in contrast to being output only. By setting up the I/O patch, you can assign input channels of your audio device to be the signal source and then route them to the appropriate output path. If you plug a microphone into the assigned input channels of your audio device, once the Mic Cue is triggered, the audio from this microphone will be the audio signal for the cue. There are a few more steps for setup but, once accomplished, the function of the Mic Cue is remarkably similar to what you have already learned in Audio Cues.

Signal Flow

Signal flow for the Mic Cue is similar to that of an Audio Cue, with the exception being there is now an external device (a microphone) inputting signal, rather than simply targeting an audio file as the input. Refer to the descriptions below in conjunction with Figure 6.1 to see the signal flow path from the Mic Cue through speaker output.

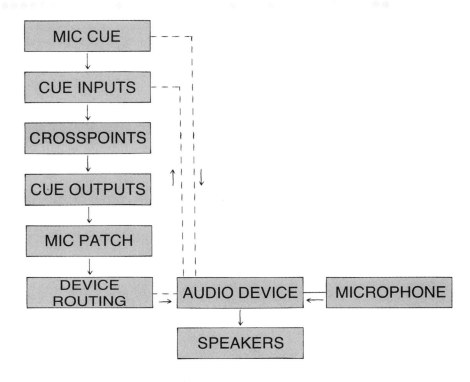

Figure 6.1
Mic Cue signal
flow chart.

1. **Mic Cue:** When triggered, the Mic Cue sends a signal that activates the assigned input channels of the audio device.
2. **Audio Device:** The audio device, once triggered, receives input signals from one or more microphones connected to its input channels. The device then samples these signals and sends them back to the computer via the digital connection (FireWire, USB, Thunderbolt, etc.)
3. **Cue Input:** The digital output from the audio device becomes the cue input for the Mic Cue.
4. **Crosspoints Matrix:** The cue input signal is bussed into all 48 channels of the crosspoints matrix. It is up to the operator to assign the amount of signal that will be routed into the corresponding levels fader. Once assigned, this signal becomes the cue output for the Mic Cue.
5. **Mic Patch:** The cue outputs are then routed through one of eight possible mic patches, which are each assigned to an individual audio device.
6. **Device Routing:** The final layer of routing is the audio device output routing. This is a signal routing within QLab that assigns the cue outputs to one or more specific device outputs on your audio device.
7. **Speakers:** Finally, the signal leaves the output device and travels out of your QLab system into external devices (i.e. mixer, signal processing, amplifier, and speaker)

Buffering

A buffer is a region of memory storage on your computer that is used to temporarily hold data while it is being moved from one place to another. All external audio devices use some level of buffering because the device must hold at least one sample of the audio going into it in order to play it back. Essentially, the buffer is how many of these samples the device holds at one time before asking the computer to provide more for playback. For this reason, buffering affects how much of your CPU is utilized when interfacing with an audio device. The lower the buffer number, the more frequently the device has to ask the computer for sampling, thus the higher drain on CPU resources. The higher the buffer, the less frequently it asks, therefore less taxing on the CPU.

While it might seem advantageous at first to use a high buffer setting, the down side to buffering is that it causes **latency** or delay in the audio signal from input source (microphone) to output source (speakers). In a live setting, it is essential that a lower buffer be used in order to reduce latency. While zero buffering is impossible, you ideally want to get as close to zero as possible. QLab accesses the buffer sizes specific to your audio device and allows for adjusting the buffer within that range of possibilities. To access these settings, click on **QLab** > **Preferences** and a window will open showing buffer size preferences for any audio device connected to your system (see Figure 6.2).

Typical range for buffer settings would be 16–1,024. This unit refers to the number of samples held as the buffer before asking the CPU another set. The process of determining which buffer size to use is simple – go with the lowest buffer setting possible that does not either create a scratchy sound or cause your device to "clip." Keep in mind, though, that for ultra-low buffer settings, it is always a good idea to use a rig with multiple core processors and lots of RAM.

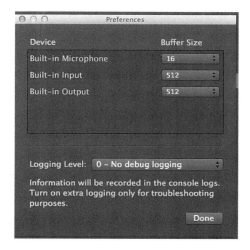

Figure 6.2
The preferences window includes device preferences and debug logging settings.

6.2 Setting Up Your Audio Device

It is worth mentioning at this point that all audio interfaces, though built to perform the same functions, do not operate in the same fashion or with the same level of dependability. There are some devices that simply do not function well in the QLab environment. Others might work perfectly well for playback, but will not be the ideal choice for microphone reinforcement purposes. This book is not intended to serve as a tool for equipment selection. My best advice for purchasing any equipment for use with your QLab system (be it audio, video, or networking) is to go to the QLab-Tested Hardware page at wiki. figure53.com to see user-submitted information about QLab-tested hardware and software. Also, visiting the QLab discussion list on the Figure 53 website is a great way to interact with the QLab community, both users and developers. Ask a question and, in most instances, you will get lots of feedback quickly.

For the purposes of microphone control, you will need an audio interface with input/output capabilities and phantom power (if you intend to use a condenser microphone). In addition, you will obviously need a microphone and at least one speaker connected to an output on your audio device. The reason for inputting and outputting from the same device is that audio input/output must use the same clock so that audio flows cleanly between the two. You can, however, create an aggregate device – the combination of multiple audio interfaces through one control – in your Audio MIDI Setup application. By doing this, you can use more than one audio interface in the same application, all sharing the same clock.

Pro-Tip ▼

Getting to Know Your Equipment

There is no overstating the importance of getting to know your equipment and understanding how its use differs from other pieces of hardware. As mentioned earlier, each audio interface tends to function in a similar way. The one aspect of each interface that tends to drastically differ is their software interfaces. Every audio interface will have software that must be installed onto your computer in order to use the interface properly. Typically, these interfaces mirror classical audio mixers in some way and allows for the control of levels, routing signals, creating sub-mixes, and adding effects. If your audio interface is not set up to route the audio signal to the correct outputs, then you will never get QLab to communicate properly with the interface. Since there are hundreds of different interfaces on the market, there is no way to cover all of the possible software interfaces in this text. Make sure to read all of the appropriate documentation that comes with your equipment and visit the manufacturer website, as well. Frequently, the manufacturer will have Frequently Asked Questions, user forums, and how to videos on their website. These resources can be invaluable to understanding how best to use their equipment.

Settings: Mic

Like the Audio Cue, the Mic Cue has a number of settings that should be established before inserting a cue into the workspace. There are three basic areas of concern to get up and running with Mic Cues: Default levels for new Mic Cues, Mic Patch assignment, and Device Routing. To access these settings, click on the gear-shaped Settings icon at the bottom right-hand corner of the workspace. This will open the Settings window. Click on the Mic icon located in the left-hand column to access Mic Settings. The window will look almost identical to the Audio Settings window explored in earlier chapters.

Default Levels for New Mic Cues

Though the look of the Default Levels window looks similar to that of the Audio Cue (see Figure 6.3), the signal flow is a bit different, as discussed earlier. There are a possible 24 inputs shown on the left side of the screen, which are the amount of microphone inputs possible for the Mic Cue. In other words, if you had an audio device with 24 available inputs, you could connect 24 separate mics to the device and control them all via a Mic Cue. Like the Audio Cue, each of these signals is then bussed down the entire row of crosspoints to its right. It is then up to the programmer to assign which crosspoints should receive which signal. These signals then become the Cue Output that will be sent into the Mic Patch.

For a simple Mic Cue setup, with only one microphone that needs to be sent out to all of the speakers in your system, a Default Levels setting would look like that shown in Figure 6.4. For this configuration, the mic input is assigned to crosspoints 1–8. This means that, for this Mic Cue, cue outputs 1–8 will receive the full audio signal sent from the microphone plugged into the first channel

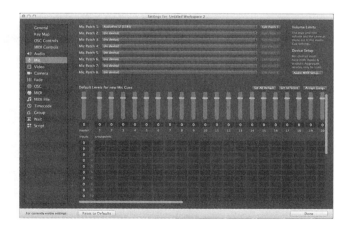

Figure 6.3
Default levels for new Mic Cues.

of the audio interface. These signals will then leave the cue and go to the next step of the signal flow: the Mic Patch.

Mic Patch

Like the Audio Cue before, the Mic Cue must be patched into a Mic Patch that sends the signal back to the audio device. Unlike the Audio Cue, though, the Mic Patch must interface with the same audio device for output as input. Select the desired audio interface by clicking on the drop-down menu shown beside Mic Patch 1. Once selected, you are ready to move on the next step: assigning the output patch for your audio device.

Device Routing

Device Routing is the final step of the Mic Cue signal flow, allowing the user to assign a path from the Mic Cue's cue outputs to one or more given device outputs. To access this interface, simply click on the Edit Patch 1 button to the end

Figure 6.4
Setting for Mic Cue assigned to cue outputs 1–8.

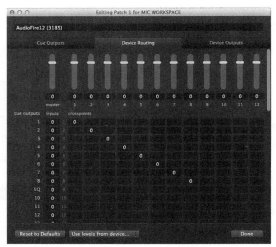

Figure 6.5
One-to-one device routing.

of the Mic Patch 1 row. This screen will look similar to the device routing interface for Audio Cues and be controlled in a similar fashion. There will be 48 possible cue outputs shown in the left-hand column, representing the 48 cue outputs of the Mic Cue. For this example, we are only concerned with the first eight, since we only assigned the signal from input 1 into crosspoints 1–8 in the Default Levels for New Audio Cues interface. As there are only eight speakers used in this configuration, the easiest thing is to set the patch in a one-to-one configuration (meaning that cue output 1 is assigned to crosspoint 1, cue output 2 to crosspoint 2, and so on) as seen in Figure 6.5. In this fashion, the sliders 1–8 in the Mic Cue's Device & Levels tab will control speakers 1–8, respectively. This will allow for the operator to choose to which of the eight speakers the signal should be assigned.

6.3 Inserting and Editing a Mic Cue

After following the steps mentioned earlier, your sound system should be set up to allow for a Mic Cue to be inserted and all basic volume controls achieved through the Device & Levels tab of the Mic Cue. To insert a new Mic Cue, click on the Mic Cue icon or drag it into the workspace. This will place a Mic Cue place keeper into your cue list in keeping with the Default Levels for new Mic Cues, established in the Mic Settings window. The following sections detail the specifics of using the Inspector Panel with a Mic Cue.

Inspector Panel: Basics

The Basics tab is almost identical for the Mic Cue as to that seen for the Audio Cue. The tab is split into two halves of the screen: Cue Info and Triggering. Again, the cue info side deals with cue numbering, assigning color to the Mic Cue, cue name, pre- and post-wait, continue status, and arm state. The only difference is that the target is not applicable to the Mic Cue, as Mic Cues don't target another file type – rather take their signal directly from a live audio input. The Triggering half of the page allows for triggering the Mic Cue via MIDI, hotkey, wall clock, or timecode.

Inspector Panel: Device & Levels

The Device & Levels tab (Figure 6.6) allows for the control of volume output from the audio device.

As the Device & Levels tab for Mic Cues is almost identical to that of Audio Cues, you should be familiar with every function in the Device & Levels panel. The following should function as a quick overview:

Audio Input & Output Patch

For the Mic Cue, the patch is referred to as the Audio Input & Output Patch, unlike the Audio Cue for which it was output only. The idea remains the same,

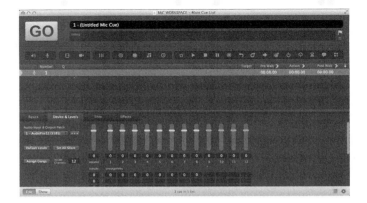

Figure 6.6
The Mic Cue
Device & Levels
tab.

though, as this patch allows you to assign which audio device you want to use for this particular Mic Cue. The button to the right of the Input and Output Patch allows for the editing of the Audio Input & Output Device.

Default Levels

By clicking on this button, you can set the levels to the pre-assigned default levels set in the Settings window.

Set All to Silent

Clicking on this button will mute all channels.

Assign Gangs

Ganging is a function that allows the linking of control of multiple cue outputs. Simply click on the Assign Gangs button and insert either a number or a letter in the open space beneath any slider (in the window where volume levels normally reside). For instance, place an "A" in the space beneath cue output channels 1 and 2, then click the Assign Gangs button again. This will now have paired output channels 1 and 2, making them move in unison. You will also notice that the two channels have a similar color. Additional gangs will have unique colors, as well.

Visible Channels

This window allows for the change in visible channels. This is an important tool for Mic Cues, as you typically only ever need to see the number of outputs available to your audio device (unless assigning an audio effect to a cue output). If, for instance, your device only has eight outputs, there is no reason to see channels 9–48. Instead, type 8 into the "Visible Channels" window and only output channels 1–8 will remain visible.

Levels and Crosspoint Matrix

This area of the window is identical to the levels settings seen in the Audio Cue earlier in the book. The Master and all audio inputs are shown in the left-hand column. The cue outputs are situated to the right of the Master, with the crosspoints matrix shown beneath for assigning an input channel to the appropriate cue output. Once patched, the sliders control volume and the Master controls the volume of all other outputs.

Had an Audio Effect been assigned to a cue output as a global effect, as detailed in Chapter 3, the slider (or sliders) for this effect would be listed (if you gave the effect a unique name).

The true ability to control microphone output resides in the Levels control panel. If you have set up the routing as described earlier in the chapter, the Levels faders will align with the control of the numbered output of your audio device (meaning fader 1 controls output 1, and so on).

Inspector Panel: Trim

Trim for the Mic Cue behaves in the same fashion as that of the Audio Cue. Mic Cues can be affected by Fade Cues in the same way that Audio Cues can. Using the Trim sliders in the Mic Cue will affect volume settings for all subsequent Fade Cues targeting the root Mic Cue.

Inspector Panel: Effects

Mic Cues can use Audio Effects in the same way as Audio Cues: either within the cue itself or globally through a cue output or device output. To assign an Audio Effect to a particular Mic Cue, simply click the "Add effect" button in the Effects tab. The chosen effect will be applied to only the selected cue. Common uses of this function might be the addition of EQ, reverb, or compression to a particular Mic Cue. Like volume settings, Mic effects can also be changed by subsequent Fade Cues.

6.4 Mic Effects

As mentioned earlier, there are a number of methods for applying an AU effect to a Mic Cue. The easiest way is by adding the effect directly to the cue by using the Effects tab in the Inspector Panel of the Mic Cue itself. This only works on that specific cue and does not affect the playback of any other Mic Cue.

While this is particularly effective, there are two other methods to globally apply AU effects to Mic Cues: by assigning it to the Cue Output or by assigning it to a Device Output.

Cue Output

Cue outputs are the signals sent out from the Audio Cue or Mic Cue that get routed into the audio patch before finally outputting from the device. The signal from an audio or mic input is routed directly into the cue output via the crosspoints matrix. For the purposes of applying a global audio effect, though, an unused cue output can have an effect assigned to it. This process of assigning an Audio Effect to a cue output was discussed in depth in Chapter 3 – Section 3.6. Assigning an audio effect to a cue output for a Mic Cue is nearly identical to that of assigning it to an Audio Cue. The complete process is described in detail in the following project.

Project 6.1 ▼

Creating a Global EQ Send in QLab

An equalizer (EQ) is used to adjust the individual frequencies of an audio signal in order to affect the resulting sound. There is any number of reasons to use an EQ on an audio signal. One might be to create a generic equalization for a male voice or one for the female voice. In the following project, we will examine how to use a cue output to create a global EQ send in your workspace. Please note that this project cannot be done without an external audio device that supports microphone input. As such, there is no project file on the companion website. Simply open an untitled workspace to begin this project.

Step One:

Make sure your audio device is properly connected to your system before starting QLab. Once in the workspace, there are two ways to access your device:

> If in Edit mode, click on Edit Device in the Device & Levels tab; if in the Mic Settings window, click on Mic Patch 1 (or whatever device you are using for Mic Cues). Once you have opened this interface, look at the first tab labeled "Cue Outputs."

Step Two:

Select an unused cue output. In this case, it would likely be the first number past the number of useable outputs on your device, so I have selected cue output 9. In order to assign an audio effect to a cue output channel, click **Add Effect** > **Apple** > **AUGraphicEQ** (see Figure 6.7).

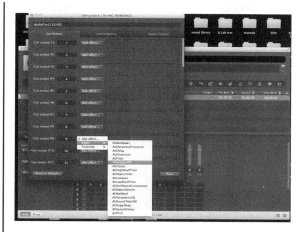

Figure 6.7
Adding a graphic EQ
through audio effects.

Step Three:

When you select AUGraphicEQ button, the control window for this AU will instantly open (see Figure 6.8). This window is not a part of QLab, rather the control window designed by Apple for this AU. This is the same window you would see in any application using the plug-in. If you are familiar with traditional graphic EQs, this window will look quite familiar to you. There are 32 sliders, each representing a section of frequency that can be either increased or decreased by the device. The sliders to the left represent lower frequencies (bass), whereas the sliders to the right represent the higher ones (treble).

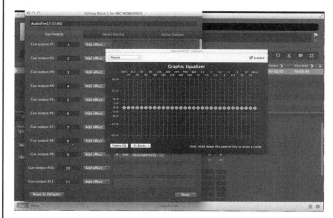

Figure 6.8
AU graphic EQ
control window.

Step Four:

One great feature of the Cue Outputs editing window is the ability to rename a cue output. Click on the black box to the right of Cue output 9 and type in

(Continued)

QLab 3 Show Control

the word "EQ." When you click enter or select an area outside the box, the number 9 will be replaced with the word EQ. This will be useful in the cueing phase, as all your sliders will now be labeled with their function. Keep in mind that a named cue output for Mic settings will not appear for Audio Cues, as this setting is dedicated to Mic Cues only. In this way, you can have distinctly different global effects sends for Mic Cues and Audio Cues.

Leave the settings window and return to the Mic Cue in your cue list. Click on the Device & Levels tab of the Inspector Panel of this cue and you will see that Cue Output 9 has been renamed "EQ" (see Figure 6.9).

Figure 6.9
The resulting labeled cue output fader.

Step Five:
The process above effectively set up cue output 9 as an EQ effects send. One final step must be done in order to enable this function. Currently, the audio effect is applied to cue output 9, but there is no input signal routed into the fader. In order to accomplish this, slide the crosspoint up to 0 for input 1 in the column located beneath the newly labeled "EQ" fader. This routes the Mic Cue signal through the EQ effects send (Figure 6.10). Now, the fader can be used to increase or decrease the amount of equalized audio sent out into the mix.

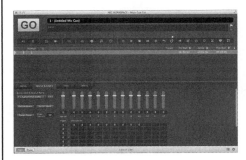

Figure 6.10
Assigning signal routing.

Step Six:
Once having gone through all of these steps, the EQ effect will be available for any subsequent Mic Cue added. This process can be replicated for any type of audio effect desired. Simply add an AU effect to another cue output, rename it, and it will also be available for all cues. It is worth noting that multiple AU effects can be applied to one given cue output. You can combine together a graphic EQ, reverb, and hi-pass filter to one cue output, if desired.

Device Output

Assigning an audio effect to a device output is the second method of applying effects in a global sense. The process of assigning the audio effect to a device output is quite similar to that of a cue output.

Project 6.2 ▼

Assigning an Audio Effect to a Device Output

One great example of an audio effect that might be used on a device output is a delay. In audio terms, a delay is a type of device that records an input sample and waits a predetermined period of time before playing it back. For many sound installations, digital delays are used to compensate for the passage of sound through air. The use of straight delays in a sound reinforcement system allow for multiple speakers to be used in a large space and make it appear as the sound is originating from the stage. This allows for adding speakers in the back of the space that provide sufficient volume without overloading the volume from the front of the hall. In the following project, we will examine how to use a device output to create a delay send for certain speakers in your sound system.

Step One:
If in Edit mode, click on Edit Device in the Device & Levels tab. If in the Mic Settings window, click on Mic Patch 1 (or whatever device you are using for Mic Cues). Once you have opened this interface, look at the first tab labeled "Device Outputs."

Step Two:
For the purposes of a reinforcement system, the goal would be to add a delay to speakers in the back of the theatre, so that the signal is perceived to be originating from the stage. For these purposes, let us assume that the device outputs 7 and 8 are the rear speakers of the theatre. In order

(Continued)

to assign an audio effect to these two channels, simply scroll down to the rows labeled Device Output 7 and Device Output 8. Click on the button to the right of the device outputs labeled "Add effect..." Select the AUDelay button.

Step Three:

When you select AUDelay button, the control window for this AU will instantly open (see Figure 6.11). This window controls the functions of the AUDelay plug-in. A delay works in one of two ways: by either delaying the signal and replaying it over itself, thereby creating an echo effect, or creating a "straight delay" by sampling the audio signal and simply waiting a period of time before playing it back. For reinforcement purposes, a straight delay is preferable. To achieve this, click on the yellow line in the grid. The line represents delay time and feedback. Delay time means how long it waits before playing back the sample. Feedback means the amount of time the sample is added onto itself. In order to achieve a straight delay, the yellow dot must be pulled all the way to the bottom of the grid, thereby changing the feedback to 0%. This will create the desired straight delay (see Figure 6.12). Play around with the actual delay time, but keep in mind that anything above 0.03 seconds will start to have an unearthly quality to it. Repeat this process identically for both device outputs 7 and 8.

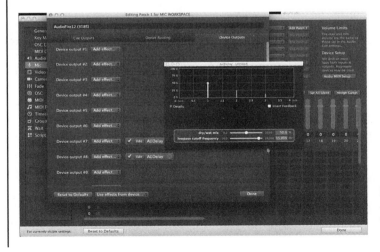

Figure 6.11
AUDelay control interface.

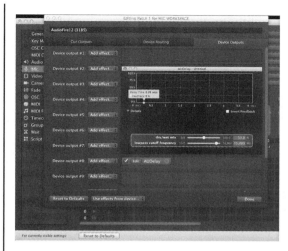

Figure 6.12
AUDelay straight delay
settings.

Step Four:

The process above effectively sets up a delay on any Mic signal outputting
through Device Outputs 7 and 8. Once having gone through all of these
steps, the delay effect will be available for any subsequent Mic Cue added.
This process can be replicated for any type of audio effect desired. Simply
add an AU effect to another device output and it will also be available for all
cues. It is worth noting that multiple AU effects can be applied to one given
cue output. You can combine together a graphic EQ, reverb, and hi-pass
filter to one cue output, if desired.

Fade Cues

The Fade Cue is a core component of controlling cues within the QLab system. A fade is generally understood to be a change in the attributes of a cue over a predetermined period of time. Initially, the purpose of the Fade Cue within QLab was simple; to change the volume settings or to stop an Audio Cue. QLab 3 vastly expands the function of Fade Cues over previous versions in that Fade Cues now have the ability to control a number of different cue types – Mic Cues, Video Cues, Camera Cues, and even Audio Effects within an Audio or Video Cue. In general, for audio-related cues a Fade Cue will affect volume levels, whereas with video-related cues a Fade Cue will affect attributes like opacity, image position, and object geometry. This versatility means that the available options for a Fade Cue will change depending on the type of a cue it targets. Since we are focusing on audio in this section of the book, this chapter will detail the differing functions of the Fade Cue for audio purposes only.

7.1 Audio Fade Cues

Audio Fade Cues are used for a number of different functions: to either increase or decrease the volume level of an Audio Cue; to change the output of the audio signal from one speaker to another (panning); or to change how audio effects are applied to an Audio Cue. Fades themselves work within a number of cue types, predominately including Audio, Mic, Video, and Camera. Once you learn the basics of how to use a Fade Cue, though, its application is similar across the different cue varieties.

An Audio Fade Cue must have an Audio Cue assigned as its target or it will not function. In order to have a Fade Cue accept an Audio Cue as its target, simply drag the Audio Cue into the Fade Cue's line on the workspace. This will automatically assign the target. Once the target has been assigned, then the Fade Cue is active. For its most basic use, simply open the Levels tab in an Audio Fade Cue and either increase or decrease the volume from that set on the targeted cue. This will either increase or decrease the volume of the cue over the Fade Cue's duration.

One important feature of note regarding the Fade Cue is that, regardless of creating a fade-in or fade-out, **the Fade Cue must always be placed after the targeted Audio Cue!** This feature often confuses first time QLab users. The reason for this is that an Audio Cue must be playing for a Fade Cue to affect its output. It has been my experience that most people intrinsically understand fade-outs, but are confused by the process of creating a fade-in. To create a fade-in, first insert an Audio Cue and set its levels at -INF (or whatever initial volume desired). Next, insert a Fade Cue and assign the Audio Cue as its target. The volume set in the Levels tab of this Fade Cue will be the final volume for the Audio Cue once faded in.

Pro·Tip ▼

One important thing to remember about the use of Fade Cues is that, without looking at the details in the Inspector Panel, it is sometimes difficult to discern the action of said cue. I find it is good to always be in the habit of naming my Fade Cues according to their function as soon as I input them into the workspace. For instance, if I have a Fade Cue that increases the volume of a police siren, I might call it "Fade up siren." Using descriptive names up front can save you lots of time later on in the tech process.

There are a number of controllable functions for a Fade Cue in addition to the basic levels setting. To change the parameters of the Fade Cue, look into the Inspector Panel. There will be four tabs shown for the Audio Fade Cue in the Inspector Panel. Similar to the Audio Cue itself, these tabs are used for changing the attributes of the Fade Cue. The attributes for each of the Inspector Panel tabs are shown later.

Inspector Panel: Basics

The Basics tab remains essentially unchanged from its layout for an Audio Cue. The functions are still split into cue information and triggering, listing pre- and post-waits, continue status, and triggering options. The only substantive difference between the Basics panel for fades is that the file name shown in the Name row is that of the file being targeted by the Fade Cue (see Figure 7.1).

Figure 7.1
The Audio Cue
Basics tab.

One of the most used functions of the Basics window is setting a pre-wait time for a Fade Cue. By using this function, the programmer can effectively create a crescendo (volume increase) or decrescendo (volume decrease) within an Audio Cue. The addition of dynamic changes such as these can add depth to an audio recording and make canned music sound a bit more realistic.

Inspector Panel: Curve Shape

The Curve Shape is the primary way of controlling your levels over the duration of the Fade Cue. For an Audio Fade Cue, the fade curve is a graphic representation of audio levels and cue duration. If perceived as a basic graph, cue duration is represented in the x-axis with audio levels (volume) represented in the y-axis. The default cue duration for a Fade Cue is 5 seconds. This duration is labeled along the top edge of the fade-curve window. Understanding this, one can see that each vertical line within the graph represents 0.5 seconds.

The default curve shape is the S-curve, a parabolic shape that resembles an "S" on its side (see Figure 7.2). The S-curve has a slower "attack," meaning that it takes longer to perceive the increase or decrease in volume. This attribute makes the S-curve suitable for most fade-ins or fade-outs of music. Looking at the curve over the 5-second duration, you can see that the volume remains fairly consistent for 0.5 seconds, and then gradually begins to increase. Once it hits 1.5 seconds, the rate of increase remains constant until around 3 seconds, then begins to slow until the 5-second mark is reached. Sliding your mouse along the S-curve shape will indicate the percentage of change versus elapsed time over the duration of the Fade Cue. You will notice that in the S-curve, both levels and duration align at the halfway mark (meaning at 2.5 seconds into the Fade Cue, increases in levels should be at 50% of their established change). Though it works for most gradual fades quite well, you will find yourself in need of fade curves that have an even faster or slower attack. In these cases, simply click on the button labeled S-Curve and select the Custom Curve setting.

Selecting the Custom Curve establishes a straight curve with a consistent rate of increase or decrease in levels over time. Like the S-curve, the level will reach the 50% change mark halfway through the Fade Cue duration. If left untouched, this straight curve can be used on its own as a fade. The true function of the Custom Curve, though, is its ability to be manipulated into a new fade-curve

Figure 7.2
Curve shape settings.

shape. By using the custom curve, the designer can create any number of unique fade curve shapes to meet the needs of the design.

To change the consistent curve into a customized shape, simply click on the curve and it will insert a control point at that location. The control point is represented as a yellow dot on the fade curve. By grabbing the control point, the operator can add either an incline or decline to the fade curve by simply pulling the control handles in any direction. Multiple control points can be inserted into one Fade Cue to create interesting fade curves. Figure 7.3 shows three different custom fade curve shapes that each behave in radically different ways.

The first fade curve illustrates a fade with a quick attack, having the sound fade to 50% by 0.25 seconds and at full by 2 seconds. This fade effect would be used to add a slight fade-in to the beginning of an audio file, making its triggering less abrupt. Sometimes this technique is useful when working from music with a slight aberration at the beginning of the track.

The second fade curve is an example of a particularly slow fade curve. In this example, the audio levels will begin to increase from the moment the Fade Cue is triggered, but at a slow rate. The rate of increase remains constant until about 3 seconds into the fade, then begins a more rapid increase, going from 12% at 3 seconds to 100% at 5 seconds. This type of fade curve might be useful for creating a sound effect in which something approaches from the distance making sound (like a police siren).

The final example illustrates the potential for adding multiple control points within one fade curve to oscillate the volume changes from increase to decrease. In this example, the audio file's volume rapidly increases to 75% over 0.5 seconds. Thereafter, the volume cycles between 75% and 25% every 0.5 second. With a consistency such as this, one could take a constant sound like a horn and make it sound more like a siren used for an alarm.

Fade Cue Duration

To this point, all of the Fade Cues discussed have had the default duration of 5 seconds. Should there be an instance for which longer or shorter fade durations are needed, simply use the Duration input on the left side of the Curve Shape panel. Input the desired time and press enter. The cue duration and fade-curve window will then be changed to match the inputted time.

Figure 7.3
Three fade curve types: Fast fade-in, slow fade-in, and an oscillating fade curve.

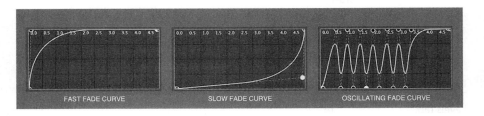

FAST FADE CURVE   SLOW FADE CURVE   OSCILLATING FADE CURVE

Stop Target When Done

It is important to understand that Fade Cues only work to affect the overall output levels of the cue. Unless explicitly stopped, an Audio Cue will remain running in the background of your workspace until it reaches the end of its duration. This is true, even if a Fade Cue has lowered the levels to 0%. This function allows for the ability to keep an Audio Cue running in the background and faded back up at a later time, thus allowing for the elapsed time to be perceived. If, upon fading out an Audio Cue, you will not be using the same cue again, it is always best to select the Stop Target When Done checkbox. This function stops the targeted cue from playing in the background after the fade duration. Keep in mind that every cue running in the background (even those which cannot be seen or heard) will continue to engage your computer's CPU. If, over the course of a show, there are multiple cues running at the same time then your computer's resources will be taxed and negatively affect its playback ability.

The Stop Target When Done checkbox appears in the Curve Shape, Levels, and Audio Effects Inspector Panel tabs. Note that activating it in any one of these tabs will activate it in all three and vice versa.

Reset to Default Shape

The Reset to Default Shape button returns the fade curve to the default setting determined in the Workspace Settings. This will replace any previous custom settings you might have created.

Inspector Panel: Levels

The Levels settings in an Audio Fade Cue control the amount of increase or decrease in output volume and mirrors the Device & Levels tab from an Audio Cue in many ways. There is no device routing, though, since the Fade Cue uses the pre-assigned device routing of the targeted Audio Cue. The following section details the many control functions and settings present in the Levels tab.

Fade Type: Absolute versus Relative

Looking at Figure 7.4, you can see the basic layout of the Levels tab. The first row on the left column of the Levels tab allows the programmer to set the Fade type to that of absolute or relative. These two terms are important to understand for the way in which they affect Audio Cues.

Figure 7.4
The Fade Cue Levels tab.

An **absolute fade** adjusts the volume of the targeted Audio Cue *to* a particular volume level. When triggered, the absolute cue will increase or decrease the volume of the targeted cue to the volume set in the Levels tab of the Fade Cue Inspector. There can only be one absolute fade assigned to one given channel at a time. In the instance of two Fade Cues targeting the same channel of audio, the second cue fired would control the volume of that channel (latest takes precedence).

A **relative fade**, in contrast, fades the volume up or down relative to the volume of the Audio Cue when triggered. In other words, whereas an absolute fade adjusts the volume *to* a particular level, the relative fade adjusts the volume *by* a particular level. Unlike the absolute fade, an unlimited number of relative fades may be applied to a given channel of audio.

The graphic interface for the levels settings of a relative fade differ from that of the absolute fade. When the relative fade is selected from the drop-down menu, the levels faders in the right column will change from their standard look to hourglass-shaped slider icons (see Figure 7.5).

One great function of the relative Fade Cue is the ability to control multiple Audio Cues at the same time. If you have created a Group Cue containing multiple Audio Cues, a relative Fade Cue can be applied to this Group Cue, thereby raising or lowering the volume of all Audio Cues within the group at once. This is particularly useful in a situation where you might have extracted a number of tracks from the same CD and the levels of the audio files are either too loud or soft for playback. In this case, you could simply target the Group Cue with a Fade Cue set to relative and increase or decrease levels, as necessary.

Levels and Crosspoint Matrix

The right column of the Levels tab is identical to the control functions for an Audio Cue. By this point, you should be exceedingly familiar with the layout and function of the levels and crosspoints matrix. The Master and all audio inputs are shown to the left, with output channels to the right of the Master and the crosspoints matrix shown beneath each corresponding cue output channel. Once patched, the sliders control volume and the Master controls the volume of all other outputs. This window is used for setting the desired

Figure 7.5
The appearance of the fade sliders changes for a relative Fade Cue.

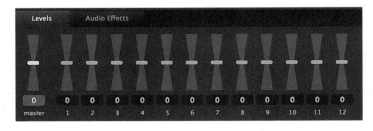

change in levels for a Fade Cue for both absolute and relative Fade Cue types. It is worth mentioning that Fades will only affect the levels that are activated – not necessarily all levels.

Set from Target/Set All Silent

The middle row of the left column allows for rapid settings of the output levels for the Fade Cue. The Set from Target button sets the levels to be identical to that of the targeted Audio Cue. This is particularly useful to set as a starting point, especially if you are working with multiple channels of audio set at different volume levels. A quick way to set a consistent fade of an Audio Cue is to click Set to Target, then either increase or decrease the Master output level as desired. Likewise, if the goal is to completely fade the volume out, then click on the Set All Silent button, which will set all of the levels faders to - INFINITY.

Assign Gangs

Fade Cue sliders can be grouped together for ease of control using the Gang function. This function is identical to the method shown in Section 5.4 for ganging channels in Audio Cues.

Inspector Panel: Audio Effects

The Audio Effects tab features two functions: changing the audio effect attributes of a targeted Audio Cue and changing the playback rate of the targeted Audio Cue. Audio effects, as discussed in Chapter 5, allow for the use of AUs to affect an Audio Cue. Fade Cues can also be used in conjunction with audio effects to change the effects settings or remove an audio effect from an Audio Cue. Audio Effects Fade Cues are always absolute fades.

To change the attributes of the Audio Effects, simply add a Fade Cue and target the desired Audio Cue. The targeted Audio Cue must have some type of audio effects applied to it already. You cannot add an audio effect on its own simply by adding a Fade Cue and adding an audio effect. Open the Audio Effects tab of the Fade Cue and check the box beside the desired audio effect and click the Edit button (see Figure 7.6). This will open the control window for the AU. Make the desired changes to the AU, and then close the window. Now, when the Fade Cue is activated, it will change the playback attributes to those you just set. The Effects Fade allows for either an increase or decrease of effects outputs and can be used for countless different purposes.

Figure 7.6
Fade audio effects window.

Fade Rate

One interesting function of the Audio Effects Fade is the ability to change the rate of playback of an Audio Cue. By selecting the Fade Rate to checkbox, the programmer can change the assigned rate of a cue. By applying a playback rate change to a Fade Cue, you can add tempo variations to an Audio Cue. Currently, the Fade Rate function does not affect the pitch of the Audio Cue, only the rate of playback.

To achieve this, click on the Fade rate button (see Figure 7.7) and set it to the desired playback rate. Increasing to a number value above 1 will speed up the playback, whereas those number values below 1 will slow playback. To make minor changes, simply click in the input window. While holding the mouse clicked down, slide your cursor up to increase the number or down to decrease it. Once the correct rate is inputted, click "enter" to finalize the number.

Stop Target When Done

Like all other Fade Cues, the Audio Effects Fade can be set to stop playback of the targeted Audio Cue when the fade action is complete. To do so, click on the Stop Target When Done checkbox on the left side of the Audio Effects tab.

Set Audio Effects from Target

This button automatically assigns the Audio Effects of the targeted Audio Cue to the selected Fade Cue. When a Fade Cue targets an Audio Cue, the Audio Effects should be automatically assigned to that fade. Sometimes, during the process of experimentation you might find that you dislike the changes made and want to return to the original state of the cue. This can be easily achieved by clicking the Set Audio Effects from Target button.

Summary

A Fade Cue has many different uses other than simply raising or lowering volume levels. Keep in mind that, even if you are only using the Fade Cue to affect Audio Effects, other attributes of the Fade Cue can be controlled through the Fade Cue Inspector Window. Curve Shape, duration, waits, and continues all apply to the Audio Effects Fade, like any other cue type.

The following project details the process of adding an audio effect through the Fade Cue in order to adjust audio effects applied to an Audio Cue. The project requires the download of Project 7.1 from the companion website.

Figure 7.7
The fade rate button can be used to change the rate of audio playback.

Project 7.1 ▼

Pitch Bend to Replicate a Reel-To-Reel Malfunction

Step One:

Open Cue 1 in the Project 7.1 workspace. This file is a recording in the style of old 1940s radio announcers. In order to affect this Audio Cue with a Fade Cue, you must first add an Audio Effect to the cue with no changes applied.

Step Two:

Click on the Audio Effects tab in the Inspector Panel. On the left side of the screen click the "add effect" button. A drop-down menu will appear. This should display any AUs installed on your computer. In this case, select the Apple button, and then select the AUPitch button. This will open the control interface for the plug-in. **Do not change any attributes!** This will simply apply the AU to the Audio Cue so that a Fade Cue can later affect it.

Step Three:

Add a Fade Cue to the workspace. Target Cue 1 with this Fade Cue.

Step Four:

Select the Fade Cue and click on the Audio Effects tab in the Inspector Panel. Click the check box beside the AUPitch effect. This will activate the AU for your Fade Cue.

Step Five:

Click on the Edit button to the left of the AUPitch label. This will open the AUPitch control interface. Slide the pitch knob to the right until it reads "1,800 Cents" (see Figure 7.8).

Figure 7.8
The AUPitch control interface allows for pitch bending and fine-tuning the effect.

Step Six:

Select the Fade Cue again and change the fade duration to 4 seconds in the Curve Shape tab of the Inspector Panel.

Step Seven:

Go back to the workspace. Trigger playback for Cue 1. After a moment, click go for Cue 2 (the Fade Cue). You should hear a rapid increase of pitch over a 4-second duration.

(Continued)

Step Six – Bonus:
As an added effect, you could find a scratch sound effect to indicate the point of malfunction. Insert this as your second Audio Cue and set it as an auto-continue with the Fade Cue next in your cue sequence. This would add the sound of a malfunction directly followed up with an increase in tape speed.

7.2 Mic Fade Cues

As addressed earlier, the Mic Cue is a great tool for adding reinforcement to your QLab sound system. In essence, the Mic Cue sends a signal to your audio interface and activates an input channel. The audio signal then passes through the Mic Patch and into the assigned device outputs on your audio interface. Once the Mic Cue has been activated, it will remain so until either a Fade Cue or another control cue such as a Stop Cue or Pause Cue affects its playback. The following section details the use of Fade Cues for affecting the playback of a Mic Cue.

Inserting a Mic Fade Cue

Like all other Fade Cue functions, the process of creating a Mic Cue fade begins with inserting a Fade Cue into the cue list. The second step is then to drag the intended Mic Cue to be affected onto the Fade Cue. This will set the Mic Cue as the target of the Fade Cue. Once you have done this, the process is all controlled from the Inspector Panel of the Fade Cue.

Basics and Curve Shape

The first two tabs in the Inspector Panel remain consistent with other types of Fade Cues. Basics offers up the basic information about the Fade Cue, pre-wait and post-wait, continue modes, and triggering options. The Curve Shape tab defaults to the standard S-curve, but also allows for adjusting the curve to a custom shape. One important element to note in this tab, though, is the "Stop Target When Done" checkbox. Like other varieties of Fades we have explored, it is essential to note that a Mic Cue will continue to run in the background until stopped. Simply muting all of the channels will not stop the cue by itself.

Levels

The Levels tab is one of the most useful when applying a fade to a Mic Cue. Like applying a fade to an Audio Cue, fading a Mic Cue will most frequently entail increasing or decreasing volume output. The process for doing so is relatively easy.

First, click on the "Set from Target" button in the left column. This will match the levels settings of the Fade Cue to that of the targeted Mic Cue. This assures that you will begin at the pre-set level of the Mic Cue. To increase or decrease the volume, select the levels fader associated with the Mic you want to change and slide it up or down. If there are changes to be applied to multiple mics, then use each of their individual sliders. Should you want to keep the balance between multiple mic levels consistent as you change the volume of the entire mix, use the master level fader and all will be affected equally.

Audio Effects

Like Audio Cues, Mic Cues can have audio effects applied to them as signal processing. As such, the Fade Cue can be used in a similar fashion to change the audio effects applied to a Mic Cue. This process is identical to the one described in Section 7.1 earlier for fading audio effects on an Audio Cue. It is important to note, once again, that audio effects cannot be added to a Fade Cue, they only display the audio effects of the targeted cue.

7.3 Manual Fades

By default, a Fade Cue inserted into a workspace is set as a manual fade, meaning that the QLab operator will trigger it. Manual Fade Cues make up a great percentage of the fades used in a typical live performance. Personally, I prefer to give the maximum amount of control to the stage manager and QLab operator in a live performance, as there is no guarantee that a performer will behave in the same fashion from night to night on stage. Any number of factors can change the timing of a performance. For me, this means that I try to limit the instances in which cues are automatically triggered to those for which are absolutely necessary.

One example that frequently pops up in live performance is an actor answering a telephone onstage. For this type of sound effect, you always want to have more rings available than what you think is necessary. What happens if you have only four rings in your audio file when the actor gets caught backstage in a quick change? For an instance like this, I always set the Audio Cue on an infinite loop so that the phone can ring until the actor picks it up. It is the action of picking up the phone, though, that requires a manual fade set to a zero count. I have seen instances of sound designers providing three ring tones, but the actor accidentally picks up after two. This creates an embarrassing situation for the actor onstage when the audience invariably laughs at being forcibly reminded that they are watching live theatre.

The following project takes you through the process of creating an infinitely looped telephone ring with a manual zero-count fade to end the ringing.

Project 7.2 ▽

Creating a Zero-Count Fade Cue

Step One:
Download Project 7.2 from the companion website and open the QLab workspace. Look at Cue 1. This is a recording of a telephone ringing.

Step Two:
Select the Time & Loops tab in the Inspector Panel. Click on the button labeled "Infinite Loop." This will set up the telephone sound to ring infinitely until stopped by QLab.

Step Three:
Using the Toolbar or Toolbox, insert a Fade Cue as Cue 2. Target Cue 1 with this Fade Cue by dragging Cue 1 over Cue 2 until it highlights the cue with a blue box.

Step Four:
Click on the Curve Shape tab of the Inspector Panel in Cue 2. Using your keypad, insert the number 0 into the Duration window. Press enter. This will make the Fade instantaneous upon pressing Go. You will notice that the words "instant fade" should be printed in the corner of your Fade-curve window (see Figure 7.9).

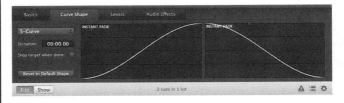

Figure 7.9
Creating an instant fade by changing the fade duration.

Step Five:
Select the Levels tab in the Inspector Panel for Cue 2. Pull the master fader all the way to the bottom of the slider. Notice that the rectangle beneath it will now read -INF and have a highlighted background color. This will make the telephone cue fade to -INF (or mute) when the Fade Cue is triggered (see Figure 7.10).

Figure 7.10
Set the master level to -INF to mute the audio levels.

Step Six:

In the area to the left of your screen, beneath the absolute fade button, select the checkbox reading "Stop Target When Done." This will stop the cue from playing in the background once the Fade Cue has been fired.

Step Seven:

Test your workspace. Fire Cue 1 and then, after a moment, fire Cue 2. It should instantly stop the telephone from ringing.

7.4 Automatic Fades

An automatic fade is one pre-programmed to fire at a predetermined time or is triggered by another cue within the workspace. These types of fades can be quite useful to automate changes of volume levels within an Audio Cue. While it is true that the integrated fade envelope on an Audio Cue can control internal level changes, it is sometimes preferable to combine together a sequence of multiple cues to accomplish an effect. The following project details how to use an automatic Fade Cue to fade-in beginning of an Audio Cue and fade-out at its end.

Project 7.3 ▼

Automated Fade-In and Fade-Out of an Audio Cue

Step One:

Download Project 7.4 from the companion website and open the QLab workspace. Look at Cue 1. This is a recording of a piece of music for which we want to create an automated fade-in at the beginning of the song and a fade-out at some interval within the Audio Cue's playback. In the Device & Levels tab of the Inspector Panel, pull the master fader down to the bottom of the slider to mute the audio. This is essential since the sound needs to start at silent in order to fade-in.

Step Two:

Using the Toobar or Toolbox, insert a Fade Cue as Cue 2. Target Cue 1 with this Fade Cue by dragging Cue 1 over Cue 2 until it highlights the cue with a blue box.

Step Three:

Click on the Curve Shape tab of the Inspector Panel in Cue 2. Using your keypad, insert the number 4 into the Duration window. Press enter. This will make the Fade's action occur over a period of 4 seconds upon pressing Go.

(Continued)

Step Four:

Click on the button labeled S-curve, and select the drop-down option labeled "Custom curve." This will enable you to create your own curve shape. The graph on the left represents the curve for a fade-in, whereas the one on the right is a fade-out. In the first graph box, click on the yellow line at the first line, labeled 0.4 seconds and pull your cursor all the way up to the upper left corner labeled 0.0 (see Figure 7.11). This will create a fade curve that curves upward fairly quickly over the course of 4 seconds.

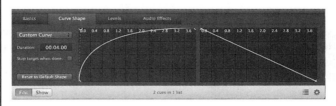

Figure 7.11
This fade curve will rise quickly over the 4-second duration.

Step Five:

In the Levels tab of Cue 2, set the available sliders to 0 (since we are working in stereo, this will be the master and faders 1 and 2). When triggered, this Fade Cue will adjust the playback volume of Cue 1 to 0, or unity, meaning it will play back at the original level of the recording. You should notice that the red x listed in the left corner of the cue row for Cue 2 will now disappear, once you have set a level for the Fade Cue.

Step Six:

As currently set, Cue 1 will play when triggered but cannot be heard since its volume is set to mute. The purpose of the Fade Cue is to bring the volume up to the desired level. In order to automate this function, you must go to Cue 1 and set the continue state to **auto-continue**. This can be done at the end of the cue row by clicking in the last column (beneath the arrow icon). Blank means no continue, the arrow icon means auto-continue (the following cue firing in unison with the first), and the arrow with a circle indicates auto-follow (the cue firing once the first cue's action is completed). Alternately, you could click on the Basics tab of Cue 1 and select auto-continue in the continue drop-down menu (located in the bottom left corner). Examine Figure 7.12 to see if your cueing matches.

Step Seven:

Test the cue sequence. If properly programmed, clicking Go for Cue 1 should trigger both Cue 1 and 2 simultaneously, and the audio signal will fade-in from silent over a 6-second interval.

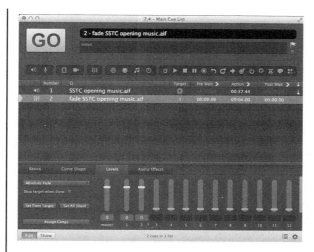

Figure 7.12
Check to see if your cueing matches.

Step Eight:

Press escape to end the playback of the cue sequence. The final desired effect is to add an automated cue that will fade-out the Audio Cue at a predetermined playback point. To do this, insert a new Fade Cue as Cue 3. Target Cue 1 with this Fade Cue by dragging Cue 1 over Cue 3 until it highlights the cue with a blue box.

Step Nine:

Set the continue state of Cue 2 as auto-continue. This will automatically fire all three cues simultaneously.

Step Ten:

Since the desired outcome of the final Fade Cue is to fade-out the volume of Cue 1, click on the Levels tab of Cue 3 and pull the master fader down to -INF. In addition, select the Stop Target When Done checkbox in the left half of the Levels tab. This will stop playback of Cue 1 once it is faded out.

Step Eleven:

Select the Curve Shape tab of Cue 3. Click on the button labeled S-curve, and select the drop-down option labeled "Custom curve." This will enable you to create your own curve shape. This time, you will use the second grid, as the desired outcome is a fade-out. In the second graph box, click on the yellow line at the last vertical graph line (4.5 seconds) and pull your cursor all the way up to the upper right corner (see Figure 7.13). This will create a fade curve that curves downward over the course of 5 seconds.

(Continued)

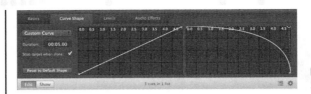

Figure 7.13
Slow fade-out.

Step Twelve:
If left in its current configuration, Cue 3 would automatically trigger resulting in audio signal almost instantly fading out. To achieve the automated fade-out, we must set a **pre-wait** for Cue 3. To accomplish this, either enter the pre-wait time in the pre-wait column of the cue row, or insert it in the Basics tab for Cue 3. Set the pre-wait as 13 seconds (00:13.00) by typing in 13 and then pressing enter.

Step Thirteen:
Test the cue sequence. If properly programmed, clicking Go for Cue 1 should trigger Cues 1–3 simultaneously, and the audio signal will fade-in from silent over a 6-second interval. After 13 seconds of audio playback, the fade-out programmed by Cue 3 should trigger, fading down to silent over a 5-second duration. This will ensure that the song will fade-out on its own before entering into the second musical phrase. Figure 7.14 shows how your finished workspace should appear.

Figure 7.14
The finished workspace.

7.5 Panning

Panning, the ability to "move" an Audio Cue from one set of speakers to another (right to left, front to back, diagonally, etc.) is one of the benchmarks of a convincing sound design. Historically, panning was either created in the studio and saved into the audio file or performed live through the audio mixer. With QLab, panning can be automated via Fade Cues and saved for playback through your workspace. The following project illustrates the process of doing so.

Project 7.4 ▼

Panning via Fade Cue

One of the best uses of panning is for the creation of "Doppler effect" sound cues, like that of a police siren approaching then passing away into the distance. The following steps detail the creation of such an effect.

Step One:

Download Project 7.5 from the companion website and open the QLab workspace. Look at Cue 1. This is a recording of a police siren without the Doppler effect added. In the Device & Levels tab of the Inspector Panel, pull the master fader down to the bottom of the slider to mute the audio. This is essential since the sound needs to start at silent in order to fade-in.

Step Two:

Using the Toolbar or Toolbox, insert four Fade Cues (Cues 2–5). Use Cue 1 as the target for all four Fade Cues. In addition, set the continue state for Cues 1–4 as auto-continue. This is the foundation of the panning effect.

Step Three:

Click on the Curve Shape tab of the Inspector Panel in Cue 2. Using your keypad, insert the number 3 into the Duration window. Press enter. This will make the Fade's action occur over a period of 3 seconds upon pressing Go. Make this the cue duration for Cues 2 and 3. Finally, set the cue duration for Cues 4 and 5 to 5 seconds. This will make for a more realistic progression of sound, rather than making each one identical.

Step Four:

Click on the button labeled S-curve, and select the drop-down option labeled "Custom curve." This will enable you to create your own curve shape. Instead of changing the curve, though, this time leave it as a straight line (see Figure 7.15). This will create a fade curve that fades in evenly over the course of the cue duration. Make this the fade curve for all of your Fade Cues (Cues 2–5).

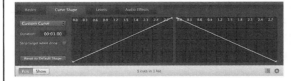

Figure 7.15
The straight curve is the default setting for all custom curves.

Step Five:

In the Levels tab of Cue 2, set the master fader and fader 1 to 0. Fader 2 should be set to -INF, as we only want the sound to come from the left channel at first.

(Continued)

Step Six:

Set volume for Cue 3 as follows: master fader +10, fader 1 at 0, fader 2 at 0. This will make the sound come from both right and left channels and increase the volume to +10 dB.

Step Seven:

Set volume for Cue 4 as follows: master fader at 0, fader 1 at -INF, fader 2 at 0. This will make the sound come from the right channel only and decrease the volume from the previous cue.

Step Eight:

Set volume for Cue 5 as follows: master fader -INF. This will mute all audio output. While in the Levels tab, select the Stop Target When Done check-box to end playback at the end of the Fade Cue sequence.

Step Nine:

Currently, all volume and panning is correct, but since they are all set to auto-continue, a pre-wait must be set for each Fade Cue in order to make sure the "domino sequence" works correctly and doesn't automatically progress to silence. For correct playback, set the pre-waits in the following sequence: Cue 3 and 4 at 3 seconds; Cue 5 at 5 seconds. You will notice that the pre-wait for each of these cues matches the cue duration of the previous Fade Cue. This creates a seamless fade sequence.

Step Ten:

Test the playback sequence. If properly programmed, clicking Go for Cue 1 should trigger Cues 1–5, and the audio signal will pan in from the left and exit to the right over a 16-second interval. See Figure 7.16 to double-check your cueing.

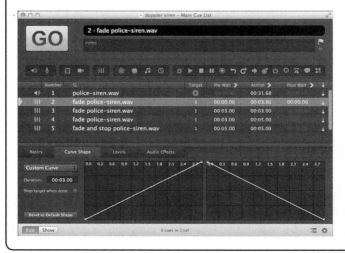

Figure 7.16
Completed workspace for Project 7.5.

7.6 Ducking Audio

Ducking is an audio effect used in music and audio production, most frequently involving the addition of voiceover. With ducking, the output volume of one audio signal is reduced in the presence of another. In most musical applications, the music will be decreased when the voiceover is added, then returned to its normal levels when the voiceover ends. In radio or television applications, ducking frequently occurs for foreign language translations. The foreign language speaker often begins at normal volume. Once the English translation is heard, the original speaker's voice is "ducked down" to keep the translation comprehensible and the foreign language speaker softly in the background. This technique is easily accomplished via QLab by inserting Fade Cues that duck audio levels down and then return them to their original state. The following project details this very process.

Project 7.5 ▼

Ducking Audio

Step One:
Download Project 7.6 from the companion website and open the QLab workspace. Look at Cue 1. This is a Group Cue containing recordings of a thunderstorm with wind and rain effects to set the mood for a scene. The continue state is set to auto-continue. This will ensure that the next cue automatically triggers when Cue 1 is fired.

Step Two:
Cue 4 is a voiceover that should play over the thunderstorm effects. In order to better hear this voiceover, though, we will need to "duck" the audio of Cue 1 down while the man speaks. In order to do so, we will need to insert Fade Cues to the workspace. Select Cue 1 and insert a Fade Cue. This should add a cue between Cues 1 and 4 (2 and 3 are hidden inside the collapsed Group Cue). Name this Cue 1.5 and assign Cue 1 as its target (see Figure 7.17).

Figure 7.17
Inserting a Fade Cue
with a group cue target.

(Continued)

Step Three:

Select the Levels tab of Cue 1.5 and set the volume in the master to −14 dB. In addition, set the pre-wait to 6 seconds and the cue duration to 1 second. Finally, set the continue state of Cue 1.5 to auto-continue. This will ensure that the sound will duck down at the same time that the audio from Cue 2 begins (See Figure 7.18). Test the cue progression.

Figure 7.18
Decreasing the output levels for the Group Cue.

Step Four:

Insert a Fade Cue following Cue 4 (Cue 5). Set Cue 1 as the target for this cue. This Fade Cue will serve the purpose of bringing the volume levels of Cue 1 back to their normal level after the voiceover ends. To do so, select the Levels tab of Cue 3 and set the volume in the master to +9. Set the duration as 1 second (see Figure 7.19).

Figure 7.19
Resetting the output levels for the Group Cue.

Step Five:
In order to automate the end of the ducking with Cue 3, set the continue state of Cue 4 to auto-follow. This will trigger Cue 5 upon the completion of Cue 4.

Step Six:
Test the cue sequence. If all of the steps were done correctly, the entire sequence should be automated to begin with the storm sound effects and duck down for the voiceover.

7.7 Copy/Paste Fade Shapes

As mentioned earlier in the book, the Tools drop-down offers a number of options for interfacing with the workspace. One of the more useful functions is the ability to copy and/or paste fade shapes from one Fade Cue to another. It can be a cumbersome process to manually set the fade shape for a number of different Fade Cues. One way to simplify this process is by the use of the Copy Fade Shape button found in the Tools drop-down menu. In addition, the quick key for this is control + ⌘c (to copy the fade shape), or control + ⌘v (to paste).

7.8 Exploring Trim

As we have already seen in the last several projects, one Audio Cue will frequently have a number of Fade Cues affecting its output levels. This instance, where a series of Fade Cues target the same Audio Cue, is referred to as a **fade series**. Trim is QLab's tool for affecting the volume of that fade series without having to individually change levels for each Fade Cue in the sequence.

Unlike the other functions explored in this chapter, Trim is located in the Inspector Panel for the targeted Audio Cue. Trim is always a manual adjustment and cannot be changed by Fade Cues. In short, the Trim settings override the levels set in the fade series and allow for an increase or decrease of volume from one convenient location.

The best example for why one might use trim is the creation of a long sequence tied to a single Audio Cue. Perhaps the play has a moment in which two people argue over the volume settings on a radio, turning it up then down a number of times in a row. Imagine then, the director wants the overall volume for the sequence to be increased. You could go through and individually change the levels of the original Audio Cue and each of the subsequent

Fade Cues in the fade series. This process, though, is quite laborious and time-consuming. Another much easier option is to simply open the Trim tab in the Inspector Panel of the Audio Cue and slide the master volume up by 20%. In this way, each Fade Cue in the fade series would be increased by 20% relative to their original settings.

Control Cues

Thus far, we have examined the use of the Audio Cue and how Fade Cues affect the playback of the Audio Cue. Control Cues are a special collection of cues that are used to affect how other cues are used and interact with one another in the workspace. When looking at the Tool bar, the Control Cues are listed in the fifth grouping located to the right of the screen. The following sections detail the use and function of each of the control cues.

8.1 Group Cue

The Group Cue is an important tool within the QLab system that holds other cues within it. In short, the Group Cue allows you to create one cue that is a composite of multiple different cues and cue types. This is why the cue has historically been represented with an icon resembling a folder (see Figure 8.1). The sole purpose of the Group Cue is to contain and organize other cues. Within the workspace, the Group Cue's contents can be hidden or expanded to show the component cues. As such, the Group Cue is frequently used to eliminate clutter from the workspace and streamline the appearance for the operator. The Group Cue is such an essential component to QLab that the next chapter is devoted entirely to its use.

8.2 Start, Stop, Pause Cues

No sound system would be considered functional without the ability to start, stop, or pause an audio file. In the case of QLab, these functions are provided in the form of three different Control Cues. When looking at the Tool bar, the icons should be easily spotted, as they are the universal symbols for start, stop, and pause found on all audio/video equipment since the 1960s.

Figure 8.1
The Group Cue icon.

Start Cue

The Start Cue is used to start playback on another cue. Like the Fade Cue, it accepts another cue as its target. Once triggered, the Start Cue will fire the targeted cue. Think of the Start Cue as another method of triggering a cue besides the GO button. It is important to note that the Start Cue will *not* relocate the playback position to the targeted cue. If you need to relocate the playback position to the targeted cue, insert a GoTo Cue following the Start Cue with an auto-continue set on the Start Cue.

Stop Cue

The Stop Cue behaves in the same fashion as the Start Cue, accepting another cue as its target, except that when fired it will stop the playback of the targeted cue rather than starting it. Stopping a Group Cue will end playback of all cues within the group. Likewise, targeting a Cue List with a Stop Cue will stop playback of all cues in that particular cue list. Once stopped, a cue is no longer active and returns to its original state for subsequent playback.

Pause Cue

The Pause Cue can be used to pause the playback of a cue, a Group Cue, or even a cue list. When a Pause Cue activates, it simply halts the playback of a cue or cue sequence, leaving all affected cues in their current state. It is important to note that if a cue is paused, you will still find it located in the Active Cues panel.

To end a Pause Cue, a Start Cue must be inserted into the cue list. It is important to note that the Start Cue should target the paused Audio Cue, *not* the Pause Cue itself. If you target the Pause Cue, then nothing will occur, as the action will essentially create a loop in which pause is pressed over and over again. Once the Start Cue is fired, it will begin playback of the paused cue in the exact location and state in which it was paused. It is important to note that these Control Cues can be used on all cue types – Audio, Mic, Video, and Camera.

8.3 Load Cue

The Load Cue (seen in Figure 8.2) can serve multiple functions in the QLab workspace. The use of the Load Cue can be both subtle and complex. Its primary function enables the programmer to load a cue or cue sequence to a certain time for playback. To insert the Load Cue, simply click on the Load Cue icon in the Tool bar thus inserting the Load Cue place keeper in your cue list. Once this has been accomplished, another cue type must be targeted. Just drag

Figure 8.2
Load Cue icon.

the desired cue onto the Load Cue's cue row and it will automatically target it. Now, once the Load Cue is fired, it loads the targeted cue to the computer's memory. The "loaded cue" status is indicated by a yellow dot placed to the left of the cue's icon (Figure 8.3a). In this case, the cue will be loaded to its start time.

In addition to simply loading a cue to its start time, the Load Cue can specify an exact start point in the targeted cue's Action time. This is incredibly useful in creating dynamic cue sequences for which you might want to start a cue at a certain point within the audio recording. In order to accomplish this function, open the Load Time tab in the Load Cue's Inspector Panel. Type in the desired load time of the Loaded Cue and, when fired, the cue will be loaded to the predetermined time. When a Load Cue is fired with an established load time, the cue row features the yellow dot as before, but also includes a yellow rectangle around the cue's Action time (see Figure 8.3b).

Another function of the Load Cue is simply loading the chosen cue into the computer's memory to ensure seamless playback. In older versions, this function was essential in creating long cue sequences, essentially loading the cues into the computer's memory to enable rapid playback. One would frequently insert a Load Cue into such longer sequences to ensure proper playback. As the software has advanced, though, this function seems less essential in most instances. One good example of the use of this type of cue, though, is if your computer sits for a long period of inactivity during the show. I have noticed that, depending on the hardware and configuration of some computers, it may take a moment to "wake up" the computer for playback in this instance. I will sometimes program a Load Cue into the cue list for just this function. Just remember to inform the stage manager or operator that the cue will perform no function that they can hear.

Figure 8.3
(a) A loaded cue with no Load Time. (b) A loaded cue with a specific Load Time.

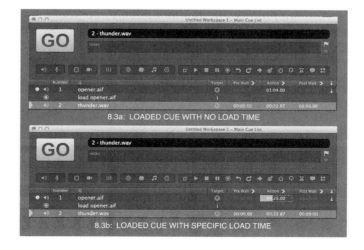

8.3a: LOADED CUE WITH NO LOAD TIME

8.3b: LOADED CUE WITH SPECIFIC LOAD TIME

Figure 8.4
The Reset Cue icon.

Pro-Tip ▼

One important thing to note is that **a Load Cue does not change the playback position of the cue list**. If you target a previous cue in your cue list, that target will be loaded and remain so until fired, but the playback position will continue to the next cue in the cue list. If you want to use a Load Cue to pre-load a previous cue and then return to it for playback, you must either manually move the playback position by clicking on the desired cue or insert a **GoTo Cue**. Essentially, a GoTo Cue is used to redirect the playback position to a different point in the cue list. The GoTo Cue is covered in detail in Section 8.6.

8.4 Reset Cue

The Reset Cue (seen in Figure 8.4) is an interesting cue in that it functions slightly differently for different cue types. For example, when looking at Audio Cues, the Reset Cue will change the targeted cue back to its original, unchanged state (resetting volume changes, trim, audio effects, etc.). When applied to an active cue (one playing), it acts as a Stop Cue and resets the targeted cue to its original state. Like the Load Cue, though, the playback position will remain unchanged and continue to the next cue in the cue list.

Some cues have what we might call "sticky" parameters – meaning that just stopping them will not reset their status. For these cue types, a Reset Cue must be used. When applied to a Cue List, a Reset Cue resets the cue list to its original playback position at the top of the list. In addition, when applied to a GoTo Cue that has been changed by a Target Cue (addressed later), the Reset Cue will reset the GoTo Cue to its original target.

8.5 Devamp Cue

The addition of the Devamp Cue (Figure 8.5) to QLab 2 was a defining feature allowing for complex compositional options in contrast to simple audio playback. In musical terms, **vamping** refers to an improvisational musical accompaniment to the solo. In musical theatre, there are frequently sections of the score written in for the musical director with the notation vamp included. These sections are easily repeatable, offering the opportunity to have musical accompaniment under sections of the show whose timing might vary from

Figure 8.5
The Devamp Cue
icon.

performance to performance. Within QLab, vamping is accomplished through looping or slices (covered in Chapter 5). When looking at the Time & Loops tab in the Inspector Panel for an Audio Cue, you have the option of looping an Audio Cue based on a predetermined play count or as an infinite loop. In addition, you could create a loop cycle based on slices in the Audio Cue. The Devamp Cue is used in conjunction with a looped Audio Cue to end a loop cycle. When fired, the targeted Audio Cue will play through its final loop and then continue to play the audio file.

The Devamp Cue allows for complex musical composition that matches the action onstage. As an example, I recently designed scenery for a production of *Richard III* at the Michigan Shakespeare Festival. In this production, many of the complex battle sequences needed musical underscoring. Since the sound designer for this production was also writing original compositions, she wanted to match the pacing of the music to that of the battle onstage. The score was heavily percussive and featured many sequences in which the drums had to align simultaneously with swords colliding or onstage deaths. In order to accomplish this feat, she created the score in hundreds of short, loop-able sections of music and used Devamp Cues to allow for the music to organically match the action onstage. The effect was stunning and truly made the actors interactive collaborators to the sound design. With QLab 3, the use of slices allows for complex vamping possibilities with even less incorporated audio tracks. A word of warning: This process is exceptionally time-consuming and requires detailed planning to pull it off. Each loop must be seamless with no "dead air" at the beginning or end, or the timing will vary making for a fake sound. When done well, though, the process is exceptionally rewarding. The project below details the process for setting up a short composition with internal vamping sequences.

Project 8.1 ▼

Vamping an Audio Cue with Loops

In previous versions of QLab, vamping of cues was accomplished via the use of loops. This process relied on creating an audio file and setting the play count to infinite loop. This creates a cycle that will continuously play until stopped or acted on by another cue. The following project details the creation of a loop sequence for these purposes. Download Project 8.1 from the companion website.

(Continued)

Step One:
Open the Project 8.1 workspace and select Cue 1.

Step Two:
Select the Time & Loops tab from the Inspector Panel. Click on the Infinite Loop button. This will create the loop sequence. Click GO to hear the Audio Cue play.

Step Three:
Now that the infinite loop is established, the Audio Cue will continue playing until stopped or acted on by another cue type. For our purposes, we will use the Devamp Cue. When fired, the targeted Audio Cue will play through its final loop and then continue to play to the end of the sequence.

Step Four:
Insert a Devamp Cue into the workspace between Cue 1 and 2. Set Cue 1 as the target for the Devamp Cue. Click on the Setting tab for the Devamp Cue and select the checkbox labeled "Start next cue when target reaches the end of the current slice." This will automatically activate playback for Cue 2 at the end of the loop.
It is worth noting that the Devamp Cue can be fired at any point during the loop cycle. In addition, you could set the Devamp Cue to simply stop the target once the loop reaches the end of its cycle without firing a subsequent cue.

Step Five:
To test the sequence, trigger playback for Cue 1 and then fire the Devamp Cue after the first loop cycle.

Project 8.2 ▽

Vamping an Audio Cue with Slices

In addition to creating loops, QLab 3 offers the opportunity to create internal vamping within Audio Cues. This process allows the sound designer to create a loopable section of a file that can vamp (useful for scene changes) until acted on by a Devamp Cue, which will end the loop and let the Audio Cue play on until the end of the file. The following project details the setup of this process, utilizing Project 8.2 downloaded from the companion website.

Step One:
Select Cue 1 from the Project 8.2 workspace.

Step Two:

Select the Time & Loops tab in the Inspector Panel. In the waveform display, click on the timeline at approximately the 5.95 second mark. Click on the "Add Slice" button to the left of the screen. You will notice a yellow line will appear with a downward pointing arrow, indicating the slice position. In addition the number "1" will appear in the slice. This indicates the loop count of the slice. Select this number and type in "inf." This will create an infinite loop cycle.

Step Three:

Insert a Devamp Cue following the cue and set Cue 1 as the target. Upon firing the Devamp Cue, the loop will end allowing the Audio Cue to play on to its end.

It is important to note that this process can be repeated any number of times. Any Audio Cue can have multiple slices within it set to infinite loop and numerous Devamp Cues may be used to exit the loop cycles.

8.6 GoTo and Target Cues

GoTo Cue

The GoTo Cue (Figure 8.6) is a simple tool that allows for changing the order of playback in a sequence. Like other control cues, it accepts another cue as a target. Once the GoTo Cue is fired, the playback position is moved to the targeted cue. Unlike Version 2, in QLab 3 a GoTo Cue cannot be used to activate playback of a cue. To achieve this in Version 3, a Start Cue must be used in conjunction with the GoTo Cue.

Target Cue

The Target Cue is a versatile cue that can manipulate any other cue that uses a cue target (i.e. Start, Stop, Pause, GoTo Cues, etc.). It is intended to work in conjunction with another cue to change the cue target, thereby allowing for even more versatility in changing the order of playback in a cue sequence. The use of a Target Cue can provide some confusion, if you are not fully versed in its application.

Like the other control cues we have look at, a Target Cue accepts another cue as its target. Once the Target Cue has been triggered, it will override the previous target of the cue and establish a new one. This new target will appear listed in brackets on the target row of the affected cue (see Figure 8.7a & b). It is important to note that the target for this cue will remain changed until using a Reset Cue to restore the cue to its original status.

Figure 8.6
GoTo and Target
Cue icons.

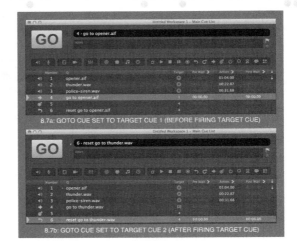

Figure 8.7
(a) GoTo Cue.
(b). GoTo Cue
after Target Cue is
fired.

8.7 Arm and Disarm Cues

The Arm Cue and Disarm Cue (Figure 8.8) are used for the simple purpose of enabling or limiting a cue's ability to perform its action when fired. When a cue is armed, it will perform all of its assigned actions when fired. When it is disarmed, it will still use pre-wait and post-wait functions, but will not perform its assigned action. Like other control cues, the Arm and Disarm Cues both require another cue as a target. Although the purpose of the cue is a simple one, it is a powerful tool that allows for organic control in complex playback situations.

Arm and Disarm Cues are frequently used as a component of the cueing and tech process. One possible use is in programming multiple cue options into the cue list before tech. You might have alternate versions of sound cues pre-programmed into your cue list that are disabled. If the director does not like your first choice, simply disable it and enable one of the other choices. This requires additional programming time up front, but makes the tech process go smoothly.

Another possibility is the use of pre-recorded materials that might need to change from night to night. Say that there is a pre-recorded voiceover for the lead role, but the understudy has to go on for one performance. In this case, the cue list could have two sets of voiceover programmed into it, with the unused files disarmed. To change from the lead role to the understudy, simply arm the understudy voiceover and disarm the lead role.

In addition to individual cues, the Arm and Disarm Cues can target a Group Cue. This is particularly useful for elaborate looping situations – such as a battle

Figure 8.8
Arm and Disarm
Cue icons.

or a thunderstorm. In both situations, it is common to create a group of discrete Audio Cues often equipped with Auto-continues and a randomized playback order. Once the Group Cue is playing, the independent cues merge to create a realistic sound effect: explosions, bullets, screams, and so on. Fading out a Group Cue such as this would make all of those independent cues fade out over the same duration. This effect would stick out like a sore thumb after the ultra-realistic approach of the previous sound effect. A much more effective technique would be the use of a Disarm Cue targeting the Group Cue. Each inactive cue would be disarmed, whereas the Active Cues would complete their playback. This effect would create a much more realistic fading of the fight sequence.

One important thing to note in this situation is how the Disarm or Arm Cues interact with a Group Cue. The cues will either arm or disarm every cue within the Group Cue. In some cases, you might have previously disarmed one cue within the group. If you disarm this group then arm it again, all cues will be armed *regardless of the fact that one of the cues was previously disarmed.*

8.8 Wait Cue

The Wait Cue (Figure 8.9) is used to insert delays between cues in the cue list. This cue performs the exact same function as the integrated pre-wait or post-wait of an individual cue. It is a matter of preference as to which method you use. Unlike other control cues, the Wait Cue does not target another cue type – it simply inserts a wait period into the cue sequence. The default wait time is set as 5 seconds (unless changed in General Settings). Notice that, upon inserting the Wait Cue, the cue will be named "wait 5 seconds." This is a handy function that lets the operator see the action of the Wait Cue. To change the wait duration, simply input the desired wait time in the Action column of the cue row. Note that, upon changing the action the name of the cue will automatically be changed to match.

8.9 Memo Cue

The Memo Cue (Figure 8.10) serves the singular function of inserting a note into your cue list without being attached to another type of cue. This cue has no action associated with it. To use the Memo Cue, insert it into the cue list and write your memo into the notes panel at the top of the screen. When in Show Mode, the Memo Cue will display the inputted notes in the notes panel.

Figure 8.9
The Wait Cue icon.

Figure 8.10
The Memo Cue icon.

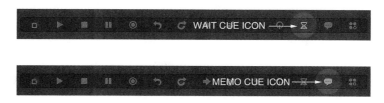

Figure 8.11
The Script Cue
icon.

Figure 8.11
The Script Cue
icon.

8.10 Script Cue

The Script Cue is a function typically reserved for advanced users, or those with previous experience in the AppleScript scripting language. AppleScript is an end-user scripting language that enables users to control applications, exchange data between applications, and automate the control of some repetitive tasks. AppleScripts can be run internally, as a Script Cue, or externally through an application such as AppleScript Editor. Within the QLab system, scripting has always been left as an option for those industrious designers who want to create some elements of customized control.

To use the scripting, insert a Script Cue into your cue list (Figure 8.11). Click on the Script tab in the Inspector Panel and it will open a Script window. This window is where you can insert an AppleScript written to perform a given task. AppleScript can be used for a number of different purposes from firing a cue in QLab to opening an Audio Cue's target file for editing in your DAW. One of the great things about the Script Cues is that you can insert a Script Cue into your cue list and assign a Hotkey Trigger for it, thereby giving yourself access to its function at any point. For instance, you could create a Script Cue that automatically muted all active cues and assign it the Hotkey of "M." After creating this cue, pressing the M key would mute all active cues.

The Figure 53 website features a wiki library of user-generated AppleScripts that have been tested for use in the QLab environment at wiki.figure53.com. Many of these scripts are simple to interpret and can be changed to suit varying purposes. For the next project, we will look at a basic but extremely useful script used to increase or decrease volume levels of a selected Audio, Mic, Video, Group, or Fade Cue. Download Project 8.3 from the companion website to examine this AppleScript at work.

Project 8.3 ▼

Creating a Hotkey Activated Script Cue

Step One:
Open Project 8.3 and select Cue 2, the Script Cue.

Step Two:
Select the Script tab in the Inspector Panel of the Script Cue. You will see in this dialog an AppleScript. This script effectively increases or decreases the Master volume settings of a selected cue, when triggered.

Step Three:

Select the Basics tab of the Script Cue. In the right side of the window, click on the Hotkey Trigger checkbox. Once this has been clicked, the next keystroke hit on your keyboard will be set as the Hotkey to trigger the Script Cue. (For mine, I use shift + 1.)

Step Four:

Select Cue 1 and then click the assigned Hotkey. This will open a dialog window reading "Insert + or − Volume Change." To increase the volume insert a + followed by a numeric value (such as +5 to increase the Master by 5 dB). After clicking ok, select Cue 1 and note that the Master volume will match the increment inserted in the window.

It is worth noting that the use of such AppleScript Cues with Hotkey assignments might be best stored in a separate cue list so as to not add clutter to your workspace. Even when the Script Cue is hidden in a second cue list, though, it can still be triggered via Hotkey.

Group Cues

Other than the Fade Cue, the Group Cue is likely the most commonly used cue type in any cue list. One reason for the prevalence of this cue is its versatility. As the Group Cue is such an essential component to dynamic cueing possibilities, the following chapter both details its use and offers up practical projects for learning how to best utilize the Group Cue in your own projects.

9.1 Understanding Group Cues

Group Cues are simple to understand, yet have the ability to be utilized to create subtle and complex effects. One key feature of the Group Cue is that grouping cues together does not change the way in which they function, it just enables the ability to control the cues by grouping them together. Though the only true function of the Group Cue is to contain other cues within it, there are many creative uses for creating a group rather than leaving cues independently organized.

1. **Organization:** One of the main reasons for using a Group Cue is the ability to "hide" some of your more complex cues. This method hides those numerous cues inside one folder on the desktop, saving the operator from having to look at a large number of cues cluttering the workspace.
2. **Complex Cue Control:** Group Cues allow for more complex cueing, enabling multiple sub-cues of differing cue types to be fired simultaneously or in sequence. For example, special effects cues are often composed of multiple different cue types with varying continue states, fades, and control cues combined to create one single effect in the show. A good example of this is a rainstorm. The stage manager might simply call one cue to trigger "go rainstorm," but the programming for that cue might entail 10–12 different combinations of Audio Cues, Fade Cues, GoTo Cues, Start Cue, or more. One great use of the Group Cue is to simply drag all of the necessary rainstorm cues into the one group and label it "rainstorm."

3. **Consolidating Control:** Fade Cues and many control cues can affect all "children" within a Group Cue (play, pause, stop). This means a simplified method of controlling one or multiple cues. Keep in mind, though, that some Group Cues will sound fake if faded out as a group.

4. **Randomized Playback:** Group Cues can be programmed to play back their internal cues in a random order. One of the most versatile functions of the Group Cue is the ability to program it to fire a random internal cue then proceed to the next cue in the workspace. By randomizing playback and adding a Play Cue to the group, an intelligent programmer can use this function to get around repetitious loop sounds for things like city street sounds or environmental sound effects.

9.2 Inserting and Editing Group Cues

Group Cues, like all other cue types, are inserted via the Toolbox or Toolbar. Click on the Group Cue icon to insert a Group Cue place keeper. If using the default hotkey configuration, pressing ⌘0 will also insert a Group Cue. Once inserted into your cue list, simply drag one or more selected cues into the cue line of the Group Cue. You will notice that the cue line for the Group Cue will be highlighted with a blue rectangle when you have positioned your cursor in the correct location. Care should always be taken when dragging and dropping files in your workspace. If you accidentally drag a cue onto another cue (besides a Group Cue), it can replace the cue or, in the case of a Fade Cue, reset the cue's target.

Once inserted, the Group Cue has a limited number of control functions compared to other cue types. The following section details Group Cue control functions found in the Inspector Panel.

Inspector Panel: Basics

The Basics panel is similar to that seen on all of the other cue types. It is split into two columns: basic information and triggering information (Figure 9.1). Basic information includes cue number, name, wait times, and continue modes. Unlike some other cue types, the target function is not applicable to the Group Cue. Triggering functions are shown in the second column. Like other cue types, Group Cues can be triggered by MIDI control, hotkey, wall clock, or timecode.

Figure 9.1
The Group Cue
basics tab.

Inspector Panel: Mode

The mode of a Group Cue determines how the cue will behave once it is triggered for playback. Figure 9.2 shows the layout of the Mode tab. One key term in discussing Group Cue modes is **child**. In Group Cues, individual cues contained within the Group Cue folder are referred to as a child. This term is fundamental to understanding Group Cue function. The four different Group Cue modes are listed below.

- The first mode is labeled, **Start first child and enter into group**. This mode establishes that when you click GO on the group, it will start playing the first child of the group, then set the playback position to the next child. This is the mode most often used and is useful for creating things like a pre-show playlist. To create a playlist, simply insert a number of cues into a Group Cue and set each audio file as Auto-Follow.
- The next mode, **Start first child and go to next cue**, allows for the playback position to move to the next cue in the cue list after the Group Cue. This is particularly useful for creating a Group Cue with lots of internal automation when you have a subsequent cue to be fired before the Group Cue completes its action. For instance, you can create a Group Cue sequence ending with a GoTo and Play Cue that would trigger the first child once the last one had finished, thereby creating an infinite loop. In order to stop this loop, you would have a Fade Cue as the next cue in the cue list. If you set the group mode as start first child and go to next cue, the playback position would be set on the Fade Cue, waiting for your trigger to fade out the infinitely looping Group Cue.
- The third mode, **Start all children simultaneously** means that, upon pressing GO, all of the children in that group will play back at the same time. This is particularly useful for special effects, such as a car crash or an offstage explosion. For the explosion effect, create a Group Cue and drag the multiple explosion sound files into the group with the mode set to start all children simultaneously. This will enable you to play back multiple audio files at once without having the operator press GO numerous times. Of course, each child can have its own pre-wait settings, if desired. This can give a more realistic effect, rather than everything beginning at exactly the same moment.
- The final mode is likely used with the least frequency, but offers flexibility for creating nuanced designs. **Start random child and go to the next cue** does just what it says – it will pick a random child within the group, activate it for playback, and then progress the playback position to the next cue in

Figure 9.2
The Group Cue
Mode tab.

the cue list. This mode is useful in creating sound loops that need to have a more random/organic feel to them. One great example, as mentioned earlier, is creating street sounds for an urban environment. Street sounds are both monotonous and random at the same time. Should you choose to use a pre-recorded sound effect for an urban background loop, you run the risk of the audience hearing the same effects looping back. Nothing kills the gravitas of a sound recording like your audience noticing the same car driving by every minute. Short of using a 30-minute long recording, the random playback Group Cue is the best way to accomplish a more realistic sounding urban landscape.

In order to accomplish this, set up a Group Cue with lots of different sound effects housed within: motorcycles, bikes, people walking, car horns, etc. Make sure that you have these recordings set up to pan from both different directions so you get a realistic interpretation of standing on a street corner. Set up a loop by adding a Play Cue at the end of the sequence and set the mode to start random child and go to next cue. This will create a randomized loop of sound effects for your urban landscape.

9.3 Workspace Function

One of the last areas of importance to understanding the Group Cue's use is its function within the cue row. There are two practical functions of the Group Cue within the cue row: notes and hiding contents. Both are simple to understand, yet essential to creating an efficient workspace.

Cue Name

Like all cue types, the cue name of Group Cues can be changed to suit the needs of the show. I find it useful to name my Group Cues in a descriptive fashion, since the Group Cue hides a number of cues within its folder. For instance, naming the Group Cue "Pre-show music" is a useful way for the operator to keep track of the group function without having the folder expanded to see its contents.

Notes

Like all other cue types, the Group Cue allows for inserting information in the Notes panel at the top of the screen (Figure 9.3a). The Notes panel allows for the creation of a note specific to the given cue that might be beneficial or informative for the QLab operator. When QLab is placed in Show Mode, the window takes up a large portion of the interface directly beneath the cue name (see Figure 9.3b). Unlike previous versions of QLab, the ability to add images has been removed in Version 3. The notes field has been relegated to plain text

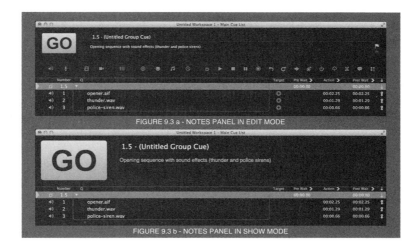

Figure 9.3
(a) The notes panel in Edit Mode. (b) The notes panel in Show Mode.

Figure 9.4
Note the rectangular box around the Group Cue contents.

formatting only. It is worth mentioning that the Show Mode window does allow for viewing more text than the Edit Mode notes panel, due to its larger size.

Hiding Group Cue Contents

Another useful function of the Group Cue is the ability to hide the contents of a Group Cue. As mentioned earlier, this is great for reducing workspace clutter. By default, any children added to a Group Cue will be shown in a cascading format beneath the parent cue. The expanded Group Cue features a blue rounded rectangle box highlighting its children (see Figure 9.4). To hide the internal cues, simply click on the downward facing arrow beside the Group Cue name in the Q column. This will change the arrow from downward facing to pointing to the right. To expand the Group Cue at a later time, simply click on the right arrow icon to re-open the folder.

9.4 Group Cue Projects

The following projects detail two common uses of the Group Cue in action: creating a playlist and using a Fade Cue to end playback; and simultaneous playback of children for creating effects cues.

Project 9.1 ▼

Using the Group Cue to Create a Playlist

One of the most common uses of the Group Cue is in creating a sequence of audio files that need to loop. Many shows have pre-show, intermission, or post-show music. Though there is no function of QLab that simply entails dropping audio files into a playlist, the combined use of the Group Cue with multiple Audio Cues and a Start Cue allows for the creation of a loop-able collection of music, which can play indefinitely until faded out. The process is quite simple and one that should be mastered, as it is used in most every production. The following project walks you through the creation of such a playlist.

Step One:
Download Project 9.1 from the companion website. This workspace features three short musical snippets that can be used for the playlist.

Step Two:
Click on the Group Cue icon to add a Group Cue to the playlist.

Step Three:
Drag the first Audio Cue into the Group Cue. Set the follow status as auto-follow.

Step Five:
Repeat step four for each of the additional Audio Cues.

Step Five:
Insert a Start Cue into the workspace and then drag it into the Group Cue as the last cue in the sequence.

Step Six:
Set Cue 1 as the target for the Start Cue. This will create a loop that will play the group indefinitely until faded out.

Step Seven:
Insert a Fade Cue outside of the Group Cue. Set the Group Cue as the target file of the Fade Cue. Under the Levels tab of the Fade Cue, pull the Master fader down to -INF and select the "Stop Target When Done" checkbox (see Figure 9.5).

Figure 9.5
Master fader levels set to -INF.

> *Step Eight:*
> Test your playlist. When the Group Cue is triggered, you will notice that the playback position will automatically jump down to the Fade Cue so you can fade out the Group Cue at any point desired.

Project 9.2 ▼

> ## Simultaneous Playback of Children
>
> Another common use of the Group Cue is the creation of effects cues in which multiple sounds play back concurrently. The benefit of using the Group Cue is unifying control wherein all cues are fired by clicking the Go button only once. Another benefit is removing clutter from your workspace, given the Group Cue's ability to collapse and hide its children. The following project details the steps necessary to create a car crash sound effect. This file contains several different Audio Cues each with its own different attributes.
>
> *Step One:*
> Download Project 9.2 from the companion website.
>
> *Step Two:*
> You will notice that there are several cues in the workspace. The first is a Group Cue that currently contains no internal cues. Pull the Audio Cues into the Group Cue, keeping them in chronological order.
>
> *Step Three:*
> Select the Mode tab in the Inspector Panel of Cue 1 and click on the button labeled "Start All Children Simultaneously." This will make all the cues fire at the same time.
>
> *Step Four:*
> Select various cues and experiment with how the car crash might sound differently with pre-waits added. For instance, add a pre-wait of 1.5 seconds to Cue 3.
>
> *Step Five:*
> Test the playback of the cue sequence.

Video Systems

Like the sound systems mentioned earlier in the text, a video system is a collection of components: media storage unit (computer), cameras, cabling/network, and output devices (monitors, projectors, televisions, and light-emitting diode [LED]/liquid crystalline display [LCD] panels). The video system deals with both audio and video combined together for the playback of still images, prerecorded video, or live video inputted from a camera. As you might assume, there are a number of different configurations one could choose, based on the needs of the project. The following chapter details the purpose of different video systems and their components.

10.1 Understanding Video Systems

As mentioned earlier in the text, QLab is a remarkable tool for a number of different production environments. In addition to live theatre, there is dance, live music, theme parks, museums, trade shows, and more. The use of the video system will invariably change, depending on the environment for which it is designed. Ultimately, there will be three basic types of video systems set up for use with QLab: an editing system, a playback system, and a reinforcement system. After reading the chapter on sound systems, these terms should be familiar to you as they are similarly used for audio and video systems alike. The following section details the types of video systems and their use with QLab.

Editing System

Though not specifically used in conjunction with QLab, the first step necessary to creating and/or editing content for playback with QLab is the editing system. As with audio, almost all content creation and editing is done through software on your computer. You could spends tens of thousands of dollars to create a high-end editing station with digital video cameras, editing software, interfaces, graphics software, and more. Likewise, if you own any Macintosh computer, you already have the beginnings of a digital video workstation in the onboard Face Time camera and iMovie.

One important thing to remember is that QLab refers to the playback of any image as video, whether it is a moving picture or a still image. This means that graphics editing programs are very handy for content creation, as well as those for video editing and sound. Graphics programs such as Adobe Photoshop, Adobe Illustrator, and Adobe After Effects have become staples in content creation for video systems. Digital video editing programs such as Final Cut Pro, Adobe Premiere, Avid Media Composer, and Sony Vegas Pro have all carved out a corner of the market, as well. Finally, no editing system would be complete without sound editing software, as well. Both Logic Pro and Pro Tools offer the ability to integrate video into the editing workspace and sync audio with your video.

For video editing considerations, the most important hardware aspects to consider are processor speed (CPU), RAM, and graphics card (GPU). Whenever possible, try to purchase a system that is upgradable like the Mac Pro tower. Hardware eventually becomes obsolete, and it is much cheaper in the long run to upgrade components of your system rather than buying a new computer (although it appears that current trends are moving away from easily upgradable systems). Another important consideration is storage. Video files are large and take up a lot of space. Make sure to have a dedicated drive for video storage with a minimum of 1 terabyte storage capacity that is separate from your startup disk. Redundant array of independent disks (RAIDs) or solid state drive drives (SSDs) are preferable, whenever possible, as they can increase both dependability and speed.

Video Playback System

Video playback systems are a combination of equipment necessary to play back prerecorded video or still images in a live performance/installation environment.

Like audio systems, the video playback system is a combination of one or more computers connected either directly to an output device(s) or into a network. It is much more common in the video system, however, to find a number of different computers each running their own QLab workspace networked into a "master computer" running its own QLab workspace as a controller for all of the component computers and devices.

Again, there are a number of different hardware options for a playback system. One major consideration is the number of video outputs available. Some graphics cards have only one video output, though there are many GPUs that offer more than one output. A playback computer might be specially built with multiple graphics cards to offer numerous video outputs. In addition, there are other hardware options, such as graphics expansion devices that use the processing power of your GPU, but spread it out across two or three outputs. The Matrox DualHead2Go or TripleHead2Go are two such options that effectively allow for the video signal from your computer to be split across multiple outputs, though there are other products on the market that perform the task as well.

Video Reinforcement System

A video reinforcement system is the combination of one or more cameras with QLab and its system of output devices in order to capture and play back live footage from the camera. The reinforcement system is identical to the playback system except in two key features: first, the input video signal comes from a camera, rather than from a video or graphics file saved on the computer's hard drive; second, Camera Cues do not include an audio signal.

The QLab video reinforcement system works with any FireWire DV, Blackmagic (a high-end cinema-quality digital video input source), or Face-Time camera attached to the system. In addition, it can accept input signals via Syphon, an open-source Mac OS X technology that allows applications to share frames— both still or full frame rate video. One main consideration in camera playback is latency. Latency will vary drastically between different camera models. As such, it is best to experiment with different cameras until you find the right device for your production needs.

10.2 Video System Components

Similar to the world of audio, the sheer amount of technology needed for video and graphic systems is amazingly high. Factor into that the frequency with which new products or upgrades to old products enter the market and it can make your head spin. Though our main focus of the text is not equipment, it is impossible to discuss many of the uses of QLab without at least taking a rudimentary look at the equipment necessary to set up a video system. The following section examines some of the basic equipment needed for a video system. While it is by no means an exhaustive list, it should be a good starting point for those new to the world of video systems.

The Digital Video Camera

Video cameras have been around for a very long time. The first video cameras functioned in an analog sense, using a lens to capture moving light, store the impulses on some type of film or tape, and then translate it into a moving image. Digital video camera hardware functions is much the same way as analog technology to capture imagery. Where they vary from their older analog counterparts is the way in which the data is stored. Digital video cameras are made up of two main components: the camera and the recorder. They use a lens to capture the moving light like traditional video cameras, and then send the light through one or more sensors to translate this captured light into images. The captured video image is then translated into computer pixels.

A **pixel** is short for the term "picture element." These tiny dots of color are the smallest element making up a digital image. Typically, thousands of pixels combine together to make an image viewed on a digital monitor. Another important term, **resolution** can be associated with pixels. Resolution, in video or graphics terms, refers to the number of pixels used to make up a digital image. The higher the pixel count, the higher the resolution, resulting in a higher-quality digital image.

These pixels are sampled by the camera at a predetermined rate and compiled into one set, representing a single still moment in time, referred to as a **frame**. Each video is made up of multiple frames, typically anywhere from 24 to 72 frames per second (fps). Playing back these still frames in rapid succession creates the illusion of movement to the human eye. These frames are either stored on the camera's memory unit or directly outputted to an external device.

Computer

For the purposes of a QLab Video System, there are only two typical uses: video playback and live video reinforcement. In either of these configurations, the next logical step in the system is the computer. If recording video for later playback, the computer will be used in conjunction with video editing software to edit audio and video components of the digital video file. Software allows for editing the digital video signal down to single frames and adding multiple effects to the image and/or audio.

If using QLab as a video reinforcement system, the camera is activated by a Camera Cue and streams live video signal directly into QLab to be outputted through the video patch and directly to one or more output devices (monitors, projectors, etc.)

Interface Connections

For any type of audio/video system, physical connections (both hardware devices and cabling) comprise a substantial amount of the necessary components. Each device in your system will require some type of cabling for input and output. Typically, this is one of the commonly overlooked costs of setting up a video system, as well. Keep in mind that each project can have considerably different needs, based on the number of input devices, computers, output devices, and the distance between each component in the system. It is often a good idea to sketch or draft out a plan that takes into consideration the distances between each component and the required physical connections between each device. This requires a thorough knowledge of all equipment and the necessary connectors, cabling, and/or adapters. Listed below are several common types of interface connections.

Interface Connection	Audio/ Video	Digital/ Analog	Connector Type
Video Graphics Array (VGA)	Video	Analog	D-subminiature 15 pin
Composite (CVBS)	Video	Analog	RCA jack
S-Video	Video	Analog	Mini-DIN 4pin
Component	Video	Analog	3 RCA jacks
Digital Visual Interface (DVI)	Video	Analog/Digital)**	DVI connector**
High-Definition Multimedia Interface (HDMI)	A/V	Digital	HDMI connector
DisplayPort	A/V	Digital	Display Port connector
Mini DisplayPort/Thunderbolt	A/V*	Digital	Mini DisplayPort connector
IEEE 1394 (FireWire)	A/V*	Digital	FireWire connector
Universal Serial Bus (USB)	A/V*	Digital	USB connector
Category 5/6 (CAT 5/CAT 6)	A/V	Digital	8P8C connector

*Indicates BUS power capability.
**Depending on cable type, the allowable signal may vary: DVI-A (analog only), DVI-D (digital only), or DVI-I (digital and analog).

Video Only – Analog

Video Graphics Array
IBM first introduced Video Graphics Array (VGA) to the market in 1987, and it quickly became an industry standard for video transmission. Typically, VGA uses the DE-15 variety of D-sub connecter, with 15 connector pins oriented in three rows (see Figure 10.1).

Composite Video
Composite video often referred to as CVBS for "color, video, blanking, and sync" is an analog video transmission across an RCA connector. It is a single channel transmission of standard definition video at either 480i or 576i resolution.

Figure 10.1
A male VGA connector. *Photo courtesy: Evan Amos.*

Figure 10.2
RCA plugs for composite video (yellow) and stereo audio (white and red). *Photo courtesy: Evan Amos.*

The standard color coding for a composite video cable is yellow. For home applications, you will frequently see this accompanied with a red and white cable, as well, for right and left audio signals, respectively (as seen in Figure 10.2).

Separate Video

Separate video (S-Video) as it is most commonly referred, is a two-channel analog video transmission of standard definition typically at 480i or 576i resolution. S-Video uses the four-pin mini-DIN connector, seen in Figure 10.3. It is a slightly higher quality than that of composite video, due to its two-channel separation of the video information.

Component Video

Component video a common term used to refer to the YP_BP_R method of transmitting analog video across component video cables (see Figure 10.4). This method transmits an analog video signal that has been split into three channels Y (which carries luminance, or brightness, information), P_B (which carries the difference between blue and luminance), and P_R (which carries the difference between red and luminance). The component video cable,

Figure 10.3
A male Mini-DIN S-Video connector. *Photo courtesy: Evan Amos.*

Figure 10.4
RCA plugs used
for YP$_B$P$_R$ analog
component video.
*Photo courtesy: Evan
Amos.*

sometimes referred to as a "yipper" cable, utilize three RCA jacks in green, blue, and red (Figure 10.4). The green cable carries the Y channel, the blue carries P$_B$, and the red carries P$_R$. Though an analog signal, component video is capable of supporting a number of resolutions up to 1080p.

Video Only – Analog/Digital

Digital Visual Interface

Digital Visual Interface (DVI) was developed in 1999 as an industry standard interface for the transfer of digital video content. The cable is used to connect a video source with an output device, such as a monitor or projector. DVI can support analog or digital signals, meaning that it is a particularly versatile interface when working with a variety of sources. Maximum resolution for DVI video signal is WUXGA (1920 × 1200).

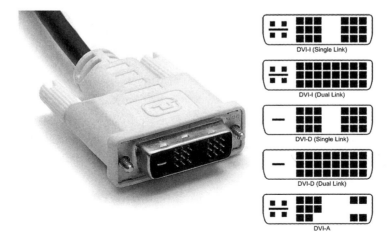

Figure 10.5
A male DVI cable
and various
connector types.
*Photo courtesy: Evan
Amos.*

There are different varieties of DVI cables for differing signal needs: DVI-A (analog only), DVI-D (digital only), and DVI-I (integrated: either analog or digital). In addition, there is another type of cable for higher video resolution bandwidth, called Dual Link DVI. The Dual Link DVI doubles the amount of TMDS pairs, effectively doubling the video bandwidth. Dual Link is only available for DVI-D and DVI-I. All of the connector types are shown in Figure 10.5.

Video and Audio – Digital

High-Definition Multimedia Interface

High-Definition Multimedia Interface (HDMI) 1.0 was developed in 2002 as a reverse compatible interface for DVI that supported both audio and video signals. Since a consortium of electronics and motion pictures producers developed HDMI, it was quickly adopted as an industry standard in hi-definition televisions and projection equipment. The cable was designed to be electrically compatible with DVI signals, so no signal conversion is required nor is there a loss of video quality for the use of a DVI-HDMI adapter. As of 2013, development began for a new HDMI 2.0 specification with the hope of supporting 4k resolution at 60 fps, improved 3d capability, and increased audio channels. There are five different types of HDMI connectors: Type A–Type E. Type A (Full size HDMI), Type C (Mini), and Type D (Micro) are the most common connectors currently used. Many Macintosh computers now feature an HDMI output as part of the video card. The HDMI Type A connector can be seen in Figure 10.6.

DisplayPort

DisplayPort was yet another graphics interface specification designed to replace VGA and DVI interfaces. DisplayPort was conceived by a consortium of electronics manufacturers in 2006 and designed to be backwards compatible with both VGA

Figure 10.6
An HDMI Type A male connector.
Photo courtesy: Evan Amos.

Figure 10.7
A DisplayPort
connector.

and DVI. This is particularly useful in that adapter devices are readily available for use with older interface types. DisplayPort can transmit both audio and video simultaneously or alone. In comparing DisplayPort to HDMI, they are quite similar in resolution, with DisplayPort having slightly more than twice the bandwidth capabilities of HDMI, enabling it to share this bandwidth with multiple streams of audio and video to separate devices. Unlike HDMI, DisplayPort was created with as a royalty-free interface, so manufacturers do not have to pay a fee to use the technology. This meant a quick industry-wide adoption across a number of computer and A/V platforms. The DisplayPort utilizes a proprietary DisplayPort connector (see Figure 10.7).

Mini DisplayPort/Thunderbolt
In 2008, Apple Inc. began development of a new Mini DisplayPort interface, built on the DisplayPort framework, but in a smaller size and with higher possible resolution (Shown in Figure 10.8). Like the DisplayPort before it, Mini

Figure 10.8
A Mini DisplayPort
connector.

DisplayPort was developed to be royalty-free to ensure a widespread industry adoption. One complication of early Mini DisplayPort use in Apple computers (pre-2010) was the inability to transmit both audio and video signals. For these earlier models, audio had to be transmitted via Universal Serial Bus (USB), FireWire, or audio line out. Later editions of Apple computers addressed this issue. Since 2011, though Apple computers have introduced a new variety of interface, still using the Mini DisplayPort connector, called Thunderbolt.

Thunderbolt

Thunderbolt is an interface developed between Intel and Apple Inc. It is electrically identical to the Mini DisplayPort, but combines the function of the PCI Express (PCIe) high-speed serial bus standard with the Mini DisplayPort to create an ultra-high-speed interface (with a data bitrate of 10 Gbit/s) capable of powering up to six external devices through one connection (via hubs or "daisy chaining" devices). Since the Thunderbolt was released in 2011, there are still a limited number of peripheral devices on the market, though adoption is rapidly increasing. The Thunderbolt connector also supplies a DC power signal for bus-powering devices.

IEEE 1394 (FireWire)

IEEE 1394 (most commonly referred to as FireWire) is a serial bus interface developed over a period from 1986 to 1995 by Apple Inc. and a small group of other engineers from other technology companies. Similar to USB, FireWire is a type of bus technology for inputting and outputting digital signals and power and the High-Definition Audio-Video Alliance (HANA) standard for communication between A/V equipment. Because of this, most digital cameras (both video and still) utilize this connector. It can be daisy chained to a remarkably high number of devices (up to 63) and used with other connector types, such as wireless, fiber optic, Ethernet, or coaxial. The most common industry connectors, though, are known as FireWire 400 or FireWire 800.

FireWire 400 (technically known as IEEE 1394-1995) was the original interface released in 1995 (Figure 10.9a). It can transfer data at rates of 100, 200, or 400 Mbit/s and carry power signals, as well.

Figure 10.9
(a) FireWire 400 cable. (b) FireWire 800 cable.

FireWire 800 (technically known as IEEE 1394b-2002) was introduced in 2002 as a specification that allowed for data transfer of up to 786.432 Mbit/s, while still remaining backwards compatible with FireWire 400 devices. Though compatible, the FireWire 800 utilizes a different connector types (Figure 10.9b), necessitating the use of an adapter to work between the two specifications.

Universal Serial Bus

Like the FireWire, the USB is a serial cable used for connecting a wide array of devices and peripherals, both for communication and power supply (Figure 10.10). Introduced in 1996, USB quickly became the industry standard for computing devices and has since become prevalent in cellular phones, video gaming consoles, audio interfaces, and more. Over the years, USB has introduced various versions: USB 1 (Full Speed) at 12 Mbit/s, USB 2.0 (High Speed) at 480 Mbit/s, and, most recently, USB 3.0 (Super Speed) at 5 Gbit/s. There are numerous connectors, as well (Type A, Type B, Mini-B, Micro-A, and Micro-B) with the Mini and Micro connectors being used most often for smaller devices such as cameras, tablets, and telephones.

Category 5/6

The final interface type that is becoming increasingly prevalent in entertainment applications is that of the Category 5/6 (CAT 5/CAT 6) (Figure 10.11). As more control systems become network capable, the use of Ethernet style Local Area Networks (LANs) or Wide Area Networks is commonplace. This development has led to the proliferation of CAT 5 and/or CAT 6 cable as an interface. One reason for the use of networking is the ability to send signals over longer cable runs than traditionally possible with the types listed above.

CAT 5, frequently referred to as Ethernet cable, is a twisted pair cable used for carrying signals (data, telephony, and video) at high-speed rates (100 MHz). CAT 6 uses the similar Ethernet connector as CAT 5, but is designed to provide a faster data transfer rate (250 MHz) and reduces crosstalk and system noise.

Figure 10.10
A standard USB Type-A connector.
Photo courtesy: Evan Amos.

Figure 10.11
A CAT 5 connector.

Though both CAT 5/6 can be used for transmitting audio, they were not originally used for this application in the entertainment industry. With new developments, though, there are signs of this becoming more commonplace. There are devices known as **baluns**, which function as converters to allow for the input and output of audio and video signals across CAT 5/6. The balun is a type of transceiver that converts the unbalanced signal from the network cable and outputs a balanced signal, suitable for audio and video applications. In addition, there are varieties of audio baluns that provide Phantom power and output via traditional audio interfaces, such as XLR.

Another common use of CAT 5/6 cable is for the creation of a LAN for control purposes. QLab 3 is designed to work across a network and communicate with multiple computers running QLab on the network. This function is highly desirable when using QLab as a Show Control system to interact with an audio system, video system, lighting control system, and so on. Today most digital control devices are equipped with some type of network port allowing them to be connected to and controlled across a network.

Output Devices

Video output devices can be any of a number of types from computer monitors, to televisions, projectors, or flat panel displays such as LCD or LED monitors. Essentially, an output device is a transducer that receives the input video signal and translates it into light impulses. The video monitor / television / projector industry is in a state of constant and rapid change, utilizing new technologies to create high-definition and 3D capable output devices. The most common devices for entertainment industry applications are digital projectors and flat panel displays. Listed below are some basic considerations to keep in mind with using these types of output devices.

Digital Projectors

Digital projectors, sometimes called video projectors, are digital outputs that accept audio and video signals from a number of different source types from computers, to DVD/Blu-ray, or live input from a video camera. Though digital projectors have been used in movie theatres for a number of years, it is still somewhat of a luxury for many live venues across the country. The cost of digital projectors has decreased at an incredible rate over the years, though, making it increasingly common in both professional and academic theatre programs, houses of worship, convention centers, and music venues.

Digital projectors work by receiving a video signal, transmitting it through a bright light source (i.e. a lamp or LED cluster) and through a lens to enlarge the image and project it across a distance, known as its **throw**. Common projector types are LCD, Digital Light Processing (DLP), and LED. The first two types utilize a high-intensity lamp, whereas the latter uses an LED cluster, creating a cooler system with less energy consumption and negating the need for lamp replacement.

Considerations for digital projectors tend to fall into two categories: brightness (lumens) and operating distance (throw ratio). Projectors are, at their heart, lighting instruments that transmit moving light. As such, using a projector in conjunction with other lighting instruments can lead to the image being "washed out" or dim, depending on the spill of other lighting instruments in use at the time. The amount of light in a given space, outside of that created by the projector, is commonly referred to as **ambient light**. The greater the amount of ambient light, the greater the need for a digital projector with high brightness output, typically referred to as "high-lumens." For most entertainment applications, there are three suitable categories of lumens: mid range (2,000–3,000 lumens), high-performance range (3,000–4,500 lumens), and ultra-bright range (4,500–12,000 lumens). For many theatrical applications, the high-performance range is the suitable and not cost-prohibitive. As throw distance and ambient light increases, though, the ultra-bright range is a must. Of course, the price of this range is incredibly high as compared to the lower range models.

Throw distance is the second consideration that will influence the type of projector necessary for a given project. All digital projectors have a given throw ratio that describes the ratio of the distance to the screen (throw) to the resulting image width. For instance, if a projector has a throw ratio or 2:1 and the projector is placed 10 feet away from the screen, then the resulting image width would be 5 feet. It is worth noting that, since most projectors have zoom lenses, most ratios will be variable in nature (i.e. 2–2.4 : 1). All decisions for projector selection should take into consideration both the need for lumens and throw distance.

Flat Panel Displays

Flat panel displays have been around for some time and now represent a significantly higher share of the market than classical televisions or cathode ray tube (CRT) models. Most flat panel displays today are LCD technology, with a thin layer of liquid crystal sandwiched between two conducting layers. Most LCD panels are backlit to make them easier to see under ambient light. Another variety of flat panel is the plasma display. A plasma display is so named for being composed of millions of tiny compartmentalized cells housed between two layers of glass. These cells each contain electrically charged ionized gas, making them glow like miniature fluorescent lamps when electrified. The plasma display produces vivid colors and deeper blacks, enabling a high contrast ratio for displayed video. Likewise, it can be manufactured in large panels and is quite thin – typically around 4".

One of the emergent trends in all areas related to lighting and media is the use of LED technology. LED displays are quite popular due to their ability to produce incredibly bright, vivid colors while using a smaller amount of electricity and having a longer life than traditional lighting fixtures or projectors. One interesting aspect of LED displays is that, depending on the project, they can function as a component of the lighting design, the projection/media design, or both. LED displays all utilize clusters of red, green, and blue diodes combined together to make what is known as a color pixel. The technology varies from conventional signage models utilizing discrete LED clusters to surface mounted devices (SMDs) that feature LEDs mounted directly to printed circuit board panels that can be readily connected to one another. One great advantage to the SMD LED display is the ability to curve the display into interesting curvilinear forms.

One final consideration with video displays is the ability to link multiple displays together to create a **video wall**. The term video wall refers to the use of multiple output sources, either contiguously or overlapped, in such a fashion as to create one large screen. This concept is important to QLab 3, as this version replaces the old model of outputting to individual screens with a new model of creating a **surface** composed of one or multiple outputs devices and transferring the data to those individual devices directly from QLab, itself. This new model makes the creation of video walls from QLab much easier than that in earlier versions.

10.3 Understanding Video Signal Flow

Like other cue types seen before, the idea of signal flow is a bit of an abstraction, considering much of the signal path is contained within QLab itself. It is important, though, to understand the path that a video signal takes from source to output. For the following examples, we will look at the signal path for both Video Cues and Camera Cues.

Video/Image File/Video Feed

The first step of any type of signal flow is always the source. In this case, the source will be a prerecorded video, a still image file, or a live video feed from a camera. In the case of the first two, a Video Cue targets the files. For the latter, a Camera Cue activates the camera for playback purposes.

Video Cue/Camera Cue

Video and Camera Cues are the place keepers within the workspace that either activate playback of the existing video or graphic file or trigger live video feed from a video camera. In either case, the signal proceeds from the cue directly into the video surface patch.

Video Surface Patch

The video surface patch controls a number of features related to how you output your video or camera signals. There are a number of differences on the video side of QLab3 compared to previous versions. If you used QLab 2, no doubt one of the first things you will notice is the use of surfaces rather than screens.

The new video engine in QLab is based around the concept of a **video surface**. A video surface is an output made up of one or more screens (video outputs). This new concept gives much more versatility. Video surfaces let you focus on what you see on the stage, rather than the signal going to each individual projector. Each "screen" attached to your QLab computer will receive its own single-screen surface by default, so if you only need simple output, these surfaces are plug and play. The versatility comes in by understanding that you can create a custom surface made up of one or more screens. In the workspace settings, you can create a master surface made up of multiple screens (i.e. projectors, or flat panel displays) and let QLab do the hard work of breaking up your signal to send it out to the screens that make up your surface!

Pro-Tip ▼

It is important to understand the distinction between the default single-screen surfaces and new surfaces made that output to the same screen (video output). Changes made to single-screen surfaces (such as corner pinning or shuttering) are unique to that surface. They **do not** carry over to other surfaces that might use the same screen for output.

In addition to parsing up digital signals into component packages, surfaces also have the ability to apply numerous powerful effects to any Video or Camera Cue outputted through a surface patch:

- **Built-in Edge Blending:** Each surface patch can automatically calculate edge blending (a decrease in the intensity of light transmitted on the edges of a projected image) for each overlapping projector on your surface. This reduces the noticeable appearance of "bright spots" where projectors overlap.

- **Global Masking:** Masking is the process of adding an image file as a frame around a video or image file. With a transparent center, the video passes through the center, but it is masked by the image on the surface edges. This is particularly beneficial for removing the look of "rectangles of light" with projections. In QLab 3, instead of taking the time to create a transparent background image, you can simply upload a graphic file with a white fill where you want video to be visible. It can be then attached to a video surface and QLab does the hard work of sending the appropriate section of the image out to the component parts of your surface. In addition, QLab watches the mask file for changes, so all you have to do is edit and save in your image editor and QLab will make sure to display the most current version. Though this may seem like a small feature, it is quite a timesaver when editing multiple files.

- **Built-in Adjustment for Ceiling and Rear Projection:** One aspect of projection that has always been troublesome is determining the placement of projectors and their configuration (rear, front, ceiling, table). For each of these changes, the required image must be different or it will be reversed or flipped. QLab 3 builds in these changes to the image file at the touch of a button by ceiling and rear checkboxes in the surface-editing menu.

- **Keystone Correction:** When a projector is not aligned perpendicularly to a projection surface, even by a few degrees, it skews the image to be smaller at the top or bottom. Most projectors have built-in keystone correction to correct this anomaly. QLab surfaces have the built-in **corner pins**, a common video editing tool that allows for grabbing a pin located in each of the four corners of the surface and moving them to create a new shape (see Figure 10.12). This resulting shape will then be imposed on the video output, skewing it to match the shape.

- **Projection Mapping:** Projection mapping, also referred to as video mapping, is the powerful process of editing a projected image to match the surface dimensions of objects (even those that are irregularly shaped with numerous dimensional planes). Through the use of mathematical equations to determine the relationship of a three-dimensional object to the exact placement of a projector, you can skew the image in such a way that the resulting image is perceived without distortion. By using the corner pinning and video grid capabilities of the surface patch, projection mapping is much easier in QLab 3 than its predecessors. In simple terms, you can shape a single surface to match the shape of the projection surface (i.e. a door). For

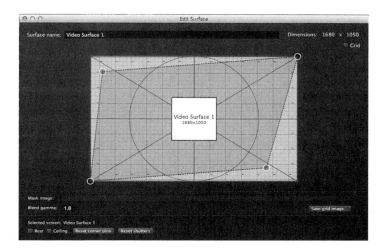

Figure 10.12
Corner pinning.

more complex three-dimensional shapes, the combination of multiple surface patches designed to fit the shape of various planes allows for projection
mapping on complex surfaces.

- **Support for Graphics Expansion Hardware:** Using the surface patch, you
  can address individual outputs of graphics expansion hardware, like the
  aforementioned Matrox TripleHead or DoubleHead2Go.

Assigned Screens

Leaving the surface patch, the next step in signal flow is to output the video
signal to the screens assigned to the surface patch. As mentioned earlier, each
display device is automatically assigned as a single-screen surface whose attributes can be individually edited. In addition, new surfaces can be created for
your display needs. Since they are all technically referred to as surfaces, this can
get a bit confusing, but with a bit of practice, it will become second nature.

Output Device

The final component of the signal flow chain is the device output (i.e. the
projectors, monitors, or flat panel displays connected to the surface patch).

Audio

Since Video Cues target video files, it is quite common that the file might
contain an audio signal in addition to the video. Audio signals attached to
video are treated in the same way as those in Audio Cues. Within the Inspector
Panel, there are tabs for Audio Levels, Audio Trim, and Audio Effects. An audio
patch is assigned in the Audio Levels tab. The signal then follows the same path
as that discussed in audio signal flow earlier in the text.

Video and Camera Preferences

In Chapter 2, we discussed audio preferences in detail. Similarly, when dealing with video, there are preferences that should be set before ever inputting a Video or Camera Cue into your workspace. Though there are many powerful functions related to video in QLab, the setup tends to be quicker than that of audio because there are significantly less preferences to address. To begin the process, click on the Settings button in the lower right-hand corner of your screen.

11.1 Workspace Settings: Video

The Settings window for video is a simple interface with complex possibilities for configuration (Figure 11.1). At the top of the screen are two drop-down menus: default mode and default surface.

Default Mode

The default mode setting allows for the determination of how new Video Cues will be inputted, as either full screen or custom geometry mode. Full screen simply means the image will fill the entirety of the surface. Custom geometry means that the Video Cue will be inserted with the ability to customize the image proportions and scale, rotate, or translate the image.

Default Surface

The default surface allows you to determine which surface in the available surfaces list will be the default output for newly created Video Cues. It can be any available surface, either single-screen or composite.

Figure 11.1
The video settings
screen.

Available Surfaces

The available surfaces window will display all possibilities for video output. As mentioned earlier, QLab will create a single-screen surface automatically for every display connected to your system. These will be the only surfaces displayed when you first open the Settings window. Each surface will have a distinct name and list its display resolution. You will notice that single-screen surfaces will list an asterisk beside a "single-screen surface" label. This indicates that single-screen surfaces are created automatically for all attached displays and cannot be removed from the list without disconnecting them.

11.2 Editing the Surface Patch

Each surface in the list can be edited by clicking on the Edit button. This is the true power of the surface-based video model. There is no limit to the number of surface patches that can be created. With the ability to edit each patch to have unique attributes, you can change the output from a single projector in complex ways from cue to cue. Likewise, you could output multiple Video Cues through separate surface patches through the same projector simultaneously. In this way, by simply changing the opacity of each Video Cue, you could accomplish some interesting layering effects.

Editing Single-Screen Surfaces

Clicking on the Edit button will open the edit surface interface assigned to your single-screen surface. There are a number of control attributes shown in this interface (see Figure 11.2).

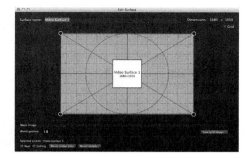

Figure 11.2
The edit surface
interface.

- **Surface Name:** There will be a generic name assigned to any display device connected to your computer, such as color LCD. If you have a number of different screens attached to your system, it can be advantageous to give each surface a unique name. To do so, simply type in the name in this slot and press enter.
- **Video Grid:** The video grid is a numbered grid that correlates to the output dimensions of your surface. The video grid is an important aspect of projection mapping and aids in correct projector placement. There is a checkbox to the right of the screen labeled "Grid." Clicking on this checkbox will display the video grid on your output device. In this way, you can move your projector into correct placement and know that the resulting projected images will align properly with projection screens, scenery, or projection surfaces.
- **Facet Window:** The Facet window is the blue-highlighted box superimposed over the video grid. It has an "x" running from the four corners with a label box in the center containing the name and resolution of the represented screen. In addition, there are yellow circles known as corner pins in each of the four corners. In short, the facet window illustrates the dimensions of a named surface and allows for skewing the resulting video output for the surface. By moving the corner pins, you will change the shape of the facet window – thereby changing the resulting shape of the projected image for that surface. Holding down shift allows for fine adjustments. Experiment with moving the corner pins and see how the surface shape can change. For single-screen surfaces, there is only one facet window, which fills the entire area of the surface. Figure 11.3 illustrates the use of corner pinning on the video grid.
- **Shutters:** One aspect of the surface window that is exceptionally useful is the ability to "shutter off" sections of the surface that you don't want to use. If you hover your cursor over the extreme edges of the surface window, the cursor will change to a vertical line with arrows protruding from each side. This allows you to shutter in the edges of the surface, creating a masked section (Figure 11.4). These shuttered areas will appear as darker than the other areas of the surface window. In Figure 11.4, the top and sides have been shuttered in, while the bottom was left untouched.

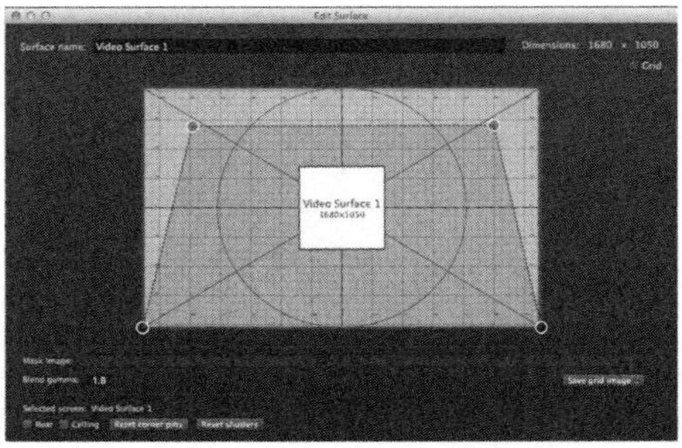

Figure 11.3
The video grid and facet window.

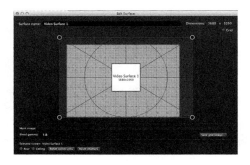

Figure 11.4
The shuttered area is represented by the "grayed-out" selection.

- **Mask Image:** As mentioned in the Chapter 10, masking is the process of adding an image file with opaque edges and a transparent center to serve as a "picture frame" of sorts around a video or graphic file. One possible use for this is the ability to "feather" the edges of an image with some type of gradation, so as to avoid "rectangles of light" with projections. In addition, you could mask out any area of the projected imagery (such as in an open doorway, where you don't want the imagery to appear). The Mask image box in the surface patch allows you to import an image to be used as a mask. To achieve this, simply use a black and white file: black will be the masking solid and white will be transparent (with video showing through it). As a bonus, QLab watches the mask file for changes, so all you have to do is edit and save in your image editor and QLab will make sure to display the most current version.
- **Save Grid Image:** This button saves a picture of the video grid to your desktop. The image is saved in the PNG format. This image is particularly useful to creating mask images. Simply open the image in your favorite image editing software and create new image masks as layers on top of the video grid. This will ensure the appropriate size and proportion of mask images.
- **Mount Position:** One particularly useful function of the surface patch is the mount position controls. The default setting in QLab assumes that you are

projecting from the front and that the projector is in the hanging position commonly referred to as desktop. Traditionally speaking, there have been many hoops to jump through if you hung a projector in a different orientation (either using the built in controls of your projector to change the projection, or to reverse or flip the image in your graphics editing program). With QLab 3, there are two checkboxes that control the image output to accommodate for rear and/or ceiling mounted projection. By clicking one or both of the checkboxes, "rear" or "ceiling," you can adjust image orientation and avoid the troublesome fixes listed earlier.

- **Reset Corner Pins:** The reset corner pins button is a quick method to return the corner pins to their original placement at the corners of the native screen resolution.
- **Reset Shutters:** The reset shutters button quickly returns the shutters to their original placement at the edge of the surface.

Creating and Editing Surfaces

To this point, we have examined the process of editing single-screen surfaces. The backbone of the entire surfaces system, though, is the creation of new and unique surfaces as patches for Video and Camera Cue output. As mentioned earlier, you can create an unlimited number of surfaces, each with unique display attributes assigned to them. The following section addresses the process of creating and editing these surfaces.

To create a new surface, open the Video Settings tab and click on the plus sign icon at the bottom left corner of the screen. This will open an interface for editing the new surface, "Untitled Surface 1." This window will look almost identical to the edit surface interface for single-screen surfaces. There are a few key differences in the operation of these two interfaces, though:

- **Screens Assigned:** In the column to the left of the screen, you will find the "screens assigned" panel. Upon creation, there are no screens assigned to a surface. This is why you will see the yellow warning sign appear to the left of all newly created surfaces. It will disappear once a screen has been assigned to the surface.

  To assign a screen to a surface, click on the plus sign icon at the bottom of the "screens assigned" panel. Upon doing so, a menu will appear listing all of the options for screens attached to your system. Simply add the screens you want to add to your surface and their facet windows will appear superimposed over the video grid for your surface. Arrange the facet windows in the appropriate positions and any Video Cue assigned to the surface patch will then automatically have its signal split across the screens and outputted to the appropriate projectors. To delete a screen, select the desired screen in the screens assigned panel and click on the minus icon at the bottom of the screen.

Pro-Tip ▼

Syphon Output

Syphon is an open-source Mac OS X technology that allows applications to share either full-frame videos or image stills with one another in real time. It is important to note that Syphon works on your computer's graphics card to share video and images between applications **on the same computer**. Syphon is *not* intended for use across a network or between separate computers.

QLab 3 offers Syphon integration in two key ways. One, which we have already covered, is the ability to use a Syphon video feed in the place of a camera for a Camera Cue. The second method is to allow the assignment of a Syphon output as a screen assigned to a surface. In other words, any surface can output its signal to a display device, as a Syphon output, or as both simultaneously. These Syphon outputs can then be routed into other Syphon-capable programs, such as Madmapper, a program designed to video map images. Visit http://syphon.v002.info for more information about Syphon-supported software.

To assign a Syphon output as a screen, click on the plus button in the same way you would add any other screen. At the bottom of the drop-down menu, though, you will see a button labeled "Syphon." Clicking on this will create a screen that mirrors the entire surface and outputs it as a Syphon signal. Note that there will be no discernable action to trigger the Video Cue with only a Syphon patch (unless you have a Syphon client running). It will simply output the cue and then proceed to the next cue in the cue sequence.

- **Dimensions:** The dimensions settings in the upper right-hand corner of the screen allows for changing the output dimensions of the surface. The default resolution is that of your native screen. You can change the dimensional format of the patch, though, by simply inputting the new resolution size in the dimensions input. This is important if you want to create a surface large enough to house multiple screens without large amounts of overlapping. Note that the first slot indicates width, while the second is height. If you change the dimensions of your surface, you will notice that the video grid size will change, but the facet window with corner pins will remain the same size and need to be moved to the appropriate section of the video grid you wish to be displayed. The video grid and facet window are important aspects of understanding how surface output works.
- **Blend Gamma:** When using multiple projectors, it is accepted that there will have to be some image overlap, so as to not have gaps of "black" between the imagery. Where two projectors overlap, however, the resulting image

will be considerably brighter than the areas around it, since two projectors produce the image simultaneously. QLab compensates for this by adding in edge blending by default. The software will automatically decrease the intensity of any overlap between multiple projector surfaces. Blend Gamma refers to the amount of edge blending that occurs for these overlapping screens. The higher the number, the brighter the brightness at the center of the blend region, and vice versa for lower numbers. Ideally speaking, you should match this number to the native gamma value of your projector, though it might be useful to actually adjust these numbers while viewing the changes on your projection surface. It is worth noting that this function does not apply to single-screen surfaces – only for created surfaces in which imagery might overlap.

- **Origin:** The origin controls sets the facet window origin in relation to the video grid. If you grab the facet window and pull it around across the video grid, you will notice that numbers appear within the two origin boxes. These numbers are a standard grid format: the first one is for the X-plane, while the second is for the Y-plane. Anything to the left of the vertical axis or below the horizontal axis is a negative number, while anything to the right of the vertical axis or above the horizontal axis are positive numbers. You can either move the facet window by hand or input the numbers directly into the origin interface. Note that there is no button to reset the origin to 0,0 so this must be done manually.

11.3 Workspace Settings: Camera

As mentioned in Chapter 10, one of the strengths to QLab video is the ability to use Camera Cues for video reinforcement. The QLab video reinforcement system works with any FireWire DV, Blackmagic (using DeckLink API), or Face-Time camera attached to the system. In addition, it can accept input signals via Syphon. The section below details the process for setting camera preferences.

Figure 11.5
Camera settings window.

Camera Patch Settings

To access the camera patch window, click on the Settings icon and then select Camera in the left column. The window shows a list of eight camera patches (see Figure 11.5). Each one should automatically have a camera assigned to them from the list of available supported cameras attached to your system. If you do not see the camera you are looking for, click on the drop-down menu to view a list of available cameras. You can move camera assignment between patches to meet your programming needs. The purpose of the camera patch is to have a readily available list of cameras that can later be assigned to a Camera Cue for input purposes.

As mentioned earlier in the text, a Camera Cue can output a live camera feed, a Syphon feed, or both simultaneously. Syphon allows a computer to share either images or live video stream from one application to another. In this case, a Syphon-capable program on your computer could function as a camera input for a Camera Cue. If you are running a Syphon server on your system, you will see this available in the drop-down menu, in addition to standard cameras.

Setting Up QLab with Your Video System

There are a number of considerations regarding setting up a video system. As seen in Chapter 10, to have a successful video system, you must consider hardware, cabling, output devices, and QLab configurations. The following chapter details many of these considerations and addresses the basic processes involved with setting up both single and multi-screen output for video playback.

12.1 Hardware Considerations

Though QLab has relatively modest minimum specifications to function, most people will find that larger video files or simultaneous file playback will quickly begin to tax a system. One of the first questions many people ask is "what kind of hardware do I need for video playback?" In short, the answer is: it depends. It depends on the type of system you want to set up. For a single screen, PowerPoint-style system you will likely be fine with the minimum system requirements. For anything beyond that, though, there are a number of factors to consider: how large of video files will you be playing back; how many files at one time will you be playing; do you intend to include live video feed via Camera Cues; what other operations will your computer be running? If the answers to these questions indicate that you will be asking your computer to complete several operations at once and play back multiple video files simultaneously, then get ready to either drop some money on performance hardware or be frustrated with your productivity.

As with any system, the strength of your video performance will be only as good as your weakest link. While there is no catchall answer for hardware needs, there are some things you can understand to help demystify the process of selecting hardware for your QLab system. The following section will address some of these concerns.

The Bottleneck Dilemma

The main problem in working with video is simple: Video files are incredibly cumbersome for your computer. The amount of data that must be transferred across computer hardware to play back even standard resolution video files is large. Add hi-definition video into the mix and change that from large to enormous. Any time you have that sheer amount of digital traffic moving across your system, there is going to be the potential for traffic jams. No matter the speed of most computer hardware, it still tends to operate in an orderly fashion from one operation to the next. When a hard drive, for instance, is asked to access multiple files simultaneously, it still only has access to one point of data at a time. While it spins away, rotating to different physical points of its drive, the other process requests start to pile up – thus the bottleneck term. The question is how can we configure hardware for your system in such a way as to limit that bottleneck? To answer that, let's look at the hardware components for your system and how they are used.

Data Path

Unlike other file types, video is processed and travels along a unique data path, utilizing specialty hardware designed to maximize video playback. Figure 12.1 illustrates the typical data path for a video file, starting with the hard drive and ending with the display device. Each step along the data path has its own unique purpose and affects the playback potential of the entire system.

- **Hard Drive/Data Storage**: The three most important questions related to data storage for video are: (1) How fast is your hard drive? (2) How fast can

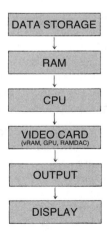

Figure 12.1
The standard data path for video.

your hard drive communicate information (i.e. bandwidth)? (3) What other data traffic is competing with your video file? The first two questions are directly tied to your choice of hard drive. The answer to the final question leads to the next logical question – is one hard drive enough?

The HDD

Every computer comes equipped with a hard drive (sometimes referred to as the hard disk). There are multiple types of hard drives on the market, but most computers still come equipped with the traditional "platter" disk drive, featuring a spinning disk upon which data is recorded and then accessed later by a reading head (see Figure 12.2). This type of drive is referred to as a hard drive disk (HDD). One of the problems with this type of hard drive is durability. Moving parts are much easier to break than non-moving ones. The fastest HDD revolves its disc at 15,000 rpm and transfers data at about 140 Mbit/s. HDDs come in very large capacity storage sizes. When equipping a playback system, it would be a good idea to get at least 1 TB.

The SSD

The second variety of hard drive commonly used in video systems is the solid state drive (SSD). An internal SSD with a Serial ATA (SATA) connection is preferable, whenever possible, for your video system. There are no moving parts to the SSD, and all data is electronically transferred (see Figure 12.3). While they vary from manufacturer to manufacturer, the maximum typical transfer rate for SSD is in the range of 100–600 Mbit/s, up to 4.25× faster than the HDD.

Figure 12.2
The inner view of a standard HDD.
Photo courtesy: Eric Gaba.

Figure 12.3
A solid state drive.

External Storage

Today, there are a number of options for external storage that can be used in conjunction with your computer from flash drives to Firewire or USB external drives. An external drive can be a great addition to any system, but keep in mind that it does present some concerns. The first concern is speed. There are a number of connector types for external storage, and the data transfer rate can vary drastically. As mentioned earlier, the rate for most hard drive, whether HDD or SSD, is in the range of 100–600 Mbit/s. Older connector types (FireWire 400/800 and USB 1/2) will clock in much slower than this. Newer connector types, USB 3.0 and Thunderbolt, clock in much faster (up to 10 Gbit/s). Obviously, whenever possible you would want to choose the faster variety. One potential problem with external drives, though, is their dependence on an external computer port. In short, they can be unplugged with relative ease. One method of getting around this is configuring a "road box" or rack mount with all external devices mounted inside, but ultimately there is no guarantee that someone will not accidentally dislodge the connector.

The Need for Multiple Drives

One question many people ask is if there is a need for more than one hard drive in their system. The short answer is yes. The more storage options in your system means you are reducing the potential for bottleneck. One main consideration for this is the number of video files playing back concurrently within QLab. The third question posed above asked what other data might be competing with the transmission of your video file. If you store your video files on the same hard drive as your OS, QLab software, and any other software that might be running (which should incidentally, always be kept to the minimum necessary), then your hard drive will have lots of reading and writing constantly occurring while trying to transmit the enormous data of your video file. Adding a separate hard drive (or more) enables storage of your media in a separate location from your system files. In the case of building a system with multiple internal drives, it might be preferable to choose a small capacity hard drive for your system files and add on one or two large-capacity drives for media storage.

Summary

Taking into account all of these variables, a best case scenario for video playback would be a computer with multiple SSD hard drives, and segregating your media files onto a separate physical drive from your system drive. More data paths mean less potential bottlenecks.

- **RAM:** RAM, or Random-Access Memory, is another type of data storage. RAM allows for data to be accessed in any random order, rather than the prede-termined method used in traditional hard disks and optical media. RAM is a temporary storage method, meaning that when power is removed from the system, all data is removed from the RAM. For our purposes, it is sufficient to say that RAM is used to serve as a temporary storage and workspace for the OS and applications. For video purposes, the more RAM the better. QLab 3 is a 64-bit program, meaning that it processes data in 64-bit (rather than 32-bit) packets. The main benefit of a 64-bit program is the ability to use a 64-bit address space, and thus use a significantly greater amount of RAM than 32-bit programs. In the past, QLab was a 32-bit program, meaning that it could not address more than 4 GB of RAM. With QLab 3, the 64-bit architecture ensures that you can utilize any RAM available to your system.

  The big question, then, is how much RAM do I need for video playback? The short answer I always give is buy as much as you can afford and your computer can hold. RAM has become harder to upgrade in newer genera-tions of laptops and some iMacs. Of course, the best option for maximum upgrade possibilities is to purchase the Mac Pro tower. This tower is a classic computer housing that allows for upgrading many of the internal compo-nents with much more ease than the iMac or MacBook lines. As of the pub-lication of this book, most iMacs start with 8 GB RAM and go up to 32 GB. It is a good rule of thumb to not purchase less than 16 GB if doing video playback.

- **CPU:** The central processing unit (CPU) is essentially the brain of your com-puter (see Figure 12.4). The purpose of the CPU is to carry out the instruc-tions of computer programs by performing mathematical, logical, and input/output operations of the system. When considering a CPU for your video system, there are two main factors to consider: the number of cores and the processor speed.

Multi-Core Processors

A multi-core processor is a type of processor that essentially combines multiple independent CPUs into one single computing component. Originally, all CPUs stood alone as a single core processor. As time progressed, the combination of

Figure 12.4
A central
processing unit.

CPUs into multi-core configurations became prevalent. Today, there are multi-core processors with up to ten independent CPUs functioning in tandem (though not in the current Mac lineup).

Processor Speed

The speed of the processor refers to the quickness with which it can operate those mathematical and logical problems mentioned earlier. High processor speeds are not always the most important factor in optimizing performance. For video editing, it is typically a good idea to get the combination of the fastest processor with the highest amount of RAM to ensure ideal video playback. Typical iMacs today feature 2.7–3.2 GHz Intel Quad Core processors. The MacPro features 2.4–3.2 GHz Intel processors with up to 12 cores (two 6-core processors).

QLab Video CPU Usage

Unlike some other applications, QLab performs much of its image processing of video in real time on your graphics processing unit (GPU). Compositing, Geometry, and edge blending are performed on the GPU, though most codecs are decoded on the CPU and many video effects use the CPU, as well. What this means is that for video purposes, the CPU speed is not the most important link in the chain. If you are in the position of deciding which is more important for your video system, CPU, or graphics card, you can spend a little less and get a medium-speed CPU in favor of getting the best graphics card available.

Regarding Codecs and Compression

A codec (derived from the terms coder-decoder) is a computer program capable of encoding or decoding a data stream, in this case a video file. Compressed video files require decompression in order to be played back. This decompressing process is generally performed in the CPU. The more the CPU has to work to decompress files, the greater a possibility for bottlenecking. Keep this in mind when creating video files for playback.

- **Video Card:** The video card is an expansion card used to generate a video feed to output to a display. The modern video card is a printed circuit board with mounted components including: vRAM, GPU, random access memory digital-to-analog converter (RAMDAC), and video output hardware (see Figure 12.5). All of these components are addressed in the following sections.

vRAM

Video RAM, more commonly called vRAM, is a dual-port variety of dynamic RAM (DRAM) housed on the video card and used specifically to improve video playback speeds and reduce latency. vRAM essentially functions as a buffer between the CPU and the video card. For video to be outputted to a display, it is first read by the CPU and then written to the vRAM. This data is converted from a digital signal to an analog one by means of a RAMDAC housed on the graphics card, before outputting to the display. Unlike typical RAM, vRAM chips contain two ports. This means that two different devices can access it simultaneously. In this way, it can receive new video data from the CPU while simultaneously outputting screen updates.

As you might have guessed, vRAM is another example of more is better. The greater the amount of vRAM, the better the processing ability of your video card, therefore the better your video output. Current high-end video cards (such as the ATI HD 5870 Eyefinity 6) feature 2 GB vRAM from fast video RAM capabilities (capable of rendering up to 1 billion pixels per second).

GPU

The GPU is a programmable logic chip that renders images, animations, and video for output to a display. The GPU is an essential component for decoding and rendering both 2D and 3D animations and video. For QLab purposes, much of the image processing is performed on the GPU in real time. The GPU

Figure 12.5
A video card with VGA, component, and DVI connections.
Photo courtesy: Evan Amos.

handles all image adjustments made by your Video Cue (resizing, opacity, rotation, etc.) and sends the frames to the display.

Output

All video cards contain some type of output hardware, such as VGA, DVI, HDMI, DisplayPort, etc. This is the final chain before connecting to the display device.

12.2 Video Card Considerations

The video card, sometimes also referred to as the graphics card, is an important component to utilizing QLab for video. There are a number of considerations when considering the appropriate video card for your rig. The ultimate question for what video card is best for you is how will you be using it? If you do not intend to be outputting to a number of different displays, then likely a mainstream consumer-level video will suffice. Should you need to incorporate multiscreen projections, or discrete video signals going to multiple surfaces, you might need to consider a higher-end video card. Again, it is becoming somewhat difficult to upgrade the video card beyond the original specs for many computers these days, so make sure to do your research before investing in too little of a computer. The following section details some necessary considerations for video card selection.

Number of Outputs

Many video cards have the option of outputting video signal to more than one display device. Currently, the ATI Radeon HD 5870 Eyefinity six features the most output possibilities for one video card. It features six Mini DisplayPort outputs, for the ability to output your video signal up to six independent displays, each with independent resolutions, refresh rates, color controls, and video overlays. Other possibilities, such as the "non-Eyefinity" ATI Radeon HD 5870 feature two DVI outputs, HDMI, and Mini DisplayPort for a potential of three independent displays, each with independent resolutions, refresh rates, color controls, and video overlays. The Mac Mini offers the potential of outputting to two displays, HDMI and Mini DisplayPort. Many other Mac computers, particularly the MacBook, offer only one video out. As you might expect, the less the output options, the less expensive the video card and vice versa.

Number of Cards

One option to consider if configuring your own system is to add multiple video cards to one computer. This is only possible for the Mac Pro tower, as other Mac units have adopted an "all in one" approach. This system, in which everything is contained in one convenient housing, makes adding additional video cards impossible. The Mac Pro, though, does offer the potential of adding up to three video cards (depending on the card size). The 2013 Mac Pro promises to offer two GPUs as a standard component of its build for support of up to three high-resolution 4k displays.

12.3 Connecting to a Video Display

One major consideration for setting up your video system will be how to physically connect your output devices to the computer or computers in your system. What types of connectors are needed? How long can you run the cable? Will you need a signal booster? With so many questions to consider, the planning of your video system will typically prove to be the most important task.

What Types of Connector(s) Are Needed?

The question of what types of connectors and cables are needed will greatly depend on the type of equipment in your system. What outputs are on your video card? What types of inputs are included on the projector or monitor you want to use? I strongly suggest doing a survey of all of your equipment and detailing the types of connectors and creating an inventory sheet. This will help you later when deciding on cables and adapters.

Typical connectors for Mac computers will be HDMI, DVI-D, DisplayPort, and Mini DisplayPort. Most projectors and monitors will feature at least VGA and DVI connectivity, though many newer projectors will feature a wide array of inputs.

Cable Runs

As you saw earlier in the text, when discussing video, there are a number of different cable and connector types. The main consideration when comparing cable types is the question of analog vs. digital signal type. The difference between an analog and digital signal is how the data is transmitted. Analog signals are mechanical representations of the sampled information, whereas digital signals are a series of number sequences of "1" and "0." Thanks to improved manufacturing techniques of analog cabling, there is little difference in the ability of analog and digital cable to transfer hi-definition video signals. The resulting difference between the two signal types is the amount of signal degradation that occurs over a run of cable.

HDMI, DVI, DisplayPort, and Mini DisplayPort are all digital video signals, capable of carrying HD signals. Since they are digital, they can carry their signals for a slightly longer distance without picking up interference. VGA is an analog cable type that can also transmit an analog HD signal. The quality is slightly less than that of the digital cabling, but it is slight and likely not noticeable by the layperson. The ultimate question of what types of cabling to use will likely depend on a few variables: How long is the required cable run? What is your budget?

Cable length is always a big concern when talking about video. Longer runs of cable can lead to interference and signal degradation, or even signal dropout. **Attenuation** is a term frequently discussed in video and/or networking conditions. It refers to the gradual loss in intensity of any signal transferring across a medium. In this case, we are typically referring to either copper cabling or fiber. Different types of cable naturally have different attributes that lead to varying maximum cable lengths. The problem in estimating this is that signal transmission is directly related to output resolution.

The smaller the output resolution, the longer the signal can run without debilitating attenuation. The larger the resolution of a video signal, the greater bandwidth utilized. Because of this, larger resolutions will encounter signal degradation at a significantly shorter span. This variable makes it difficult for a manufacturer to list firm rules for the maximum lengths of cable, since it is greatly dependent on the resolution of your signal and other hardware factors. Listed in the table below are a few references for cable length, but keep in mind every situation has variables that no quick-reference can account for like cable quality, environmental interference, and hardware quality. The following should be viewed as more of a starting point. Always rigorously test your system before going into a tech setting! Also note that the types of cables listed below are the standard consumer variety.

Cable Type	Digital/ Analog	Distance (Low Res*)	Distance (High Res*)
Video Graphics Array (VGA)	Analog	65'	25'
Composite (CVBS)	Analog	50'	N/A
S-Video	Analog	65'	N/A
Component	Analog	25'	10'
Digital Visual Interface (DVI)	Digital	50'	20'
High-Definition Multimedia Interface (HDMI)	Digital	50'	25'
DisplayPort/Mini DisplayPort	Digital	50'	10'
Thunderbolt	Digital	10'	10'
IEEE 1394 (FireWire)	Digital	15'	15'
Universal Serial Bus (USB1)	Digital	10'	10'
Universal Serial Bus (USB2)	Digital	15'	15'
Universal Serial Bus (USB3)	Digital	10'	10'

*Low resolution is defined as 480i/VGA (640 × 480).

**High resolution is 1,080p (1,920 × 1,080).

Use of cable runs greater than these might work, given the environment, but would not be recommended. It should be noted that the single greatest determining factor for cable length recommendations is the quality of the manufactured cable. There are a number of professional grade cable options that can be made using coax, category cable, or fiber-optic cable with any number of connector types attached. Using these cable types will expand your options from the tens of feet to the hundreds of feet range. For specs on these, see the individual manufacturer and always request to see a specifications sheet, whenever possible. For ultra-long cable run requirements, fiber-optic cables might be a good consideration since they can transmit data over thousands of feet.

Signal Amplifiers and Baluns

Sometimes you might find yourself in a situation where you have to exceed the maximum cable run length for a video system. In these cases, you will need to rely on certain devices designed to boost the video signal to travel over longer distances. One such device, a **distribution amplifier** takes the video signal and amplifies it to travel over a longer run. These devices are constructed for all types of cabling listed earlier. In all cases, the amplifier requires an external power supply.

A **balun**, as mentioned in earlier chapters, serves to change the data transmission from one type of cabling to another and balance unbalanced signals. The most common use of a balun in a video setting would be to convert VGA signal transmission to travel over category cable (5e, 6, 6a). The benefit of this is a dramatically increased capability for cable run lengths. As always, the transmitted video resolution affects the distance a signal can travel before debilitating attenuation. Cat5 can carry VGA (640 × 480) for 400–450′, SVGA (800 × 600) for 300–350′, XGA (1,024 × 768) for 100–250′, and SXGA (1,280 × 1,024) for 50–200′. With runs of this length capable, you can see why this is an attractive option for some video systems.

12.4 Graphics Expansion Devices

For many installations, you will find yourself in need of outputting to multiple display devices. As mentioned earlier, you could outfit a rig with multiple video cards, or a single card with multiple outputs. If buying a new computer or upgrading is not in your budget, though, one option remains for multi-screen output: a graphics expansion device. The graphics expansion device is an external electronic device that splits the video output from your computer across two or more outputs. There are a number of devices on the market that accomplish this goal, though the brand that seems to be the most prevalent at this point is the DualHead2Go or TripleHead2Go graphics expansion modules manufactured by Matrox. The following section details the process of setting up a graphics expansion device for video output.

Setting Up a Graphics Expansion Device with QLab

The physical attributes of expansion devices tend to be quite simple. It uses the standard video output of your computer as its input source. It might be DVI, VGA, DisplayPort, Mini DisplayPort, or even HDMI. In addition to connecting to your computer's video output, many expansion devices use a USB cable to power the device and connect to software running on your computer. For older analog models, it might need to connect to an AC power source in addition to these two connections.

The graphics expansion device creates a virtual display that is two or three times wider than the resolution of your display. In the case of the TripleHead2Go, the output dimensions are three times wider than the resolution of your monitor. For instance, if your monitor were set to SXGA resolution (1,280 × 1,024), then the device output would be three times wider for a resulting resolution of 3,840 × 1,024. An image or video designed to fit these dimensions would be equally split over all of the three separate outputs; the left third going to output 1, the center to output 2, and the right third to output 3 (see Figure 12.6). As seen in Figure 12.6, all images will not necessarily fit within this triple-wide aspect ratio without having some cropping occur or shrinking the image down to fit. This is the basic "plug-and-play" method covered below. This method is best used when combining multiple projectors or output devices to create a single unified surface (i.e. a video wall).

Plug-and-Play Setup

1. With QLab closed, connect the graphics expansion device to your computer. Make sure to follow the manufacturer's guidelines for installation. Some outputs are "hot pluggable," while others will not function in this process.
2. After your device is connected, open QLab. Click on the Workspace Settings icon in the lower right corner and select the Video Settings button. You will see a list on the right side of the screen labeled "available surfaces." Your

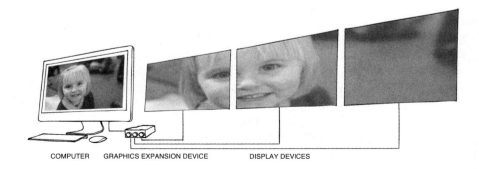

Figure 12.6
Multi-screen output.

COMPUTER   GRAPHICS EXPANSION DEVICE   DISPLAY DEVICES

graphics expansion device should be listed here in addition to any monitors connected to your system. This will likely be labeled as "display." It is important to note that QLab will not recognize any displays connected to your expansion device as individual surfaces, as they are simply outputs from your expansion device.

3. You will notice that the dimensions of your expansion device will be proportionate to your computer's built-in display resolution. As mentioned above, if your display resolution were 1,280 × 1,024, then the resulting output for a triple-wide expansion device would be 3,840 × 1,024 (Figure 12.7). Likewise, if you have used and named this surface before, QLab will remember the established name. In my case, I named my laptop's monitor "LCD Display" and my expansion device "Triple-wide."

4. Click on the "edit" button beside your display. This will open the settings panel for the expansion device. The first attribute to edit should be the surface name. I find it is a good idea to re-name the surface name as something descriptive, like "triple-wide." After typing in the new name, click "enter" and changes will be assigned.

5. Once you have changed the name, you are ready to use this surface as a video surface patch. Any Video Cue sent to this video surface will be outputted to all three displays as if they were one big screen. Images can be displayed on any one or all of the output displays.

The process described earlier is ideal if you only ever want to use the three outputs as one large display. There are, however, many functions such as individual keystone control for displays, edge-blending, and projector orientation that cannot be used through this single-screen surface method. For maximum control of each individual display output, follow the process listed below.

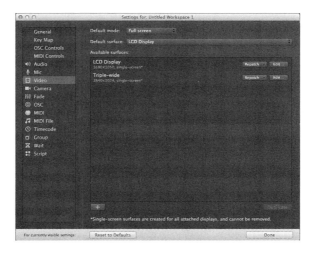

Figure 12.7
The available surfaces menu.

Multi-Display Setup

1. After having followed the steps above, go back to the Video settings and click the + button at the bottom of the screen to create a new surface.
2. The "Edit Surface" window will appear for creating a new surface. Name the new surface "multi-display." Press enter and it will save the name. This will be the new surface patch used to output to the three outputs of your graphics expansion device.
3. In the upper right corner, there will be two slots for inputting the dimensions of your surface. In this area, input dimensions that match that of your expansion device's output (for this example, 3,840 × 1,024). Inputting these dimensions will create a new surface called "multi-display" that matches the output dimensions of your expansion device (Figure 12.8).
4. The process to this point essentially created a new surface that matches the output of your three projectors combined, but without the ability to control each projector individually. That is where the screen function comes in.

   In the left column of the screen, you will see a box labeled "screens assigned." Click on the + button at the bottom of this column to add a screen. Instead of using one of the single-screen surfaces listed, click on the line labeled "partial screens." There will be a dropdown line that features the name of your graphics expansion device created above "Triple-wide." Click on that and then select the number of outputs your device features. In my case, that is "3 wide."

   There will be three choices following this: virtual screen 1, virtual screen 2, and virtual screen 3. Click on virtual screen 1 and a blue facet screen will appear superimposed over your "multi-display" surface (see Figure 12.9). It will be labeled "Triple-wide (1/3)" indicating that this is the first of three virtual screens derived from the screen called "Triple-wide." The blue facet screen is the visual representation of the projector connected to output one of your expansion device. It will automatically be placed in the left third of your surface. This means that output 1 of your expansion device will display the left portion of the video output.
5. Repeat the process above and insert virtual screen 2. This will then place a new partial screen called "Triple-wide (2/3)" superimposed over the first

Figure 12.8
The "multi-display" surface is three times the width of our standard output resolution.

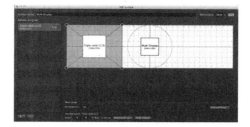

Figure 12.9
The facet screen
is superimposed
over the surface
window.

virtual screen. This virtual screen will have a green facet screen. Grab it and move it over until it is aligned in the center of the "multi-display" surface. This means that output 2 of your expansion device will display the center portion of the video output. To make sure the facet window is aligned properly, input an origin of 1,281 and 0 at the bottom of the screen.

6. Finally, repeat this process a third time for the final virtual screen, "Triple-wide (3/3)." Move the facet screen, a red one this time, all the way to the right third of the "multi-display" surface. The origin settings for this screen should be 2,561 and 0. This means that output 3 of your expansion device will display the right portion of the video output. At this point, your surface output should look like that seen in Figure 12.10.

7. By following the process detailed in the steps above, you will have three individual screens that can be controlled by your surface patch. Select any of the three screens on the left of the screen and you can control many of the attributes for each screen such as origin, projector orientation, or corner pin control. Please note that masking, gamma, and shutters affect only the overall surface not the individual screens. Specific details are listed below for each of these controls.

Mask Image

As discussed in Chapter 10, masking is the process of adding an image file as a frame around a video or image file or blocking out other parts of the image. With a white area, the video passes through the white color fill, but is masked by the non-white pixels. To assign a mask image to the surface, simply double-click in the mask image input window. This will open a finder screen to allow

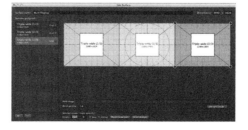

Figure 12.10
All three facet
screens are now
appropriately
placed.

you to select the desired image. In past versions of QLab, a mask had to be an actual Video Cue created with a transparent background that always stayed on the top layer of the video output. In version 3, though, there is a new feature that allows inputting image as a mask attached to the specific surface. In addition, rather than requiring a transparent background, any black and white image can be used as a mask – with a white fill set as the desired transparent area. QLab will automatically multiply the cue pixels by the mask pixels value to remove the white fill and create this as a transparent area through which the Video Cue can be seen. QLab tracks any changes made to the file so that you can edit it without having to remember to reinsert the source file into your workspace.

Blend Gamma

If any of your screens do overlap, QLab automatically factors in edge-blending to reduce the brightness of the overlapping areas on both projectors so the resulting image does not have a bright spot.

Origin Control

Each virtual screen has its own precise origin control settings that affect where the screen gets placed on the surface. Using the x, y coordinate system, you can place the screens precisely without any guess work. In this case, the first screen should have an origin of 0, 0. The second one should be placed at 1,280, 0 and the third screen at 2,560, 0. This interval uses a spacing of 1,280 pixels, the width of each screen.

Projector Orientation

One big benefit of using virtual screens is the ability to assign projector orientation to each screen separately. If using the expansion device as one plug-and-play output, each projector must be oriented in exactly the same fashion (either front or rear and ceiling or table). By controlling each screen separately, you have the potential to have each projector oriented in different ways and simply change the orientation on the screen to match that of the projector. For instance, what if your first projector is front projection from the ceiling and your second is rear projection from a table mount? With this method, simply select screen one and click the "ceiling" checkbox. For screen two, select the "rear" checkbox. This simple process will guarantee that QLab does all of the video processing for you and you don't have to change it ahead of time in your image processing software.

Corner Pin Control

Finally, one of the greatest strengths of the virtual display system is the ability to use corner pins to re-shape the video output of each separate screen. The corner pins are the yellow circles in each of the four corners of the facet screen. By moving these pins, the resulting image will be skewed to match the newly created shape. This process compensates for the keystone effect that occurs due to placing the projector at an angle less or greater than perpendicular to the projection surface. This is also particularly useful for reshaping images for projection mapping applications. To adjust corner pins in real time, I suggest clicking on the "grid" checkbox located to the right of your screen in the "screens assigned" window. This will send the grid as a video image from your projector, so that you can re-shape the screen in real time and see the effects of moving the corner pins. Holding down the shift key during this process allows for finer adjustments. Should you want to reset the corner pins, simply click on the "reset corner pins" button at the bottom of the screen. Just make sure that you have the correct screen selected.

Video and Camera Cues

Video Cues are the foundation for QLab's video playback capabilities. They allow you to display either movies or still images on any display attached to your system. Over the years, many changes have been made to the video component of the software. Version 1 featured Video Cues. Version 2 expanded the possibilities of Video Cues by adding the video stage and a custom graphic user interface (GUI) for manipulating the output across multiple screens. In addition, Animation Cues were introduced to change the output options of a Video Cue. Version 3 has reinvented the way in which QLab interacts with Video Cues and expanded on many of the functions introduced in past versions.

Though you can experiment with all of the video tools in the free version, a video license is required to access all of the functions available. Full screen video, however, can be played to the default single-screen surface from the free version. A final note before jumping into Video Cues: video editing and playback is a taxing process for most computers. A number of the video functions of QLab will require a lot of processing power. Look over the hardware concerns listed in previous chapters if your computer is having difficulty keeping pace.

13.1 Inserting a Video Cue

Video Cues are QLab cues specially designed to play video or image files through a video patch. QLab 3 uses AVFoundation to render video, which is a distinct change from previous versions. In addition to simple playback, there are a number of built-in filters and video effects that can be applied to the video or image files to affect their appearance and behavior. Like any other cue, a Video Cue can be inserted via the Toolbar, Tool Box, or via dragging a video file directly into the cue list. Since video files frequently have imbedded audio, the cue will feature a number of settings for audio in addition to video. The following section details the numerous tabs found in the Video Cue's Inspector Panel.

Before delving into the finer details of the Video Cue, though, it is wise to look at one final setting. QLab outputs video atop of the desktop of attached displays, meaning that if there is no video output the default image shown would be your computer's desktop. To disable this, you want to use a useful built-in feature that blacks out the desktop background. Click on **Tools > Black out Desktop Backgrounds.** After activating this function, your desktop background will be replaced with a plain black background, thus ensuring that when all videos are done there will be no visible desktop image.

13.2 Inspector Panel: Basics

Once a Video Cue is inserted into your cue list, the Inspector Panel can be used to access a wide range of control functions related to the cue. There are seven tabs within the Inspector Panel that house a number of these functions: Basics, Display & Geometry, Time & Loops, Audio Levels, Audio Trim, Audio Effects, and Video Effects. Each of these tabs contains specific control functions that affect the playback of the given Video Cue. The first tab, Basics, allows the same basic function seen in examining the Audio Cue. Like the Audio Cue, Video Cue Basics deals with cue info and triggering.

Cue Info

Aligned to the left half of the screen, cue basics deals with information related to cue numbering, naming, targeting, and playback. The inputs in this area are identical to that of the Audio Cue.

Triggering

Again, the triggering functions of the Video Cue match that of the Audio Cue. The triggering window allows the programmer to establish MIDI, hotkey, wall clock, or Timecode triggering.

13.3 Inspector Panel: Display & Geometry

Display & Geometry deals specifically with video surface assignment and affecting the display geometry of the video output. At first glance, much of this tab visually resembles the layout of QLab 2. Digging beneath the surface, though, you will find that the new video engine for QLab 3 features a number of powerful new tools for realizing your artistic vision. Looking at Figure 13.1, you will notice that the tab is divided into two columns. The left column contains the video surface assignment and video mode, whereas the right side contains the video stage, a graphic representation of your assigned video surface.

Figure 13.1
The Display &
Geometry tab.

The Video Stage

The Video Stage is a great tool for seeing your image placement on the video surface in real time. The translucent blue shape on the Video Stage represents your assigned Video Surface. Even though the surface might be composed of several individual screens, these screens will not be shown, only the surface. The translucent yellow area on the stage represents your Video Cue and should show the assigned image inside its boundary box. This Video Cue can be moved anywhere inside, or even outside of the assigned surface by simply grabbing it and moving it with your mouse. There are a few interesting multi-touch gestures imbedded into the video stage, as well. For instance, the scale can be zoomed in or out by doing a "two-finger scroll" up or down. By using the two-finger scroll from right to left, the z rotation can be easily toggled.

Video Surface

As addressed in Chapter 11, the new video engine allows for the use of video surfaces, rather than simple screen patches. A surface is a user-defined area of a predetermined size that can have one or more screens assigned to it. The idea of the video surface is that it frees you up to think about your design in a more artistic and holistic sense, rather than focusing on the nuts and bolts of screen output.

When an output device is attached to your system, a single-screen surface will automatically be created and added to your list of available video surfaces (in the Video Settings window). Depending on your design needs, you can either output a Video Cue to a single screen or create a multi-screen surface composed of multiple screens and send the signal to that surface. If you choose to do this, QLab will do all of the necessary calculations behind the scenes to route the video components out the appropriate display devices. Either method, the output patch is selected in the Video Surface drop-down menu.

If you want to edit the assigned video surface, just click on the edit surface button (the button with three dots to the right of the video surface) and it will open up the Edit Surface window. This window allows for naming the surface, changing its dimensions, assigning screens, masks, edge blending, and more. All the details for this are covered in depth in Chapter 11, Section 11.2 – Editing the Surface Patch.

Mode: Full Screen

The "Mode" control, located beneath the video surface controls, addresses the geometry for controlling image output. When a Video Cue is assigned to a video surface, it can either be full screen or custom geometry. Full screen does exactly what you might suspect – it enlarges or reduces the image or video file to fill the entire width of your surface. In choosing full screen, you can either select "preserve the aspect ratio" (to keep the original proportion of the image upon enlarging or reducing) or deselect this checkbox (to disregard the original proportion of the image and stretch it to fill the entirety of the surface).

Mode: Custom Geometry

Upon selecting the Custom Geometry button in the drop-down menu of the Mode control, a new set of input windows will appear (see Figure 13.2) that allow for adjusting the placement, size, and rotation of the video or image file in the surface output. These controls offer a wide range of tools to affect the image output in a number of ways.

- **Translation:** Translation refers to the placement of the image or video file in the surface. It is important to think of the concept of a graph for video controls. In translation, the first input represents placement in the horizontal plane (or the x-axis). The second input represents placement in the vertical plane (or the y-axis). The center of your surface represents the 0,0 position. Movement up or to the right of this is a positive number, whereas movement down or to the left is a negative number. There are two methods for changing translation. You can either input the numbers manually, or simply grab the image in the video stage and move it to the desired position.

- **Scale:** Scale refers to the size of the image. The default scale is 1 for any image. To enlarge the image, change the scale to a number greater than 1. To reduce the image, change the scale to a number less than 1. Again, the first input represents the x-plane (width), while the second one represents the y-plane (height). You will notice that changing one will also change the other. This is because the lock icon is set to lock, meaning the aspect ratio

Figure 13.2
The custom geometry window is used for resizing the output image.

is set so that a change in width affects a change in height and vice versa. To disable this function, simply click on the padlock icon, unlocking the fixed aspect ratio. As mentioned earlier, a quick method for zooming in and out of scale is the two-finger scroll up to enlarge or down to reduce scale.

- **Rotation:** Rotation refers to the image placement in relation to the x, y, and z coordinates of the surface. Until this point, we have only discussed the x and y-axes. In a 2-dimensional drawing, x and y coordinates refer to right and left or up and down. In a 3-dimensional drawing, a third axis, the z-axis, refers to the vertical coordinates lifted above the surface. For QLab, these coordinates refer specifically to the way in which an image can be rotated on the surface.

By clicking on any of the three inputs (x, y, or z), a dialog window will pop up asking for rotation coordinates. The x-rotation tool rotates the image on the x-axis ("flipping" the image head over foot). The y-rotation tool rotates the image on the y-axis ("spinning" the image like a top). Finally, the z-rotation tool rotates the image on the z-axis (turning it in a clockwise or counter-clockwise fashion). To input rotation changes, click in the input box and slide your mouse up for a positive number or down for a negative one. As you do so, look to the image in your video stage to the right and you will see how the numbers affect the image output. To return the Video Cue to its original rotation state, simply click on the reset button and all axis rotations will be set back to 0.

Pro-Tip ▽

Rotation Options

The Rotation settings for a Video Cue refer specifically to the original placement of an image. Rotation does not indicate an animated movement. In order to accomplish this, a Fade Cue must be used in conjunction with a Video Cue in order to allow for 3D rotation around the X, Y, or Z-axes. For more information on using these options, look at Project 13.2.

- Layer: This function allows for the "stacking" of multiple Video Cues atop one another. The lower numbers remain on the bottom of the stack, while higher numbers are arranged above. There are 999 numbered layers to choose from. In addition, you can assign any Video Cue to be "bottom" or "top" by selecting this in the Layer drop-down menu.
- Opacity: Finally, opacity is the setting that allows the programmer to change the video image from opaque to translucent. Hundred percent opacity means that the image is perceived as "solid." As the numbers decrease, the resulting image becomes more translucent, allowing the layers or background behind it to be visible through the image. This setting is useful for creating interesting layered imagery seen in tandem. Likewise, combining opacity settings with a Fade Cue creates a fade-in or fade-out of a Video Cue.

Project 13.1 ▼

Fade Controls for Video Cues

One of the most common requests for Video Cues is the ability to fade in at the beginning or fade to black at the end of the cue. With QLab 3, these functions are accomplished via Fade Cues. The following project takes you through the process of creating a fade-in and fade-out for a Video Cue.

Step One:
Download Project 13.1 from the companion website.

Step Two:
Select Cue 1 from the workspace. Click Shift + Command + A to open the Audition Window. Click GO to fire the Video Cue featuring a young girl on the beach. Press escape to end the playback.

Step Three:
Insert two Fade Cues following the Video Cue and assign Cue 1 as the target for both.

Step Four:
Select Cue 1 and open the Display & Geometry tab in the Inspector Panel. Set the opacity to 0.0%. This will make the Video Cue invisible when fired, showing only the black background.

Step Five:
Select Cue 2 and open the Geometry tab in the Inspector Panel. Click on the opacity checkbox and set the opacity to 100%. You will notice that the red x will disappear from this Fade Cue's status.

Step Six:
Set the opacity for Cue 3 to 0.0% in the same fashion as Step Five. Likewise, the red x should disappear from the cue row.

Step Seven:
Test your programming. Clicking Cue 1 should activate the Video Cue (though you will not see it). Firing Cue 2 will fade-in the image, and firing Cue 3 will fade to black.

Step Eight:
In order to automate this cue sequence and eliminate the need for extra GO clicks, set the continue status of Cue 1 to Auto-continue. This will make the image fade-in when the first cue is fired. To further clean up your workspace you could even place both of these cues into one group so as to hide the unnecessary programming.

Step Nine:
The final step is to make sure the Video Cue will stop playing once faded to black. Remember, like Audio Cues, a Video Cue will continue to play until stopped. In order to free up system resources, remember to click the "stop target when done" checkbox on Cue 3. This will assure that the cue will stop playing once faded out.

Project 13.2 ▼

Animating Image Rotation through Fade Cues

In QLab 2, there was only one option for rotating the image – the z-axis. In QLab 3, there are many different options for rotation. The first method, 3D rotation, allows for rotation of one image along the X, Y, and Z-axes simultaneously. This method is excellent for doing basic 3D changes of image rotation, so long as you do not need multiple spins around any given axis. It is important to note that there is currently no method for creating a 3D rotation that revolves around an axis more than one rotation.

For instances in which multiple spins around one axis is required, you can choose either X, Y, or Z-axes for individual axis rotation. This is effective for rotation effects that revolve numerous times around one axis (like the spinning newspaper effects of classic black-and-white films).

The Spinning Headlines Newspaper
Step One:
Download Project 13.2 from the companion website.

Step Two:
Select Cue 1 from the workspace. This is an image of a classic newspaper headline. Click Shift + Command + A to open the Audition Window.

Step Three:
To create the desired effect of the newspaper zooming in from the distance, we must first start with the Display & Geometry tab. Select the drop-down menu labeled "Full Screen" and change it to "Custom Geometry." After doing this, change the scale from 1 to 0. This will shrink the image so much as to make the image disappear. Your settings should mirror those seen in Figure 13.3.

Figure 13.3
The Display & Geometry tab settings.

(Continued)

Step Four:

Set the continue status of Cue 1 to Auto-continue, so that it will automatically fire Cue 2.

Step Five:

Insert a Fade Cue and set Cue 1 as its target. Select the Geometry tab in the Inspector Panel. First, click on the Scale button and slowly slide the scale up until the image almost fills the screen of your video stage (see Figure 13.4)

Figure 13.4
Scaling the image.

Step Six:

Test the sequence by firing Cue 1. The resulting effect should be the newspaper zooming in from the distance.

Step Seven:

In order to get the newspaper to spin, you must once more select the Geometry tab of Cue 2. This time click on the drop-down menu beside rotation and select "Z rotation." Type in -1080 in the box and make sure to remember to select the checkbox to the left of "rotation." Figure 13.5 illustrates how your screen should look.

Figure 13.5
Inputting image rotation.

Step Eight:

Test your cue sequence. It should now successfully spin in from the distance. One last option to tinker with might be customizing your fade curve settings. To do this, select Curve Shape from the Fade Cue's Inspector Panel and click on "custom curve" in the drop-down menu instead of "S-curve." Play around with different curve shapes until you feel comfortable that you understand their use.

13.4 Inspector Panel: Time & Loops

The Time & Loops panel for Video Cues is identical to that in Audio Cues in all but one way. Video Cues includes an additional control to hold the final frame up on the screen when the video cycle is complete. Beyond that, the layout of Time & Loops mirrors the one seen in Chapter 5 (Figure 13.6).

Waveform Display

The waveform display is blank for Video Cues with image files or silent video targets. When using a video file with an audio track, the waveform will display in the same fashion as that for an Audio Cue. Likewise, the start time/end time of the Video Cue can be changed by simply grabbing either of the handles at the beginning or end of the Video Cue and scrubbing them to the desired start or end point. Again, this is a non-destructive process that can be changed as frequently as necessary without damaging the target file.

Preview Cue

For the Video Cue, it is especially important to master the use of the **Audition Window** for previewing cues. Click on ⌘ + shift + A to open the audition window, a special window that serves as a temporary surface for viewing Video Cues or listening to Audio Cues. While you can press the preview button for Video Cues, the problem arises when the computer is not connected to your additional output devices. If your computer does not have an external display, the Video Cue will play in full screen mode and cover up your workspace. This makes it impossible to edit the cue, as you cannot see the controls. By using the Audition Window, the Video Cue preview will be exported to the Audition Window and can be resized or moved anywhere on the desktop for preview purposes.

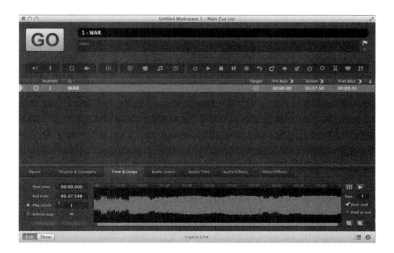

Figure 13.6
The Time & Loops
tab for Video Cues.

Times, Loops, and Slices

Again, the column to the left of the Time & Loops tab mirrors that seen in the Audio Cue. There is a start and end time dialog for inserting the times manually. In addition, there is a play count dialog for the amount of times the Video Cue will play (looping). Likewise, the infinite loop enables an infinite number of playback loops.

Slices are enabled for video playback, as well as audio. Like the Audio Cue, slices allow for the looping of internal sections of a Video Cue. In many ways, video looping is much more complicated to achieve than audio, due to the visual nature of videos. The video must be created in such a way that it can loop back to a point without a noticeable "hiccup."

In order to insert a loop into a cue, simply click the location in the waveform to place the end of your slice. Likewise, if you created the file in a video editing software with markers, those markers will translate into slices automatically when imported to QLab. If you want the first three seconds of a Video Cue to repeat, place your cursor at the 3-second position in the waveform viewer and click the "add Slice" button. Once you have done this, you will notice a handle appears at the top of the waveform timeline similar to the playback position icon in your cue list. This indicates the end of the slice. To fine-tune the ending position, simply grab the slice position icon in the timeline and slide it to the desired location.

Once a slice is inserted, two numbers will appear at the bottom of the waveform, both reading 1. This indicates the number of times your slice will loop before proceeding to the next slice. Click on the first number and change it to 2. This will create a slice that plays back twice before progressing to the next section in the Audio Cue. Likewise, if you want to make the loop repeat an infinite number of times, simply insert "inf" instead of a number and the infinity symbol ∞ will replace it.

If you wish to remove a single slice, simply change the number back to 1 and it will function like it is not there. Likewise, you can grab the handle and pull it out of the workspace to delete it. If you wish to delete all slices, click on the button labeled "Delete All."

To end an infinite loop cycle, you must use the DeVamp Cue in conjunction with your Video Cue. Once triggered, a DeVamp Cue tells a cue to stop repeating and progress to the next slice once the next loop cycle has completed. This is addressed in depth in Chapter 8, Control Cues.

Like in Audio Cues, the slices can also function as a visual marker in your waveform that makes it easier to identify key spots during tech. If, for instance, there is a spot in the middle of a song where a certain effect occurs and you want to note that location simply insert a slice and keep the loop number set to 1. There will be no function to the slice, other than serving as a visual marker for your own use at a later time.

Integrated Fade Envelope & Playback Rate

The integrated fade envelope allows for inserting fade curves attached to the audio component of your Video Cue. When you click on the "toggle integrated fade envelope" button, a yellow line will appear placed horizontally across the top of your waveform with a circle at the beginning and end of the line. This is the fade line that allows for inserting level increases or decreases to automate volume changes.

The rate control changes the rate of playback for the Video Cue in the same manner as the Audio Cue. Likewise, the pitch shift button can be deselected to keep the pitch unchanged as the rate increases.

13.5 Inspector Panel: Audio Levels, Audio Trim, and Audio Effects

The following three tabs in the Video Cue Inspector Panel are identical in function to those seen in the Audio Cue Inspector Panel, though the tab names are slightly different.

Audio Levels for the Video Cue functions in the exact same fashion as Device & Levels tab in the Audio Cue Inspector Panel. The purpose of this tab remains the assignment of the audio output patch, setting volume levels, and ganging outputs.

Audio Trim mirrors the Trim tab in the Audio Cue. As with the Audio Cue, the trim controls allow for the increase or decrease of volume across a series of Fade Cues that target the same cue. In this case, it is specifically related to the audio track of a Video Cue, though, rather than an Audio Cue.

Finally, the Audio Effects tab shares both the name and function of that seen in the Audio Cue Inspector Panel. Again, this tab allows for the addition of audio effects to change the audio output of a Video Cue. All of the same AUs are available for a Video Cue as that for the Audio Cue.

All three of these control tabs offer a great amount of flexibility to how a Video Cue can be used in your workspace. By using these in conjunction with Fade Cues, you can truly create dynamic playback effects and offer a wide array of non-destructive editing effects built-in to your Video Cue.

13.6 Inspector Panel: Video Effects

One of the biggest changes to the Video Cue structure for QLab 3 comes in the introduction of a wide array of built-in video effects available in the Inspector Panel. For those used to working with graphics and video editing programs, many of these effects will already be a part of your working vocabulary.

Currently, each Video Cue can apply only one video effect to its output and these effects cannot be changed via Fade Cues in the same way that audio effects can. Nonetheless, the addition of these video effects adds great versatility to Video Cue options.

To access the video effects, click on the Video Effects tab in the Inspector Panel and click on the drop-down menu beside the "Apply effects" button. You will notice that the drop-down menu features a number of effects, each separated into seven different groups (see Figure 13.7). Listed below are the video effects categories and basic descriptions of their use. Video effects are such a large component of the Video Cue structure that Chapter 14 is dedicated to fully exploring their functions.

- **Color and Exposure Effects:** The first category of video effects offers up a number of options in changing the video output related to color, gamma, exposure, and more. Included in this group are features like creating a sepia or monochromatic image.
- **Titles:** The title effect allows for the insertion of text as an overlay on your Video Cue. There are a number of options such as font type, font color, size, and blend mode that affect the look of inserted titles.
- **Blur/Sharpen Effects:** This category of video effects allows for a number of blurring effects (box, disc, Gaussian, motion, and zoom), and sharpening effects.
- **Texture & Edge Effects:** Texture effects such as pixelation, halftones, pointillize, and comic effect allow for a drastic change to the appearance of the video or image file.
- **Distortion Effects:** This category of effects all deal with warping the image output in some fashion to make the image appear to be wrapped in a three-dimensional form.

Figure 13.7
The video effects drop-down menu features many options for affecting video output.

- **Tile Effects:** Tiling is the duplication of your image feed across multiple areas or "tiles" within your video surface. There are five tile effects, each with numerous output variables for creating interesting tiles.
- **Custom Compositions:** Quartz Composer is visual programming environment created by Apple that allows for sophisticated motion graphics compositions. QLab has long allowed the use of custom Quartz Compositions for image output. In QLab 3, this function is included as part of the Video Effects tab. Quartz compositions are used as image filters, as QLab is actually in control of the final rendering of images. Quartz Composition renderers such as sprites, billboards, and meshes will not work (a difference from earlier versions).

13.7 Camera Cues

In addition to playing back prerecorded video, QLab also has the capability to insert a live video feed directly into the workspace via the Camera Cue. A Camera Cue functions in exactly the same fashion as a Video Cue, except it does not have an audio feed. The QLab video system works with any FireWire DV camera, Blackmagic devices that use the DeckLink API, or Face-Time camera attached to the system. In addition, it can accept input signals via Syphon. Once the camera patch is set up, pressing go will activate the camera, sending a video feed out to the assigned video surface. The following section details the setup and application of the Camera Cue.

Camera Cues are QLab cues specially designed to activate an external camera connected to the video system and send its signal out through a video surface patch. In addition to simple playback, there are also a number of built-in filters and effects that can be applied to the video feed to affect its appearance and behavior. Like any other cue, a Camera Cue can be inserted via the Cue bar or Tool Box. Unlike Video Cues, though, a Camera Cue does not feature audio feed. Since the video feed does not feature audio, the Camera Cue has fewer options within the Inspector Panel than the Audio or Video Cues. It is possible to run a Camera Cue in conjunction with a Mic Cue to have both audio and video feed, though there are a number of difficulties in making the audio line up correctly with the video feed due to latency and clocking issues between separate interfaces. The following section details the functions of the tabs found in the Camera Cue's Inspector Panel.

13.8 Inspector Panel: Basics

Once a Camera Cue is inserted into the cue list, the Inspector Panel is used to examine the control functions and settings related to the cue. Unlike the Video Cue, the Inspector Panel for the Camera Cue features only three tabs: Basics, Display & Geometry, and Video Effects. The Camera Cue Basics tab is identical in appearance and function to that of the Video Cue. The first tab, Basics, allows the same basic function seen in examining the Audio and Video Cue. Like those other cue types, Camera Cue Basics deals with cue numbering, naming, targeting, and playback options. In addition, triggering options such as MIDI, hotkey, wall clock, and Timecode triggering are also controlled in this tab.

13.9 Inspector Panel: Display & Geometry

Like the Video Cue, Display and Geometry for the Camera Cue deals with input assignment (camera patch) and output assignment (video surface patch). As seen in Figure 13.8 the Display & Geometry tab contains both patch and geometry functions (on the left side of the screen) and the video stage on the right side of the screen.

Camera Patch

The camera patch is the first menu located on the left column of the screen. By clicking on the drop-down menu, you will see all of the available cameras attached to your video system. Select the desired camera and it will automatically be assigned as the input source for your Camera Cue.

Video Surface

The video surface patch is located directly beneath the camera patch and is used to assign the display output for your Camera Cue. Like the Video Cue, you can either output the video feed to a single screen, or to a multi-screen surface. If you choose to do this, QLab will do all of the necessary calculations behind the scenes to route the video feed out the appropriate display devices. With either method, the output patch is selected in the Video Surface drop-down menu.

Video Display Modes: Full Screen and Custom Geometry

The "Mode" control, located beneath the video surface controls, addresses the geometry for controlling image output. When a Camera Cue is assigned to a video surface, it can either be full screen or custom geometry. For full screen,

Figure 13.8
The Display & Geometry tab for camera cues.

the image is either reduced or enlarged to the correct size to fill the entire width or height of the assigned surface. By selecting or deselecting "preserve aspect ratio" you can keep the original proportion in mind or disregard it, giving you the ability to stretch the image's height or width disproportionately to completely fill the surface. Custom geometry allows for changing the size, shape, and geometric rotation of the image around the x, y, and z planes. For detailed exploration of this process, look at Section 13.3.

Layer and Opacity

Again, the layer settings for a Camera Cue determine the order in which video frames get stacked. A cue with a higher number will always be stacked atop a layer with a lower number (0-999). Assigning "Top" means that this cue will be layered above any previous Video or Camera Cues. The most recent cue labeled top will always be displayed on top.

Finally, opacity is the setting that allows the programmer to change the video feed from opaque to translucent. Hundred percent opacity means that the image is perceived as "solid." As the numbers decrease, the resulting image becomes more translucent, allowing the layers or background behind it to be visible through the image. This setting is useful when combined with the layers function. Imagine the possibility of overlaying a Camera Cue atop a second Camera or Video Cue. This would be particularly useful in the creation of a "ghostly apparition" effect. The following project details the process of tackling this effect.

Project 13.3 ▽

Creating a Ghostly Effect

As a reminder, Camera Cues must use a camera connected to your system. Without a FireWire, Blackmagic, or Face-Time camera you cannot do this project.

Step One:
Download Project 13.3 from the companion website.

Step Two:
You will notice the workspace contains only one cue. Cue 1 is a Video Cue featuring a crinkled paper background. This will be the background image. Open the Audition window (Command+Shift+A) so you can preview the cues live.

Step Three:
Insert a Camera Cue into the workspace as Cue 2. Check your camera patch under the Display & Geometry tab to ensure the appropriate camera

(Continued)

is patched to your cue. Also, while in this tab, set your opacity to 48%. Finally, ensure that the Camera Cue is set to the Top layer (see Figure 13.9).

Figure 13.9
The camera patch is used to assign the camera input.

Step Four:

As currently programmed, the Camera Cue will play atop the paper background, but it will hardly look ghostly. In order to accomplish this goal, there will be some requirements of both lighting and Video Effects settings. As for lighting, make certain to darken the room to black and use a bright light at a harsh angle on your actor (if sitting at your laptop, this will be particularly easy to experiment with – simply turn off the lights and use a flashlight beneath the chin).

Step Five:

Open the Video Effects tab in Cue 2 and select "Bloom and Gloom" from the drop-down menu. Click on the checkbox beside apply effects to ensure the effect will be applied. Finally, set Bloom as the effect with Radius at 17.500 and Intensity at 1.000 (see Figure 13.10).

Figure 13.10
Bloom and gloom settings.

Step Six:

Test the cue sequence. If programmed properly, a ghostly face should appear superimposed atop the paper texture (see Figure 13.11).

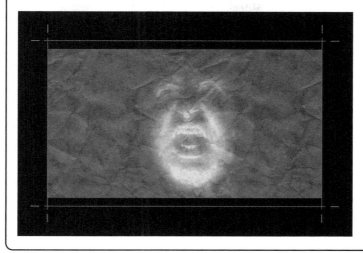

Figure 13.11
The resulting ghostly figure.

13.10 Inspector Panel: Video Effects

The final tab in the Camera Cue Inspector Panel is called video effects. The video effects for Camera Cues function in exactly the same fashion as that for Video Cues. To access the video effects, click on the drop-down menu beside the "Apply effects" button. You will notice that the drop-down menu features a number of effects, each separated into seven different groups as seen in Figure 13.3. Once you are familiar with the use of video effects in Video Cues, the execution for Camera Cues is identical.

Quartz Composer Integration

QLab 3 allows for the use of a custom Quartz Composer file as an image filter for the camera feed. An original composition can apply Core Image filters, apply complex animations, and more to your live video feed. QLab provides Quartz Composition frames to your video feed in real time to affect the image output.

Video Effects

As mentioned in previous chapters, one of the biggest advances in QLab video is the addition of video effects to both Video and Camera Cues. Essentially, each Video or Camera Cue has a library of video effects to choose from that can be applied to the image/video file or camera feed. There are a number of built-in effects to choose from, all as simple as selecting the effects, applying it to the cue, and changing the video effect control settings. With so many different effects to choose from, the process can be a bit overwhelming for a first-time user. This chapter details the purpose and process of the seven groups of video effects presets.

For the following sections, download Project 14.1 from the companion website. Open your Audition Window, so that you can preview the effects without covering up your workspace. Select the first cue and then click on the Video effects tab in the Inspector Panel. We will use this cue list to examine the various video effects presets.

14.1 Video Effects Presets: Color and Exposure

The first set of video effects presets deal primarily with changing the color, exposure, gamma, or contrast of the cue output. There are six video effects in the color and exposure grouping. For all effects, you must both select the desired video effect in the drop-down menu and click on the "Apply Effects" button. This will then list the effect controls in the effect inputs window at the bottom of the screen.

Color Controls

The first option listed in the drop-down menu is called color controls. Color controls offers basic video/image editing options of saturation, brightness, contrast, and hue angle (see Figure 14.1). Select Cue 1 from Project 14.1 and press the space bar. This will play your Video Cue in the Audition window. Click on the "Apply Effects" button to activate the color controls, if you have not already done so. You should notice an immediate, if slight, change to your image. Let's now examine the sliders in the effect inputs panel.

Saturation refers to the amount of color present in the image. Increasing the saturation will make the image have much more vibrant colors, whereas decreasing it will make it look like a black and white photo. **Brightness** refers to the amount of light or shadow present in the image. Increasing it will make the image go to a completely white screen. Decreasing it will move toward a completely black screen. **Contrast** refers to the difference perceived between the darks and lights in your image. By increasing the contrast, you will get deep blacks and vivid, glowing highlights. By decreasing it, you will get a washed-out, gray image with little difference between highlights and shadows. Finally, **Hue Angle** allows you to enhance the colors present in your image in one range of the color spectrum. Sliding across the scale from –180 to 180 will change the color output from blue (–180) to more cyan tones (180).

Exposure

Selecting exposure in the drop-down menu will activate the exposure video effects preset. **Exposure** is a photography term that relates to the amount of light that is allowed to transfer onto the film. Exposure is linked to the shutter speed of a camera – the longer the shutter stays open, the more light that is allowed onto the film and vice versa. In QLab terms, exposure refers to the method of using a digital effect to simulate film exposure.

Figure 14.1
The color controls subset of video effects.

Experiment by adjusting the exposure of Cue 1. The **Exposure Value** slides from –10 to 10, with values below zero being underexposed (overly dark) and those above zero being overexposed (overly bright white). Figure 14.2 shows the exposure value slider.

Gamma

Moving one step down the list in the drop-down menu, you will arrive at the third effect in the color and exposure grouping, Gamma. **Gamma** refers to a digital method of coding and decoding the brightness values of both still and moving images. In terms of output, each pixel of a digital image is assigned a gamma value. QLab allows for the adjustment of the gamma value from the power of 0.100–3.000. In this case, sliding the gamma power slider down to its lowest setting will brighten the image output, whereas raising it will darken the image (see Figure 14.3). Go ahead and adjust the gamma power slider and see the ways in which the image is affected.

Figure 14.2
The Exposure
Value slider.

Figure 14.3
(a) The Gamma
Power slider at a
low setting. (b)
The Gamma Power
slider at a high
setting.

Sepia Monochrome

This fourth effect gives the option to change the image output for your Video or Camera Cue to be either sepia or monochromatic. When you first select the Sepia Monochrome effect, the default setting will be sepia. To change to the monochrome effect, select the drop-down menu and you will see monochrome as the other choice (Figure 14.4).

Sepia refers to the reddish-brown color of antique photographs. To control the amount of sepia tones added to the image, use the Intensity slider. The intensity scale (0.000–1.000) represents the amount of original color that will read after the effect is applied. 0.000–0.500 will have some of the original color remaining, whereas anything above this will gradually replace all original hues with sepia colors.

Monochrome, or "one chroma," refers to an image in which everything is presented in different values of one color. To use the monochrome effect, simply click on the drop-down menu to select monochrome. After doing this, click on the color block at the bottom of the screen. This will open up the Mac OS X Color Picker that gives you several different options from which to choose your color (see Figures 14.5–14.9). The intensity slider will function in the same fashion for monochrome as it did for sepia – meaning the lower half of the slider will allow some of the original colors to bleed through, where anything above the 50% mark will begin to replace all original colors with your selected hue.

Min Max Invert

The Min Max Invert effects preset is actually a collection of three separate video effects: Minimum Component, Maximum Component, and Color Invert.

Minimum Component creates a gray scale version of your image that emphasizes the darker tones by examining the minimum RGB values. **Maximum Component** also creates a gray scale version but focuses instead on the brighter tones of the image by examining the maximum RGB values. **Color Invert** does exactly what the name implies; it creates an inverted image in which the colors are reversed from those in the original file. There are no variables to these three effects, simply on or off. Click through these three different presets to see the way in which the video output for Cue 1 is affected.

Figure 14.4
The sepia monochrome drop-down menu.

Pro-Tip ▽

The Mac OS X Color Picker is a handy tool that was introduced with the first version of Mac OS X. There are a number of different options, but they all serve the same basic purpose of helping you select a color within an application. Along the top of the interface, you will see five icons. Each of these icons represents a different method of selecting colors. The first icon, **Color Wheel**, allows you to select the hue and saturation with the color wheel, and the value (or relative lightness or darkness of the color) by using the slider on the right side of the window (Figure 14.5). In the color wheel, moving toward the center of the circle will de-saturate your hue selection.

The second icon represents the **Sliders** panel of the Color Picker (Figure 14.6), where there is a series of sliders useful for creating your own color schemes: Gray Scale, Red-Green-Blue (RGB), Cyan-Magenta-Yellow-Black (CMYK), and Hue-Saturation-Brightness (HSB). One very useful function in this window is the magnifying glass tool in the left corner. This tool allows you to select the color from any pixel on your screen, no matter what program is running it. By clicking on a color, it will be selected and placed into your color selection window.

The next icon, the **Palette** picker, is a selection tool for using pre-existing color palettes and creating palettes of your own (Figure 14.7). The palette

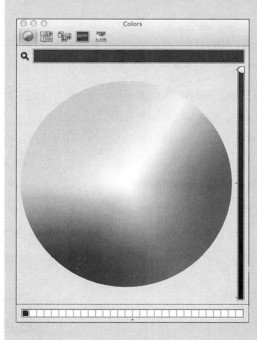

Figure 14.5
The color wheel
color-picking tab.

(Continued)

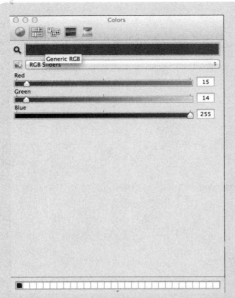

Figure 14.6
The sliders
color-picking tab.

picker features four palettes: Web Safe Colors, Crayons, Developer, and Apple. In addition to this, you can use this menu to create your own palettes for a project that needs to use a consistent set of colors. To add a color to your original color palette, simply drag that color down into the row of squares at the bottom of the screen

Figure 14.7
The palette
color-picking tab.

The fourth icon is the **Image Palette**. By default, when you select the image palette, it will open a spectrum showing all the colors within the visible spectrum. This is useful by itself, but a truly useful function within this picker is its ability to add any image from your hard drive as a color palette. Click on the Palette drop-down menu, and then select New from File (Figure 14.8). If you have an image on your clipboard, you can also paste it in by using New from Clipboard. To select a color within the image, simply click on the desired color within the image, and it will be added to the color box. Drag that color down into the row of squares at the bottom of the screen to create your own custom palette.

The fifth and final icon is the **Crayon Box**. It is a simplistic representation of colors with easy to remember color names (Figure 14.9). It has much fewer functions than the other pickers yet is a quick and easy reference at times.

One final thing to keep in mind is that Color Picker is expandable with the addition of plug-ins – some freeware or shareware. Many of these additional Color Pickers can be added on to use with QLab and allow for a truly customized approach to how you select your colors within the software. Just do a quick search for "mac color selector plug-ins" and you will find a number of options!

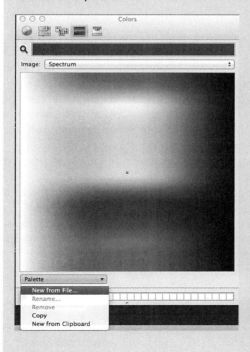

Figure 14.8
Selecting New
from file.

(Continued)

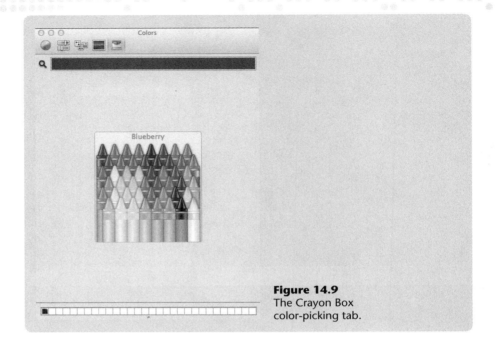

Figure 14.9
The Crayon Box
color-picking tab.

White Point

The final effects preset in the color and exposure section of the drop-down menu is called white point. In photography terms, the **white point** is the color value within the photo that is determined to be neutral. This is a key factor that plays into lighting modes on cameras, like incandescent, outdoors, fluorescent, etc. Each of these light sources produces a drastically different color temperature; therefore, shooting an indoor scene with an outdoor camera setting will result in an oddly discolored photo. White point conversions have been around in photo editing software for years. Essentially, it allows you to select a hue that should be substituted for white. In QLab, once you have selected white point, a color tool will appear in the effects input, allowing you to open the OS X Color Picker and select your white point color. Doing so will create a color overlay that changes your light areas to various values of the chosen hue. Try out this effect by selecting a number of different hues, saturations, and values to see how it affects the image output.

14.2 Video Effects Presets: Titles

The next section of video effects presets has only one effect included: titles. The titles video effect is a simple, yet powerful interface for adding text to a Video or Camera Cue. In the past, any text had to be inserted into the image or video file upon creation, or by using a custom Quartz Composition. With the addition of the titles effect, the integration of text into any Video or Camera Cue is a snap.

Once more, select Cue 1 and trigger it for playback. To insert titles, click on the "Titles" button in the effects drop-down menu. An interface will appear featuring a number of options (see Figure 14.10). Unlike in the color settings, QLab does not integrate an OS X text selection box; rather it provides its own menu of options in the effect inputs panel. The following section details the control options for titles.

Title Content and Font

The "text" window is used exclusively for inserting text for title display. In Cue 1, click on the text window and insert any word or words you want to display. Next, you need to indicate the desired font. Type in the name of the desired font in the "Font_Name" window. QLab will allow you to input any font in your computer's font library. At this point, there is no type of interface that lists the fonts available on your system, so it might be useful to experiment in a Font Book (a standard OS X application) beforehand to determine the desired font. I recommend Font Book, as it not only will let you preview fonts but, more importantly, also tells you the PostScript name of the font. QLab requires the PostScript name in the "Font_Name" window. Once you have inputted the content and selected the font name, either press "stop all" or click escape to end playback of the Video Cue, then select it once more and press the spacebar. Your title should now be displayed.

Font Size and Placement

The three sliders shown in the effect inputs window controls the font size and placement. Font size is on a sliding scale from 1 (almost invisible) to 600 (so large that it will likely extend off the borders of your video surface). Input X and Input Y refer to the placement of the text within your video surface. One thing you will notice is that titles do not appear in the video stage under the

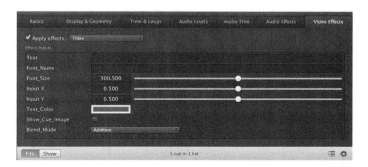

Figure 14.10
The Titles menu in QLab.

Display & Geometry tab. Because of this, there is no way to simply grab and move the text. Input X and Y controls are the only way to reposition the text placement. Go ahead and adjust the values of each slider to see how they manipulate the size and placement of your title.

Color

Text color is a simple matter of clicking on the text color box. This will then open the OS X Color Picker for your use in selecting a font color.

Show Cue Image

One of the interesting functions of the title effect is that you can choose to either show or hide the cue's image output. This could be particularly useful if you had a reason to project only text with no image for a background. Of course, you could create a neutral background image to be used for this purpose, but another option is to simply unclick the "Show_Cue_Image" checkbox, which will make the cue image disappear, leaving only the title behind.

Blend Mode

The final text control is likely the one that will be the greatest source of confusion for those unfamiliar with graphics editing programs. **Blend Mode** simply refers to how one object interacts or "blends" with the background when placed atop another layer. There are a number of different options available in the Blend Mode drop-down menu and each slightly varies from the other (Figure 14.11).

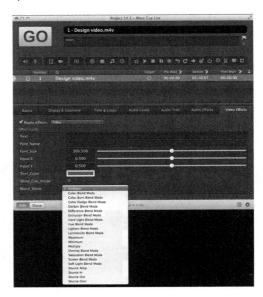

Figure 14.11
Blend modes.

One thing that can lead to a bit of confusion for the beginner is that the blending modes are listed in alphabetical order, rather than being grouped by their function. Below is a list of the modes grouped into their functions. It is important to note that working with blending modes is almost always an experimental process. They are, at their core, mathematical processes that change the pixels of your image. The following list will, by no means, make you an expert at blend modes. Rather, it is intended to be a springboard that enables you to better understand where to begin your own experimentation.

Darken Modes are so named because they have the effect of darkening the text. Those blending modes in the **Lighten Modes** category lighten the text overlay. Each blend mode in the Darken category has an opposite in the Lighten category. These opposites perform the reverse function of their pair in the other category. For instance, in the Darken Blend Mode, if pixels of your text are darker than the ones in the layer below it, they are kept in the text. For Lighten Blend Mode, it is the opposite in that the lighter pixels of the text will remain.

Contrast Modes work by lightening the lightest pixels, darkening the darkest pixels, and eliminating the mid-tones of the overlaid text altogether. These blend modes will create a text overlay that is translucent, showing the base image through it.

Darken Modes	Darken Blend Mode Multiply Color Burn Blend Mode
Lighten Modes	Lighten Blend Mode Screen Blend Mode Color Dodge Blend Mode
Contrast Modes	Overlay Blend Mode Soft Light Blend Mode Hard Light Blend Mode
Inversion Modes	Difference Blend Mode Exclusion Blend Mode
Component Modes	Hue Blend Mode Saturation Blend Mode Color Blend Mode Luminosity Blend Mode
Min Max Modes	Minimum Maximum
Source Modes	Source Atop Source In Source Out Source Over

Inversion Modes are named so for the way in which overlapping colors of multiple layers are treated. For Difference Blend Mode, similar colors that overlap are processed, so that the matching colors in the top layer (the text) will be changed to an inverted color. In Exclusion Blending Mode, similar colors cancel each other out and the resulting color on the top layer will be gray.

Component Modes (sometimes called HSL Mode for Hue, Saturation, and Luminance) are blending modes that address the hue, saturation, and luminosity of the overlapping layers.

The **Min Max Modes** are an interesting set of blending modes that allow for the use of text as a mask. When using the Minimum function, the color of the font becomes a cutout and the area outside the text functions as a black mask. The resulting effect is that the Video or Camera Cue will be seen through the mask of whatever text is on the screen.

Finally, the last category of blending modes is the **Source Mode.** There are four types of source modes, each of which performing a slightly different function. **Source Atop** places the text over the background image and then uses the luminance of the background to determine what to show. **Source In** uses the background image to define what to leave of the text and sometimes cropping off areas of the text. **Source Out** uses the background image to define what to take out of the text. **Source Over** places the text over the background image. These four modes can be somewhat confusing at first, so I recommend experimentation to see how to best utilize them in your QLab workspace.

14.3 Video Effects Presets: Blur/ Sharpen

Blurs are specific types of image filters that create a blurry image, whereas sharpen does the opposite. Unlike an actual camera, QLab uses a series of algorithms to recreate a traditional blurred look. The following video effects are all used to either blur or sharpen the video output.

Box/Disc/Gaussian Blurs

The first choice in the list of blur/sharpen effects is a series of three basic blurs: the box blur, disc blur, and Gaussian blur. Using Cue 1 in Project 14.1, select the Box/Disc/Gaussian Blurs preset from the drop-down menu. You will see that the effect inputs panel features a second drop-down menu to select which blur type you want to utilize and a "radius" slider (see Figure 14.12). The radius slider controls the amount of blurriness for each of the three blur types. In each case, the setting of 0.000 (all the way to the left) indicates no blur, and sliding it upwards begins to add more blur effect.

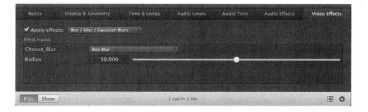

Figure 14.12
The Box/Disc/
Gaussian Blur
controls.

The **Box Blur** creates a hazy quality that does not distort the image shape too greatly. The **Disc Blur** distorts the image quality more than the box blur but may also add a level of latency to moving image output as the effect is increased; slowing the resulting image feed and adding a "jumpy" quality to it. CPU load is a factor here; faster machines may not experience this issue, but slower machines likely will. Finally, the **Gaussian Blur** adds the greatest level of "haziness" to the image, resulting in an incredibly blurred image that lacks in definition.

Motion Blur

Simply put, the motion blur adds a blur to your Video or Camera Cue in a given direction and radius. When the motion blur is selected, there are two sliders in the effect inputs panel: Angle and Radius. The easiest way to perceive how the motion blur works is to increase the radius all the way to 100.000 and then slowly start sliding your Angle slider to how this affects the direction of the motion blur.

Sharpen Luminance

In video terminology, **luma** is the signal that represents the brightness of an image, whereas **chroma** refers to the signal that conveys the color information. The sharpen luminance effect increases the image detail of the luma without affecting the chrominance. There is only one slider used to operate the sharpen luminance effect, labeled "Sharpness." Sliding the sharpness to the right will increase image detail, whereas sliding it to the left will decrease it. The default level is 1.000, in the center of the slider (Figure 14.13).

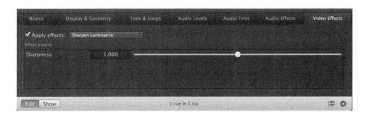

Figure 14.13
The Sharpness
slider.

Unsharp Mask

The name unsharp mask has confused many beginners into thinking that the purpose of the effect is to "unsharpen" an image. In fact, the opposite is true. The purpose of the unsharp mask is to increase a new image that is less blurry than the one you started with. The effect takes a negative copy of the blurry image and superimposes it atop the original, creating a resulting clearer image. To activate the unsharp mask, select it in the drop-down menu. You will notice that there are two sliders for controlling unsharp masking: radius and intensity (Figure 14.14). The first slider, **radius**, affects the size of the edges to be enhanced; the smaller the radius, the greater is the detail. High radii can lead to halos around the edges of your image. The **intensity** slider controls how much contrast is added to image edges. Radius and intensity are inversely connected, as decreasing one allows for increasing the other. Increasing both to high intensities will create a darker image.

Zoom Blur

In photography terms, a **zoom blur** is an effect achieved by activating the zoom on your lens while the shutter is open. The resulting image tends to have one central point of focus, around which the surrounding imagery seems to be moving somewhat. In QLab, the zoom blur video effect recreates this look for you. Selecting Zoom Blur from the drop-down menu will reveal three sliders in the effect inputs panel: Input X, Input Y, and Amount (see Figure 14.15). Input X and Input Y control the direction of the blur on the *x, y* planes. Amount represents the amount of zoom blur desired in the resulting image. This effect can be used with some success to create interesting movement effects.

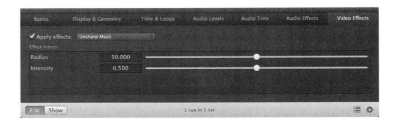

Figure 14.14
Unsharp mask controls.

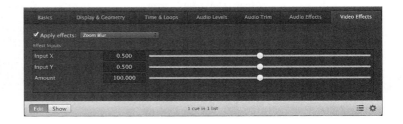

Figure 14.15
Zoom Blur controls.

14.4 Video Effects Presets: Textures and Edge Effects

For most users, the textures and edge effects will be one of the most useful effects sets and will require the least amount of explanation to use. Essentially, this group of effects takes the image feed and either applies a texture to it or emulates a classic look (like a computer monitor, comic book, or kaleidoscope). This group of effects is the third grouping in the drop-down menu and starts with pixelation.

Pixelation

Pixelation is an effect that breaks down the image feed into a series of square or hexagons for output. There are four sets of controls: effect, input x, input y, and scale. Effect allows you to choose either a square or a hexagonal pixel shape from its drop-down menu. Figure 14.16 shows the same image presented in both pixel types. The scale slider changes the overall size of pixels. Smaller pixels give increased image detail, whereas larger pixels add more image distortion.

Screen

The next video effects preset, **screen**, imitates the look of various half toning methods used in printing. This effect features a number of control sliders in the effect inputs (Figure 14.17). The first control function is a drop-down menu that allows for the selection between the different screen types: Dot Screen, Line Screen, Hatched Screen, or Circular Screen. Using Cue 1, cycle through the four options to get a feel of their different looks. The **Dot Screen**, when first activated, resembles a classic pixelated black and white monitor. **Line Screen** features a series of lines running in one direction, whereas **Hatched Screen** has two sets of lines cross-hatching one another for the creation of a moiré pattern. The **Circle Screen** features a series of concentric circles originating from a central point on the screen.

Figure 14.16
Both square (left) and hexagonal (right) pixel types.

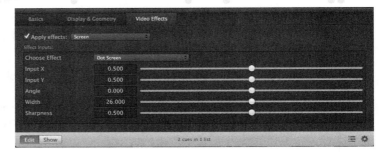

Figure 14.17
Screen control
sliders.

For each of these effects, the five sliders change the appearance of the pattern to some degree. The first two sliders (**input x and input y**) have little function for any of the effects except for circle screen. In circle screen, these sliders will move the point of origin for the circles around on the screen. Conversely, the **Angle** slider has no visible effect on the circle screen, but it will rotate the patterns around the z-axis for the other three presets. The final two sliders are applicable for all four presets. **Width** controls the size of the pattern and drastically changes the appearance of the effect. For example, the dots screen resembles an older computer monitor in a small scale, but when enlarged tales on more of a pop art look. Finally, the **Sharpness** slider controls the sharpness/softness of the screen textures. Using Cue 1, again, take some time to navigate through these different effects and how the control sliders change their appearance.

Bloom and Gloom

The third set of texture and edge effects presets is called Bloom and Gloom. This effect preset is made up of two different effects: Bloom and Gloom. **Bloom** is an effect that creates a glow emanating from light objects in your image feed. This glow will bleed over to other aspects of the image. **Gloom** creates the opposite effect of having a darkness invade from the outer edges of the image and "gray out" the luminance in your image, thus creating a gloomy look. The only two control sliders for both effects are radius and intensity.

CMYK Halftone

Halftone is a reprographic technique used to simulate variations in shade and color in the printed image. The idea is that several halftones are printed, each in a single color. These tones are composed of thousands of circular dots in varying sizes. When combined together, this creates the illusion of a continuous range of colors. The CMYK Halftone effect in QLab breaks down your Video or Camera Cue and imposes a CMYK (Cyan, Magenta, Yellow, and Black) halftone process to the image output. Like many of the other effects in this category, there are the input x, input y, width, angle, and sharpness sliders. By this point, you have no doubt familiar with their use. The final two sliders, **Grey Component Removal** and **Under Color Removal,** affect the amount of black dots versus color in the composition. Sliding both to the right will create an image that is mostly composed of black dots and less CMYK (see Figure 14.18).

Color Posterize

Posterization is a classic photographic process used to distill a complex image down to a series of several small regions of color with abrupt changes from one to another. This technique was originally used for the creation of color posters. The **Color Posterize** effect in QLab is a simple interface, featuring only one slider called "Levels." The levels slider determines how complex the posterization will be for your video feed. The slider works on a scale from 2.000 to 30.000. The lower end of the scale will feature fewer layers of tones, whereas sliding it to the upper end will result in thousands of layers of tones (see Figure 14.19).

Crystallize and Pointillize

The sixth video effect is a combination of two effects quite similar to those seen in Pixelation. Again, you choose the effect between two choices on a drop-down menu. **Crystallize** takes your image feed and imposes a crystalline structure to it, similar to the hexagonal pixelation except that each crystalline pixel is a different shape from its neighbors. **Pointillize** does the same with a series of overlapping circular dots on a white background. Both of these effects have a "shimmering" look to them as individual random pixels have a slight color flickering to them. Again, the radius slider controls the size of the individual pixels, with a smaller value indicating more detail to the image output.

Figure 14.18
Using high Grey Component Removal and Under Color Removal settings.

Figure 14.19
Low posterization levels.

Edge Work

The next effect preset has two options: one called Edge Work and the other Edges. **Edge Work** creates a simple black and white outlined image of your video output. Dark tones are outputted as black and light tones as white with the edges of every object featuring a white outline. One interesting aspect of this effect is that, for moving images, there is a constant flickering on white dots (similar to the "snow" seen on old television screens without a signal). This creates an interesting visual effect. In this effect preset, the radius slider controls the level of detail and color. The radius slider operates on a scale from 0.000 to 20.000. The lower ends of the scale produce quite detailed images with an "x-ray" appearance to them. As you slide further up the scale, edges become less defined, and the resulting image is more of a series of black and white blobs.

The second option, **Edges** creates highly complex images in dark blacks and blues, with the outlines done in various shades of light colors. It also has the "flickery" quality to the image output and resembles a somewhat colorful version of an x-ray. Figure 14.20 shows the same image seen in both Edge Work and Edges.

Kaleidoscope

A real kaleidoscope uses a series of mirrors placed at angles from one another inside a cylinder to create a bizarre fractured and colorful representation of the world. For the kaleidoscope effect in QLab, the image is mirrored on the x- and y-axes without the addition of colorful reflections. This effect preset uses three control sliders: input x, input y, and count. The count slider controls

Figure 14.20
The top image illustrates Edge Works, while the bottom is Edges.

the number of planes upon which the image is mirrored. Sliding it all the way down to 1.000 would result in the image being mirrored across one plane; the x-axis only. Sliding it to 2.000 mirrors the image across two planes: the x-axis and y-axis. Increasing the number begins to create the more recognizable circular kaleidoscope pattern. The input x and input y sliders affect the distance of spread from their axes. This is one of those effects that will truly require spending some time experimenting to find the exact desired look, but the resulting images can be quite stunning.

Median and Comic Effect

The Median and Comic effects are both simple on/off effects that create a predetermined look for your image. **Median** is an effect that replaces each pixel with a new pixel having the median value of neighboring pixels. This tends to somewhat darken the image and reduce some levels of noise. The **Comic** effect applies a halftone effect to the image in limited color range somewhat similar to classic comic book print, but with significantly fewer details (see Figure 14.21).

Noise Reduction

Image noise is the appearance of tiny spots of variant color in a digital image, similar to film grain that appeared in pre-digital cameras. Typically speaking, noise is an undesired effect, as it detracts from the image and degrades the overall

Figure 14.21
An image with
comic effect
applied.

image quality. The **Noise Reduction** effect allows for manipulating the noise levels and sharpness of an image in order to boost or reduce noise in a cue. There are only two sliders for this effect: noise level and sharpness.

14.5 Video Effects Presets: Distortion Effects

As the name implies, distortion effects are a set of effects that distort the image output in a number of different ways. These effects are particularly useful in creating dynamic video applications for QLab.

Circle Splash/Hole Distortion

Both the circle splash and hole distortion serve the same basic purpose, to create a circular selection around which the image will be distorted. For **circle splash**, the image inside circular selection remains unchanged, whereas the imagery outside it gets an effect similar to the motion blur applied to it. The **hole distortion**, on the other hand, removes any image information inside the circular selection and creates a "black hole" in its place. The imagery outside this hole is warped in a cylindrical fashion. The three controls for both effects presets are input x, input y, and radius.

Pinch/Bump Distortion

The pinch/bump distortion effect presets have three effects options: pinch, bump, and bump linear. Essentially, these three effects create the appearance that the image is being either pushed down upon to create a depression or pushed up against from the backside, bulging the surface out. **Pinch** is the effect of pushing down on the center of the image to make a depression. **Bump** is the circular appearance of something pushing either up or down onto the image, while **bump linear** creates an effect that resembles the ripple of a flag in the wind. As in others, input x and input y move the point of incident around on the surface. Radius and scale relate to the overall size of the effect. This effect preset also features a slider called "angle_bump_linear" that controls the placement of the linear bump effect.

Torus/Lens Distortion

A torus is best described as a three-dimensional form shaped like a donut (with a hole or, in some cases, a concave dimple in the center). The purpose of this video effect is to simulate the look of the refractive quality of light passing through a torus-shaped lens (Figure 14.22). There are numerous control sliders for this effect, but the only new one is the refraction slider. This slider controls the refracted quality of the image viewed through the torus. The effects are not easily described, and this is another of the features best understood through experimentation.

Twirl/Circular Wrap/Vortex

This effect tab actually has three separate effect presets imbedded within it: twirl, circular wrap, and vortex. All the three effects feature the same control sliders; input x and y for moving the effect placement, and radius and angle for controlling the size and direction of the effect. Essentially, they are all similar

Figure 14.22
The torus effect applied to an image.

Figure 14.23
The lozenge shape is an interesting effect for creating refracted looks.

effects in that they all deal with distorting the image in a circular or cylindrical fashion. **Twirl** creates a circular selection of the image and spins the contents in either a clockwise or a counterclockwise direction, creating a hurricane appearance. **Circular Wrap** creates the appearance of wrapping the image around itself, like rolling a drawing into a tube shape. **Vortex** places a small circular selection at some point on the screen and creates a vortex reaching out from that point to all edges of the image. This creates a strong swirl pattern at the placement and a slight warping of imagery as it reaches the perimeter.

Glass Lozenge

The glass lozenge effect is one of the stranger presets in which it creates a pill-shaped lens through which the image is refracted (see Figure 14.23). When first selecting the effect, you will likely notice a small black semi-circle in the upper right corner of your image. This is one edge of the lozenge. By manipulating the placement of four independent x/y sliders, you can create the desired size and placement of the lozenge. Note that there are two sliders for the x-plane and two for the y-plane. Experiment by moving these sliders around to see what kind of unique sizes and angles you can create. For this effect, the radius slider controls how thick or thin the lozenge becomes. The refraction slider controls the appearance of the refracted image, as seen in the torus/lens distortion effect.

14.6 Video Effects Presets: Tiles

Of all the effects presets, tiles are the hardest to explain. The best way to experience them is to experiment with their use and see yourself what kinds of interesting effects emerge. For this reason, the following section will entail only a brief description of each effect and its use. I strongly encourage you to open Project 14.1 and go through each of the effects to see firsthand how they respond. All the following effects are tiles because they take samples of your image and reconstruct it into some type of tiled fashion. The biggest difference between most of them is the shape or mathematical rearrangement of the tiles for output.

Op Tile

The op tile effect segments the cue image, applies scaling and rotation as inputted in the control sliders, and then reassembles the image to give it an op art appearance.

Perspective Tile

The perspective tile effect applies a transformation to the cue image to give the illusion of perspective and then tiles the result. This effect requires a great number of control sliders, as there are eight interfaces to control the x/y placement.

Quad Tiles

The quad tiles category contains three effects presets bundled into it: fourfold translated tile, fourfold reflected tile, and parallelogram tile. The **fourfold translated tile** effect produces a tiled image from the source by applying four translation operations (x/y placement, angle, acute angle, and width). The **fourfold reflected tile** produces a tiled image from the source by applying a four-way reflected symmetry. Finally, the **parallelogram tile** effect warps an image by reflecting it on a parallelogram, then tiling the resulting image.

Reflected Tiles

The Reflected tiles category contains four subcategories: glide, sixfold, eightfold, and twelvefold reflected tile. Each of them differs only in the planes of symmetry across which the image is reflected. For instance, eightfold reflected symmetry produces a tiled image from the cue source by applying four-way reflected symmetry to the image. Depending on the original image, the resulting image tiles might resemble square tiles, snowflakes, or complex mosaic tile arrangements.

Rotated Tiles

The rotating tile effect looks somewhat similar to the reflected tile effect, but the mathematics to produce it is different. The rotated tile effect is achieved by reproducing a source image multiple times at increments of a common degree.

For instance, the sixfold-rotated tile reproduces the image in increments of 60 degrees, thereby creating a resulting hexagonal image output. Within the rotated tiles category, there are three effects: triangle tile, fourfold-rotated tile, and sixfold-rotated tile.

14.7 Video Effects Presets: Custom Compositions

One of the greatest strengths of QLab is its inclusion of the OS X native graphic and audio frameworks that enable it to handle graphics, animations, and video effects. Quartz Composer is one of these OS X technologies that work hand-in-hand with QLab. Quartz Composer is a visual programming environment that allows for sophisticated motion graphics compositions without actually writing code. The software includes pre-installed building blocks of graphics processing that can be combined together to create dynamic visualizations and effects. Once completed, these compositions can be inserted into your QLab workspace to render the video from a Video or Camera Cue.

The custom compositions tab under video effects is the location to insert these compositions. Simply copy and paste the composition into the effect inputs panel at the bottom of the page and that's it. QLab will provide the Quartz Composer frames from the video file as it plays.

Although addressing programming is not the central aim of this text, it should be noted that Quartz Composer is a fantastic toolset for anyone seriously interested in projection design through QLab. The software is part of a download called Graphics Tools for Xcode. It is not on the App Store but can be downloaded from developer.apple.com/downloads (free Apple developer account required). Xcode is a toolkit of applications needed to create software for the Mac, iPhone, and iPad. To learn more about Quartz Composer and its uses, check out www.quartzcomposer.com. It is an independent website unaffiliated with Apple Inc. featuring a number of compositions, patches, and plug-ins that can be used in the QLab environment.

14.8 Video Effects Projects

Video Effects present a wide range of new opportunities for those using QLab for projection design/integrated media. Although there are numerous applications for this aspect of the software, there are only two areas which I would like to cover in projects, as much of the other functions you discover will be based on the foundation of these two techniques. This first technique is using Fade Cues to fade in or out from a Video/Camera Cue with an applied effect. The second is the ability to stack two or more Video/Camera Cues atop one another to create a unique new effect.

Project 14.2 ▽

Video Effects and Fade Cues

One important feature to recognize is the inability to control video effects through Fade Cues. Unlike Audio Effects, Video Effects cannot be faded in or out while the Video Cue continues to play. That does not mean, however, that a Video Cue with video effects applied to it cannot be faded in or out. The following project details how to fade in a Camera Cue featuring the Zoom Blur effect. This effect is particularly useful for creating hazy, dream-like effects. Imagine a production in which you needed a live feed of an actor portraying a ghost speaking from the spiritual plane. The following project takes you through the steps necessary to set up such an effect.

Step One:
Download Project 14.2 from the companion website. Once the project is open, activate the Audition Window to preview your effects.

Step Two:
This project includes one Camera Cue. You will need to have a camera attached to your system to test its application. Select Cue 1 and click on the Video Effects tab in the Inspector Panel. Select Zoom Blur and click the Apply Effects checkbox.

Step Three:
Click GO to preview the Camera Cue feed with the applied effect. Manipulate the Input X, Input Y, and Amount sliders until you achieve the desired ghostly effect on your video feed.

Step Four:
Select the Display & Geometry tab in the Inspector Panel and set the opacity to 0.0%. This will ensure the Camera Cue starts with no opacity, so as to create a fade-in.

Step Five:
Insert a Fade Cue after Cue 1 and assign Cue 1 as its target. In the Geometry tab, input an opacity of 100%. This will create the fade-in.

Step Six:
Select Cue 1 and change the continue status to auto-continue. This will fire Cue 1 and Cue 2 concurrently. If you test Cue 1, you should now see the video feed slowly fade-in from a black screen to a ghostly figure.

Project 14.3 ▼

Combining Video Effects

One interesting feature of Video and Camera Cues is the ability to layer multiple cues atop one another. In the case of the Camera Cue, the feed is identical thereby enabling the creation of a feed that appears to have multiple video effects applied to one video stream. For the project below, imagine a production with a stylized comic book design aesthetic in which a character is visited by a vision from God. For this production, it might be useful to combine together more than one video effect to achieve the appropriate comic book deity.

Step One:
Download Project 14.3 from the companion website. Once the project is open, activate the Audition Window to preview your effects.

Step Two:
This project includes two Camera Cues. You will need to have a camera attached to your system to test its application. Select Cue 1 and click on the Video Effects tab in the Inspector Panel. Select Zoom Blur and click the Apply Effects checkbox.

Step Three:
Click GO to preview the Camera Cue feed with the applied effect. Manipulate the Input X, Input Y, and Amount sliders until you achieve the desired ghostly effect on your video feed.

Step Four:
Select the Display & Geometry tab in the Inspector Panel and set the opacity to 0.0%. This will ensure the Camera Cue starts with no opacity, so as to create a fade-in. In addition, set the Layer to 1. This will place the camera feed on a lower layer.

Step Five:
Insert a Fade Cue (Cue 1.5) after Cue 1 and assign Cue 1 as its target. In the Geometry tab, input an opacity of 100%. This will create the fade in. Set the continue state to auto-continue.

Step Six:
Select Cue 1 and change the continue status to auto-continue. This will fire Cue 1 and 2 concurrently. If you test Cue 1, you should now see the video feed slowly fade in from a black screen to a ghostly figure.

Step Seven:
Select Cue 2 and activate the Median and Comic Effect setting in the Video Effects tab. In the Choose Effect drop-down menu, select Comic Effect.

Step Eight:

In the Display & Geometry tab of Cue 2, set the opacity to 0%. In addition, set its Layer to 2. This will place the comic effect Camera Cue on a layer above the first camera feed. Finally, set the continue state to auto-continue.

Step Nine:

Insert a Fade Cue (Cue 2.5) after Cue 2 and assign Cue 2 as its target. In the Geometry tab, input an opacity of 20%. This will create the fade in for Cue 2 and set the opacity to a low level so it is semi-transparent.

Step Ten:

Test the cue sequence. Your programming should match that seen in Figure 14.24.

Figure 14.24
A workspace utilizing camera cues and video effects.

Show Control Systems

The entertainment design and technology industry has evolved over the years to include practices from a number of different fields. Each area brings its own unique equipment and control systems into the mix, requiring today's practitioners to have a working vocabulary of many disparate fields and the ability to collaborate with more production members than ever before. As production technology has evolved, so has the need for simplifying methods of control across this wide range of production elements. This is the nature of show control, the method of centralizing control for a number of different production elements.

15.1 Terminology

The discussion of show control can be a confusing endeavor without a basic introduction to terminology. The following section covers some of the fundamental terms in understanding show control.

Entertainment Control Systems

For every production, there are a number of different elements that must work together seamlessly: sound, lighting, projections, special effects, etc. For each of these different areas, there will be one or more **systems**, or a set of elements working together as parts of an interconnecting network. An **entertainment control system** is the combination of all the necessary equipment required to control a live production area. For instance, a lighting control system is the combination of a lighting console, dimmers, circuits, and cabling necessary to power conventional lighting equipment and send control signals to intelligent lighting and accessories.

Standards

When talking about entertainment control systems, we are referring to literally thousands of unique proprietary systems created to work with specialized equipment. This equipment can be anything from sound mixers to lighting consoles, moving lights, confetti cannons, projectors, foggers, automated scenery/rigging control, or more. Each of these areas also has numerous manufacturers creating equipment that has its own individualized control system architecture.

The one thing that enables all of these systems to work together is standards. Regarding control systems, a **standard** refers to a commonly accepted working practice or protocol that governs how different manufacturers can create products that interact well with one another. The most important type of standard concerning show control is the **open standard**, a standard commonly created by bringing together a group of industry professionals to create a mutually beneficial standard practice publicly available for the market. This standard may relate to how hardware is created or, in the case of a **communication standard**, what type of language is used to communicate between varying pieces of hardware. In the early days of entertainment control, there were many proprietary standards created by and for individual manufacturers that did not work well with equipment from other manufacturers. This practice became costly and frustrating for the end-user, as you would never be guaranteed that equipment would work together at different venues (or sometimes even at the same venue). This led to the creation of entertainment industry standards such as MIDI, MSC, DMX 512-A, and OSC. In addition to standards created for our industry, we obviously benefit from industry standards in the telecommunications and computer industry regarding networking, data transmission, and more. The following table lists some of the most common standards for the entertainment industry, all of which you should familiarize yourself with.

MIDI	**Musical Instrument Digital Interface.** One of the most widely utilized standards for communication within entertainment control systems. Standard maintained by the MIDI Manufacturers Association. www.midi.org.
MSC	**MIDI Show Control.** A subset of the MIDI protocol dealing specifically with triggering and controlling entertainment control systems from a remote source. www.midi.org.
DMX 512-A	**Digital MultipleX.** Developed by the United States Institute for Theatre Technology (USITT), this standard describes a method of digital transmission between lighting consoles and equipment. Though originally intended as lighting exclusive, the standard has been adopted for use in special effects (smoke, fog, and haze), video systems, animatronics, and more (www.usitt.org).
OSC	**Open Sound Control.** OSC is a protocol for communication between computers, sound synthesizers, and multimedia devices that is optimized for real-time control over networks (www.opensoundcontrol.org).

Show Control

In short, show control is the method of linking together multiple entertainment control systems into a master system. It is basically a system that controls other systems. It can be software-based or dedicated hardware.

Network

In basic terms, a network refers to a system of interconnected people or objects that share resources in some way. For technology purposes, we usually refer to a network as a connection of one or more computers that are linked together in order to share files, resources, and allow communication/command signals to be transferred in both directions. In the most basic type of connection, a **point-to-point** interface, each device would be physically connected to any device it needed to share information with. This obviously creates a wiring nightmare and is cost-prohibitive. A more common approach would be to create a true network, in which each system device or **node** connects to a centralized data pathway to communicate with the **host**, a networked computer that communicates data out the nodes.

There are a number of terms you have likely heard like LAN (Local Area Networks) or WLAN (Wireless Local Area Networks) referring to networks. These are common in entertainment networks, as well. Most of our day-to-day experience with networking comes from the Internet. Whether you use an Ethernet cable or a wireless router to connect the Internet, you are connecting to a network in order to do so. With the world of entertainment control systems, it is equally common to see our equipment networked through DMX and MIDI cables in addition to Ethernet cable runs. This leads to our next big concept to understanding show control: entertainment control systems.

15.2 Entertainment Control Systems

Since there are so many different categories of entertainment control systems, it might be beneficial to examine a few of the most common types that can be used in conjunction with QLab. The following section covers three such areas and offers a basic introduction to terminology associated with each system. This is by no means an exhaustive study of these areas but should serve as useful platform to discuss control system architecture before delving into show control.

Sound Control Systems

Since much of the first half of the book was dedicated to sound systems, you should already be familiar with many of the basic concepts of the sound system. As we have already seen, QLab serves as a powerful controller for both reinforcement and playback systems. In addition to QLab and a digital audio interface, there might be a number of different pieces of equipment connected to your sound system like a mixer, microphones, signal processing, amplifiers, and speakers. Listed below is some of the most common equipment with which QLab might communicate.

MIDI Keyboards/Sequencers

QLab can both receive and send MIDI signals from various sources. In this fashion, QLab can either trigger an effect on an external MIDI device or be triggered by a MIDI signal sent from the device.

Sound Mixers

Most digital sound mixers can both send and receive MIDI signals. One great method of utilizing this function is to send a MIDI signal from QLab to change a pre-programmed attribute of your mixer. For instance, you can send a signal from QLab to your mixer to recall a scene from its memory with presets like EQ, reverb, compressions, etc.

Timecode

Timecode is a method of ensuring multiple devices sync with one another for playback. QLab allows for all cues to be triggered by an incoming timecode. In addition, the Timecode Cue allows for QLab to send a timecode out to any MIDI device.

Lighting Control Systems

Lighting control systems can vary in a number of ways, but all share many common attributes. For every system, there will be a lighting controller, dimmers, circuits, and lighting instruments. Lighting control systems utilize the DMX-512 standard practice for communication. In addition, most lighting consoles also have the ability to send and receive MIDI signals.

Lighting Controller

The lighting controller can be a dedicated console or a piece of software running on a computer. The controller sends DMX control signals that interface with the dimmers and, in some instances, lighting fixtures and accessories.

Dimmers

Dimmers are specialized devices that regulate the flow of voltage out to a circuit. The control signal from the lighting controller tells the dimmers what percentage of voltage to output to the circuits.

Circuits

A circuit is the physical connection through which a lighting instrument receives electricity. There are a number of different connector types from Edison to stage pin, or twist lock.

Lighting Instruments

Lighting instruments can be either conventional or intelligent in nature. **Conventional lighting fixtures** allow for control of intensity (brightness). These lighting instruments only need electricity to operate. **Intelligent Lighting Fixtures** feature a wide range of control features such as angle, rotation, intensity, color, strobe, textures, and beam shaping. These intelligent fixtures require both electricity and a DMX control signal from the lighting controller to operate. In addition to lighting instruments, there may also be **lighting accessories**, such as color scrollers, gobo spinners, or irises that are also controlled by DMX signals.

Video/Projections Systems

Most video systems are comprised of one or more computers working in tandem to output a video signal to one or more displays or projectors. Video systems typically utilize IP/Ethernet connections for control.

Video Playback Software

Control software like QLab is often used for video playback in video systems. When used as a stand-alone method, the software triggers playback and outputs it through the computer's video card(s).

Video Servers

Video servers are computer-based hardware dedicated to providing video signals. Unlike a typical computer, the video server is utilized for only one function. A high-end video server can play back multiple simultaneous video streams synchronized with one another.

Timecode

Since most video systems must offer synchronized playback with audio feeds, timecode is an essential component. If using an external time clock, QLab audio playback can be triggered via timecode to sync with external video playback.

Additional Control Systems

Though the three entertainment control systems listed earlier are most commonly associated with QLab, there are a number of other control systems that could be controlled by QLab. For example, a number of additional control systems (automated scenery, fog, haze, pyrotechnics, confetti cannons, etc.) are readily controlled by DMX-512. While QLab does not natively send DMX signals, it can interface with another computer or console on the network via MIDI and trigger its control, which would then activate the control system. One example of this might be sending a MIDI signal to a lighting console that would control both lights and special effects via DMX signal transmission. Another possibility might be networking to a second computer running a DMX emulator program and using a USB to DMX output to trigger the control system.

15.3 Show Control Systems

QLab show control covers a wide array of possibilities and, as such, features a number of variables regarding how a show control network might be set up. Depending on the nature of your show control needs, you might have one or more additional systems connected to you QLab control computer. At the heart of QLab's show control abilities are two main cue types: the OSC Cue and the MIDI Cue. Through the use of these two cue types, QLab can control a wide array of devices. Listed below are some of the common configurations that might be used to set up a QLab show control network for various entertainment control systems.

Sound Control Systems

Regarding sound, QLab has the potential to function as its own sound system or to interface with other sound equipment or computers. The two main methods of control are OSC and MIDI. To control another computer running QLab, network the two computers together via Ethernet and send an OSC cue to trigger a specific cue number and command type. To interface with other MIDI hardware, you can send a MIDI message across either MIDI cable or Ethernet. Many USB or Firewire audio devices also have built-in MIDI ports for sending MIDI messages. For both OSC and MIDI, a destination must be established in the cue settings to assign which device the signal will be routed to.

Lighting Control Systems

As shown earlier, most lighting control systems have the ability to input and output MIDI messages. This means that these lighting consoles have the ability to both be triggered by QLab and send MIDI messages to QLab for triggering cues within the workspace. Most lighting consoles feature a standard MIDI connector for both input and output. In addition, some lighting manufacturers like ETC (Electronic Theatre Controls) have created specialized network

Figure 15.1
The NET3 show
control gateway
from ETC.
*Photo courtesy: ETC
(Electronic Theatre
Controls Inc.).*

gateways to interface with their lighting consoles. ETC's NET3 Show Control Gateway (Figure 15.1) is an Ethernet device that allows for bi-directional communication (unlike standard MIDI cabling which only communicates in one direction) of MIDI and timecode over a lighting network. In this case, QLab could be networked to an EOS family lighting console to send and receive MIDI and timecode control signals.

Video/Projections Control Systems

Video control systems could be a number of different configurations from using QLab to control displays to networking several computers running QLab together, or even sending a control signal to a video server. For all but the most basic needs, your video control system will send and receive messages across an Ethernet network between computers.

15.4 Show Control Considerations

As seen earlier, there are a number of different ways that QLab can interface with various entertainment control systems. The bottom line is assessing the needs for your individual project and considering all the variables: equipment owned by the producing entity, budget to acquire necessary equipment, personnel available for running the show, amount of space available at the performance space for said personnel, and union contracts stipulating personnel numbers. Not every project is the same, and just because you *can* centralize show control to one computer, it does not always mean that you *should*.

For educational theatre, there are often numerous crewmembers available to man control systems, and though it might be tempting to streamline control, it is beneficial for students to learn how to operate the equipment. For the small storefront theatre, there is often no space for multiple board operators and you will find one stage manager controlling all control systems from one small booth. In this case, using QLab to control multiple aspects might be desirable. Should you decide that a show control setup is the right choice for your production, there will be a number of steps necessary to integrate control into one network.

The most important step to create a successfully integrated show control system is planning. Ideally, all designers will meet with stage management and create a thorough list of all cues in the appropriate order. Once all of these cues have been organized, this will be the foundation for creating a master QLab workspace that sends control signals out to various entertainment control systems across the network. As changes occur during the tech process, they must be meticulously noted and changed in the workspace, else one change might throw off the sequence for the entire system. A word of caution is that a completely automated show control systems seem to work best in rigidly choreographed productions like dance concerts. In more organic or improvisational productions, this method may not work as well. There are many challenges in creating a successful show control system, but the rewards are well worth it in the long run.

QLab and MIDI

MIDI is one of the most versatile and enduring forms of communication languages written over the past 30 years. Likely, you have heard the term MIDI before but perhaps not understood exactly what it is or how it is utilized. This chapter details both the basics of MIDI and how QLab utilizes it as an important component of its show control engine.

16.1 MIDI Basics

In the early 1980s, a team of engineers and synthesizer designers from various manufacturers devised a method of direct communication between electronic keyboards called **Musical Instrument Digital Interface**, or **MIDI**. Over the time, manufacturers adopted this method as a standard, making it a component of most electronic keyboards. In short, MIDI is a digital language that allows musical instruments to communicate with each other, thereby allowing one instrument to control another. Instead of being a musical recording, the MIDI signal is a numeric set of codes arranged to send instructions from one device to another. MIDI signals, amazingly compact in size, travel in one direction from one device to another. Within a short time of its introduction to the market, digital musicians quickly branched out to using MIDI with other types of digital devices like personal computers. By the mid-1980s, MIDI was utilized in music production across several computer platforms.

16.2 What Is MIDI Show Control

In 1986, Charlie Richmond debuted one of the first computerized sound control systems for live theatre called Command/Cue. In addition to running Richmond Sound Designs Ltd, a company dedicated to producing a range of commercial theatre sound consoles, Mr. Richmond also served as the sound design editor for *TD&T*, the quarterly publication of The United States Institute for Theatre

Technology (USITT). It was during this time that he started a MIDI forum through USITT's Callboard network, which used the resources of the early Internet to allow people around the world to communicate. After these early communications, Richmond and roughly two-dozen other individuals from across the world (mostly from the lighting manufacturing sector) took on the task of creating a show control standard and what emerged was **MIDI Show Control (MSC)**. The introduction to the MSC 1.0 Standard defined the purpose of MSC as "to allow MIDI systems to communicate with and to control dedicated intelligent control equipment in theatrical, live performance, multi-media, audio-visual and similar environments." In short, a MIDI interface could send command messages to one or multiple devices in a system, allowing for synchronization in control. The benefits to such a system were reliable and repeatable controls that lacked the errors and inconsistent timing of human controllers. In addition to the immediate application for live performance, MSC quickly became a logical solution for playback and automation in museum installations and audio animatronic shows.

In 1991, both the MIDI Manufacturers Association and the Japan MIDI Standards Committee ratified MSC as an international standard. According to Richmond, this was one of the first international standards created without the members having a single physical meeting, since all communication was done virtually. This was certainly a sign of things to come.

16.3 QLab and MIDI

MIDI has always been an essential component of QLab, both for its use in sound systems and for its show control capabilities. In QLab 3, there are only two MIDI cue types: a MIDI Cue and a MIDI File Cue. Embedded within the MIDI Cue are a number of different message types from "musical MIDI," to MSC, or MIDI System Exclusive (MIDI SysEx). The first step to harnessing the ability of these MIDI Cues is in MIDI setup within the QLab Workspace Settings window. The basic information on MIDI setup is listed below.

Workspace Settings: MIDI Controls

You will find three tabs in the Workspace Settings window related to MIDI, the first of which is called MIDI Controls. By clicking on the MIDI Controls tab, you will open a window to the right of the page that is used to activate MIDI control preferences (see Figure 16.1). There are two rows: one for MSC and the other for "Musical" MIDI controls. The functions for both are quite similar. By clicking the checkbox to the left of the control, you are allowing your workspace to be controlled by one or both of the MIDI control categories.

The first row, MIDI Show Control, explains that by checking the box, you are enabling QLab to respond to the MSC commands: Go, Stop, Resume, Load, All_Off, Standby +/-, Sequence +/-, and Reset. To the right side of the row is

Figure 16.1
MIDI controls
preferences.

a menu for establishing the Device ID for your individual QLab computer. In MSC, there is a possible range of Device IDs from 0 to 126. Each device in your show control system will have its own unique Device ID. In some cases, you can give two devices the same Device ID, but you would lose the ability to individually control either without controlling the other. If an MSC control message with an ID of 127 is sent along the show control network, all devices will respond to the message (if they support the command format). This is a nice "fire all" option.

The second row of control settings is dedicated to "Musical" MIDI Controls. This refers to the type of signal sent out by a MIDI keyboard or device called a message. By clicking the checkbox to the left, you enable the control of certain QLab commands to assigned MIDI messages. Like the Key Map, you can pre-program QLab to respond to certain messages received across the network. To do this, simply click on the drop-down menu to the right of the desired QLab command. After clicking on the drop-down menu, you will see a list of choices featuring: Note On, Note Off, Program Change, and Control Change. These are the four types of MIDI messages that can be sent by a MIDI device or emulator. Note On refers to the message sent when a note (key) is depressed. Note Off is the message sent when a note is released (ended). Control Change is the message sent when a controller (such as a foot pedal) changes its value. Finally, a Program Change is the message sent when the patch number changes on the MIDI device.

The middle windows, labeled Byte 1 and Byte 2, allow for the insertion of the eight-digit binary code that represents the pertinent data of the note being triggered on the MIDI device. Another method is clicking on the "capture" button to the right of the row. Once depressed, the message "waiting" will appear in the windows for Byte 1 and Byte 2. Once a note is triggered on a MIDI keyboard attached to the system, QLab will record its values and insert them into the row. Thereafter, once that note is triggered under the same conditions, the QLab command will be triggered.

Workspace Settings: MIDI

The MIDI tab for workspace settings serves two functions: setting the default MIDI message type and establishing the MIDI patch for MIDI output through QLab. The top row of the screen establishes the default type of MIDI message sent through QLab's MIDI Cue as a MIDI Voice message, MSC message, or MIDI SysEx message.

The second row in the MIDI workspace settings tab allows for assigning MIDI devices to one of eight different patches. Any MIDI capable device attached to your system will automatically appear on this list. You can change the order of devices to re-order the arrangement as desired.

Pro-Tip ▼

MIDI Across Network
One of the great benefits of the Apple computer has long been its native ability to send MIDI across Internet Protocol (IP). For QLab, this is a particularly useful application. MIDI interconnect cables are, by their nature, one-way communication. If you want two-way communication between devices, you will have to run two sets of cabling to allow this. In the case of MIDI over IP, though, signals can travel in both directions making the network an ideal solution for instances of MSC. For this application, a program called ipMIDI is indispensible.

ipMIDI is a freeware program for Mac computers that allows the routing of MIDI across an Ethernet network, using ipMIDI ports to send and receive data between computers connected to your network. The driver for the software produces results with less latency than traditional MIDI interconnect cables and eliminates the need for additional cabling between devices. To download the software, visit www.nerds.de/en/ipmidi_osx.html. Once installed, ipMIDI will be available as a MIDI patch for QLab.

Workspace Settings: MIDI File

Standard MIDI files (SMF) are digital codes that contain all the necessary instructions for notes, volume, voice assignment, and effects. Unlike a WAV or AIF file, MIDI files do not contain an audio recording – only the numeric information necessary for a software or hardware player to play back the file with the appropriate voicing and effects. QLab can send MIDI File Cues but cannot synthesize them. In order to actually hear the song file, you must send the MIDI file to a player of some sort with a sound engine connected to it.

In the Workspace Settings, there is a tab for assigning MIDI file output. This MIDI File settings tab is identical to the MIDI patch in every way, except that the purpose for this setting is to assign the device patch for outputting a MIDI File Cue.

16.4 MIDI Cues

Once the workspace settings have been established for MIDI control, you are now ready to utilize MIDI Cues. A MIDI Cue can be used in a number of different ways. It could send a control signal to a MIDI device to trigger playback. It could be used as for MSC to trigger other entertainment control systems, like lighting. There are many options. The following sections detail the process of utilizing the MIDI Cue for such purposes. To insert a MIDI Cue, simply click on the MIDI Cue icon in the tool bar or drag it into your workspace. From there, you can examine all the various functions of the cue in the Inspector Panel.

Inspector Panel: Basics

The Basics tab for a MIDI Cue is identical to that seen in many of the other QLab Cue types. The screen is divided into basic cue information on the left side of the screen with triggering information on the right half of the screen. These functions do not differ in any way from those seen in other cue types.

Inspector Panel: Settings

The Settings tab is the heart of the control system for MIDI Cues. It is important to recognize that the MIDI Cue function contains three different MIDI Message types imbedded within its control architecture. The look and functions of the settings tab will differ between these three message types. For each of the three message types, the Settings tab is divided into two rows. The top row will always remain the same for every message type (see Figure 16.2).

MIDI Destination

The first button on the top row is labeled "MIDI Destination." This drop-down menu allows you to select one of eight different MIDI patches from the MIDI tab in Workspace Settings. This allows you to determine which MIDI device will receive the MIDI Cue.

Figure 16.2
The MIDI settings tab in the Inspector Panel.

Message Type

This drop-down menu allows for the selection between the three different MIDI Message types: MIDI Voice Message ("Musical" MIDI), MSC, and MIDI SysEx Message. Depending on the workspace settings established for MIDI, all MIDI Cues inserted into the workspace are default to one of these three:

- **MIDI Voice Messages** (also referred to as channel voice messages) are used to carry musical performance data, such a triggering or stopping a sound, selecting a particular instrument, bending the pitch, sustaining a note, etc. In addition to sending information to MIDI instruments, this type of message can also be used to control certain sound devices, such as a digital mixer.
- **MIDI Show Control Messages** are a specific subset of MIDI messaging used to interact with a wide array of devices in the entertainment industry. These messages include command formats for equipment (lighting, sound, machinery, video, projection, process control, and pyro) paired with specific commands like go, stop, resume, etc. The purpose of these controls is to decrease the likelihood of errors in cueing and give more precise timing for playback.
- **MIDI SysEx Messages** are one of the biggest reasons for MIDI's longevity. SysEx messages are a subset of MIDI messaging that give versatility to manufacturers of MIDI devices. Most manufacturers have created their own proprietary messaging system that is more thorough than standard MIDI and written specifically for one piece of equipment. SysEx messages are addressed to a specific device in the system and are ignored by other devices in the same system.

Each of the three message types listed above is contained within the cue architecture for a MIDI Cue. Now that we have explored the difference between these three message types, it is useful to examine how each of the three can be used. The following sections address the controls featured in the Settings tab for each message type.

16.5 MIDI Voice Message

The MIDI Voice Message, sometimes referred to as "Musical" MIDI, can be used for a number of different control functions interacting with MIDI devices in your system. Since MIDI is such an exhaustive category unto itself, it is perhaps best to address a few of the basics in this area. The MIDI Voice message is in a category of MIDI called "channel messages" or MIDI messages that apply only to a specific channel. MIDI has a possibility of 16 channels, so in a MIDI voice message, a channel number is included with the status byte for the message to indicate which channel should receive the command. In QLab, the MIDI Voice Message has seven commands that can be sent. Each one has its own attributes listed below.

- **Note On:** The Note On command is the data sent when a key is pressed on a MIDI keyboard. It contains the information of which key is pushed and with what velocity (how hard the key was hit). The QLab parameters include channel, note number, and velocity (Figure 16.3). By assigning a note number and velocity, QLab can send a MIDI command across the system to trigger a note on an attached MIDI keyboard.
- **Note Off:** The Note Off command serves the same function as the Note On, except that it sends the message to release a key on the keyboard. The Note Off interface is identical to the Note On.
- **Program Change:** Most MIDI devices have a number of different instrument sounds programmed for playback. The Program Change is a MIDI message that tells the device which instrument to use for playback. There are 128 possible program numbers (0–127). In some cases, some MIDI devices may not have instrument sounds, but use program change to shift between functions. One example of this might be a drum machine that will change the drum beat when it receives a program change command. In QLab, the Program Change command window includes parameters for Channel and Program Number (see Figure 16.4).

Figure 16.3
The Note On command window.

Figure 16.4
The Program Change command window.

- **Control Change:** A controller is a type of musical device that implements a function other than starting or stopping notes, such as a sustain pedal, modulation wheel, volume pedal, etc. A Control Change command is the MIDI command associated with the changes created by that device. As with all MIDI commands, the details are strictly defined in the MIDI Specification. For a Control Change, QLab can send a Channel, Control Number, and Control Value. The control number references 128 different possible controller types, whereas the control value is the level (0–127) at which the controller is operating. One interesting function of the Control Change command in QLab is the ability to fade over duration (Figure 16.5). In the right corner of the control window, you will see a fade curve window with a time and "fade to control value" setting. This allows for more gradual control changes.
- **Key Pressure (AfterTouch):** The Key Pressure command deals with the ability of MIDI to communicate information regarding the amount of pressure applied to an individual key on the keyboard *after it has been depressed*, leading to the term **AfterTouch**. These messages can be used to vary the pressure on a given key to create a vibrato effect. For the Key Pressure command in QLab, the control window features Channel, Note Number, and Pressure Value. Like the Control Change command, this command can be faded over time (Figure 16.6).
- **Channel Pressure:** Unlike Key Pressure, which generates AfterTouch information for each individual key, the Channel Pressure command generates AfterTouch information for *every* key on the keyboard simultaneously. As such, the only difference between the Key Pressure and Channel Pressure interfaces for QLab is that Channel Pressure does not list a note number.

Figure 16.5
The Control Change command window.

Figure 16.6
The Key Pressure command window.

- **Pitch Bend Change:** On a MIDI keyboard, the Pitch Bend Change command is normally sent by the instrument's pitch bend wheel. As the name implies, this command will bend the pitch either higher or lower, depending on the byte value entered in the MIDI command. For QLab, the Pitch Bend Change command features two control attributes: Channel and Velocity (see Figure 16.7). The velocity can be viewed as a binary representation of sliding the pitch bend wheel up or down. Pitch bend data have a possible 16,383 values with -8,192 being the lowest bend, 0 being no pitch bend, and 8,192 being the highest bend.

Each of the MIDI Voice Messages above can be used in a number of creative ways to interact with other MIDI equipment in your sound system. I recommend a thorough examination of the user's manuals of your equipment, as each different manufacturer uses slightly different systems for MIDI communication.

16.6 MIDI Show Control

The MSC is a useful subset of MIDI dedicated to communication between entertainment controllers and devices in a system. Like MIDI itself, the documentation for MSC is thorough and recommended reading for anyone interested in pursuing show control. The complete document can be obtained from the MIDI Manufacturers Association at www.midi.org. For general understanding, we will look at some of the basics below. To specify your MIDI Cue as MSC, simply click on the Message Type drop-down menu and select MSC. You will notice that, upon changing the message type, the bottom row will change to feature new options (Figure 16.8). These options are addressed below.

Figure 16.7
The Pitch Bend Change command window.

Figure 16.8
The MIDI Show Control message window.

Though the top row of the Settings tab remains unchanged between MIDI Voice Message and MSC, there are a few key differences to the bottom row for different message types. The first item listed is **Command Format**. In MSC, there are categories to commands specified for different types of equipment. Command Formats fall into three categories: General, Specific, and All-types. For example, in dealing with lighting commands the general command format sent out would be called "Lighting." Within the category of lighting, there are a number of other specific command formats like moving lights, color changers, strobes, lasers, or chasers. The command format "All-types" is reserved for a system-wide broadcast of commands to all devices in the system.

All MSC-capable devices can be assigned a **Device ID**, a number specific to that device so that each can be individually controlled without fear of accidentally triggering the wrong device. That is why each MSC message has a device id drop-down menu for assigning its patch. Likewise, each cue has the ability to specify Q number, Q List, and Q Path for detailed interaction with other entertainment control systems.

The last term of importance in the Setting tab is **Command**, which indicates the type of control signal to be sent out to a device (such as Go, Stop, Resume, etc.). Like the MIDI Voice Message, MSC features a number of different commands (26 in all) for communicating with devices. The first 11 commands are categorized as general commands that can be used with a range of different entertainment control systems. The final 15 commands are specific to sound control. The following list briefly explains each command type and its use.

General Commands

- **Go:** This command starts a cue. Once triggered, the cue will play until complete or until acted upon to stop with another command. If the controlled device has multiple cue numbers or cue lists, this information can be stipulated in the command. If no cue number is indicated, then the next cue in sequence will play back.
- **Stop:** Halts the playback of the running cue. If no specific cue is specified, then all running cues will be stopped. If a specific cue number is given, only that cue will stop.
- **Resume:** Begins the playback of a halted cue at the stop point. If no specific cue is specified, then all stopped cues will resume. If a specific cue number is given, only that cue will resume.
- **Timed-Go:** Starts a cue at a specific point in time, using the standard time specification with subframes (Timecode). Once triggered, the cue will play until complete or until acted upon to stop with another command. If the controlled device has multiple cue numbers or cue lists, this information can be stipulated in the command. If no cue number is indicated, then the next cue in sequence will play back. When the Timed-Go command is selected,

a Timecode window will pop up in the right half of the screen for inputting start time.

- **Load:** Places a specified cue into a standby position. If the controlled device has multiple cue lists, a specific cue list must be specified or all similar cue numbers will be loaded to standby.
- **Set:** This command defines the value of a Generic Control on a controlled device and the time in which these changes should occur. Depending on the manufacturer, almost any attributes can be established as a Generic Control (levels, subs, channels, rates, etc.). When using the Set command in QLab, the variables are control number, control value, and send Timecode.
- **Fire:** The Fire command triggers a pre-programmed Macro on the controlled device. QLab features a Macro menu for selecting the desired Macro to trigger.
- **All-Off:** This command disables all functions and outputs of the controlled device without changing control settings.
- **Restore:** Restores the operating status of controlled device to that as it was before the All-Off command.
- **Reset:** This command terminates all running cues and resets them to their original state. The cue order will also be reset, loading the first cue in the sequence.
- **Go-Off:** Starts a cue and immediately places the cue into the off state. If no cue number is indicated, then the next cue in sequence will go. If the controlled device has multiple cue lists, a specific cue list must be specified or all similar cue numbers will go off.

Sound Control Commands

- **Go/Jam-Clock:** Starts a cue and simultaneously forces the clock to the "Go Time" if that cue is set as auto-follow. If the cue is manual, then Jam-Clock is ignored. If no cue number is indicated, then the next cue in sequence will go. If a cue number is specified, that cue goes and the clock of the appropriate cue list is "jammed" to that "Go Time."
- **Standby_+:** Places the next cue in the cue list into standby. If no cue list is noted, the current cue list will be used. If more than one cue list contains the same number, then these matching cue numbers will be placed on standby for each cue list.
- **Standby_-:** Places the previous cue in the cue list into standby. If no cue list is noted, the current cue list will be used. If more than one cue list contains the same number, then these matching cue numbers will be placed on standby for each cue list.
- **Sequence_+:** Places the next parent cue in the cue list into standby. If no cue list is noted, the current cue list will be used. If more than one cue list contains the same number, then these matching cue numbers will be placed on standby for each cue list.

- **Sequence_-:** Places the lowest numbered parent cue in the previous parent sequence into standby. If no cue list is noted, the current cue list will be used. If more than one cue list contains the same number, then these matching cue numbers will be placed on standby for each cue list.
- **Start_Clock:** Starts the "auto-follow" clock timer. The clock will start from any previous value from which it was stopped. If no cue list is noted, the clocks for all cue lists will start.
- **Stop_Clock:** Stops the "auto-follow" clock timer. When stopped, the clock will retain its value. If no cue list is noted, the clocks for all cue lists will stop.
- **Zero_Clock:** Sets the clock to a value of 00:00:00:00:00 whether or not it is running. Zeroing the clock will not affect its running status. If no cue list is noted, the clocks for all cue lists will be zero.
- **Set_Clock:** Sets the clock to a value sent by QLab whether or not it is running. Zeroing the clock will not affect its running status. If no cue list is noted, the clocks for all cue lists will be set to the value sent by QLab.
- **MTC_Chase_On:** Causes the clock to be set identically to incoming MIDI Timecode. If no cue list is noted, the clocks for all cue lists will chase.
- **MTC_Chase_Off:** Causes the clock to stop receiving the MIDI Timecode. It does not reset the clock value. If no cue list is noted, the clocks for all cue lists will stop chasing.
- **Open_Cue_List:** Opens a stipulated cue list and makes it active so that the controlled device can access it.
- **Close_Cue_List:** Closes a stipulated cue list and makes it inactive so that the controlled device cannot access it.
- **Open_Cue_Path:** Opens a stipulated cue path and makes it active so that the controlled device can access it.
- **Close_Cue_Path:** Closes a stipulated cue path and makes it inactive so that the controlled device cannot access it.

16.7 MIDI SysEx Cue

MIDI SysEx commands, short for System Exclusive, are a type of command used specifically to communicate proprietary information to one particular model of equipment. No two devices use the same SysEx commands, meaning that you need to have access to the owner's manual for your particular device to best understand how to send it commands. The only common factor between all manufacturers SysEx commands is that they must begin with a 0xF0 status and end with a 0xF7 status. This is the only type of MIDI command that has both a beginning and end status byte. When sending SysEx commands in QLab, there is only an input window for typing in the raw MIDI code (see Figure 16.9).

Figure 16.9
The MIDI SysEx command window.

16.8 MIDI File Cue

One final aspect of QLab's MIDI control is the ability to play back a MIDI file. MIDI files are a collection of binary code that communicates a vast amount of information including instrument voice, note duration, velocity, volume, and more. Though QLab does not have a built-in synthesizer for hearing MIDI playback, it can send the MIDI file information across its system to another MIDI synthesizer for playback. When the MIDI file is inserted as a MIDI File Cue, you can see the file information in the Settings tab of the Inspector Panel (Figure 16.10). There are no control parameters for the MIDI File Cue other than playback rate.

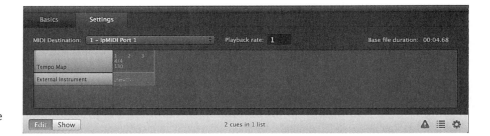

Figure 16.10
A MIDI file displayed in the Settings tab of the Inspector Panel.

QLab and OSC

One of QLab's greatest strengths is its ability to control and/or be controlled by other instances of QLab running on multiple computers. By creating a network between multiple QLab computers, they each can communicate with one another and share information. Before Version 3, MSC was the common method of controlling one QLab workspace by another. If controlling QLab over a network, this meant the use of the ipMIDI software mentioned earlier in the text for sending MIDI across Ethernet. With the introduction of QLab 3, there is a new stand-alone method of communicating between QLab workspaces over a network, the OSC Cue.

17.1 What Is OSC?

Open Sound Control (OSC) is a protocol for communicating between computers, sound synthesizers, and other multimedia devices across a network. Though somewhat similar to MIDI in function, OSC is a high-resolution content format with a dynamic, URL-style naming convention for versatile control. One of its greatest advantages is the ability to enact real-time sound and media control over both local area and wide area networks (LAN/WAN). OSC was created at the University of California, Berkley's Center for New Music and Audio Technologies (CNMAT) and had since branched out as a content format used in numerous applications outside of digital music. To read more about the OSC Specification, visit opensoundcontrol.org.

17.2 OSC Settings

Settings: OSC Controls

Like many other cue types examined earlier in the text, OSC Cues Settings are found by clicking on the Workspace Settings icon in the lower right hand corner of the screen. Once you have opened this, select the OSC Controls button to the left of the screen. When you click on the OSC Controls button, a window will open to the right that features a number of control parameters (see Figure 17.1).

Like Hotkeys and MIDI controls, your QLab workspace can be programmed to respond to certain OSC commands. To enable this function, click on the checkbox labeled "Use OSC Controls." Without selecting this box, your workspace will not respond to incoming OSC commands. You can assign an optional passcode by clicking on the "Use Passcode" checkbox. When selected, all clients wishing to access your workspace will be required to give the four-digit passcode. In addition, by clicking the "new" button, QLab will generate a random code.

One important aspect of the OSC Controls window is the display of your computer's current Internet Protocol (IP) address. Knowing this address is essential to setting up OSC patches. In addition to the IP address, this area also tells some important information about ports. When using QLab OSC Controls, QLab will listen to Transmission Control Protocol (TCP) and User Datagram Protocol (UDP) port 53000. If using UDP, QLab will respond using port 53001.

At the bottom of the OSC Controls window, you will see a list of controls that can all be set to respond to OSC commands. In order to assign the desired OSC command, either the code can be written directly into the slot to the right of the control or you can click the "Capture" button and then send the desired command from the OSC host running on your system. Once QLab "hears" the

Figure 17.1
The OSC controls settings.

command, it will be recorded and the QLab command will be triggered if the message is sent again.

Settings: OSC

The second OSC setting is located roughly halfway down the list on the left of the screen and is simply called "OSC." The OSC settings tab controls the output patch for OSC Cues in your workspace. In order to send OSC commands from one QLab computer to another, you must set up an OSC patch in the OSC settings window (Figure 17.2). Your local computer running QLab will be listed as "localhost" by default with a port of 53000. In order to set up the patch to communicate with other QLab computers, you will need to open the OSC Controls panel in QLab for each additional computer and note the IP address. In addition, note whether the computer has a passcode assigned. Input the IP addresses into the OSC patch row with the port of 53000. If a passcode is required, input this into the passcode column. Once you have managed your list of networked computers, click on the done button and return to your workspace.

17.3 OSC Cues

We have looked at how QLab can be configured to respond to OSC commands, but one of the greatest strengths of QLab 3 is its ability to natively send OSC Cues from one computer to another. The OSC Cue allows QLab to send either QLab OSC messages or raw OSC messages. This fundamentally

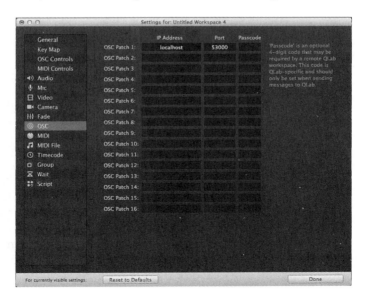

Figure 17.2
The OSC settings window.

Pro-Tip ▼

Networking Options

Ethernet Connection

There are a number of options for networking together different QLab computers. When using just two computers, the easiest method is to simply connect them with an Ethernet cable. An interconnect cable is unnecessary for newer Macs. In order to network the two computers together, you should turn off the Wi-Fi on both computers to limit interference. After connecting the two computers with the Ethernet cable and inputting the appropriate IP addresses in the OSC Settings patch, you will be able to send OSC controls from one QLab computer to another.

Networking via Router

For instances of multiple computers that need to interact with one another, the best method to connect the computers is via a router. A router is a small device that joins together multiple networks together, typically using a wireless or wired IP. Essentially, a router works as a gateway device to link together multiple computers in order to communicate with one another on the same system.

One important aspect to remember about routers is that many utilize Dynamic Host Configuration Protocol (DHCP), a network protocol that can change the IP address of devices logged into it from time to time. Since QLab depends on the computers always utilizing the same IP address, it is a good idea to disable DHCP settings on your router, or to use manually assigned IP addresses outside of the router's DHCP range. This will guarantee that each QLab machine will have a consistent IP address each time it is booted.

Wireless Networking

Another method for networking is to create a wireless computer-to-computer network (often referred to as an Ad-hoc wireless network). In order to do so, click on the Airport status icon in your Mac's Menu Bar (upper right corner). Click on the Create Network button. A pop-up menu will appear reading, "Create a computer-to-computer network." The network name will default to your computer's name or serial number. I recommend creating a specific name for your purposes, like "QLab." If you want to add a password, click on the security button and select either 40-bit Wired Equivalent Privacy (WEP) or 128-bit WEP. Input a password that fits the parameters listed and then click the button labeled "create." This will create a wireless network that can be logged onto from other computers. After all computers are logged into the same wireless network you will be able to send OSC controls from one QLab computer to another.

replaces the need for sending MSC Cues across an ipMIDI network to control one QLab workspace with another. Click on the OSC Cue button to insert the cue into your workspace.

Inspector Panel: Basics

Like most other cue types, the Basics tab in the Inspector Panel features the common naming, pre/post-wait, continue status, and triggering information. These controls do not differ from the ones we covered in earlier chapters.

Inspector Panel: Settings

The Settings tab for OSC Cues is the main method for editing your OSC Cue. The first interface listed in the Settings tab is "OSC Destination." By clicking on this drop-down menu, you can choose the routing of your OSC signal from the entire list of network devices running on your system. Each one will be listed as a unique name, coinciding with the name given to the QLab workspace in the OSC Settings window.

The second interface, message type, is a drop-down menu that allows for the selection of two message types: QLab message or Custom OSC message. Depending on the message type chosen, the bottom row of the window will change. For QLab message, there will be a cue number slot and command type. If Custom message is chosen, then a blank input window will appear in which the OSC address and arguments should be inserted. Finally, there is a "send message" button that can be clicked to send a test signal out without actually firing the OSC Cue.

QLab Messages

QLab 3 has done the heavy lifting for you in creating a control architecture of pre-programmed OSC commands for communicating with other computers running QLab. Instead of having to research on how OSC works and learning how to code it, you can simply click on a drop-down menu, select the desired message type, and QLab does the rest. The following section details the use of the QLab message within OSC Cues.

Playback Control Commands

When you click on the Command drop-down menu, you will find two types of commands separated by a divider (Figure 17.3). At the top of the menu is what I refer to as playback control commands, as they are used to control some aspect of QLab playback. The list of commands includes Start, Stop, Hard Stop, Pause, Resume, Toggle Pause, Load, Preview, Reset, and Panic. These commands are simple to use. Simply select the command type and

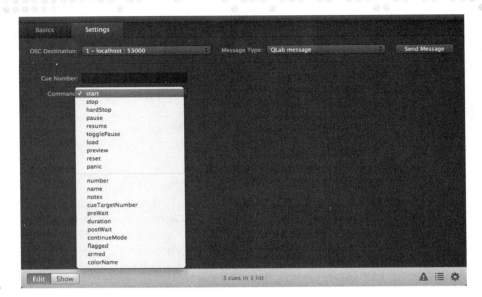

Figure 17.3
The OSC
command
drop-down menu.

input the cue number you want to control. Once the OSC Cue is fired, it will automatically find the cue number in the patched workspace and trigger the command.

Parameter-Change Commands

The second section of commands listed in the drop-down menu functions to change some parameter of another cue. By inputting the desired cue number and command, you can then input a parameter to change some aspects of a cue such as Cue Number, Cue Name, Notes, Cue Target Number, Pre-wait, Duration, Post-wait, Continue Mode, Flagged, Armed, and Color Name. This is an incredibly useful method for changing aspects of a remote workspace without having to actually access it in person.

Timecode

Timecode has origins tied to the earliest video recorders in the 1960s. The recording of moving images on magnetic tape created a number of problems related to editing video and aligning audio with video. In film-based recordings, each picture on the film was aligned with guide holes that could be counted exactly to clearly define the location of frames. With magnetic tape, there were no such guide holes, creating a difficulty in clearly tracking the alignment of frames. By 1967, the Society of Motion Picture and Television Engineers (SMPTE) had created a standardized system for sending audio impulses for recording a picture number parallel to every video picture, thus creating an "electronic guide hole" system. This method was the first Timecode. In the years since the creation of Timecode, a number of interesting uses have emerged including aligning video and audio signals and triggering cues from a Timecode signal. QLab 3 has the ability to both transmit and receive Timecode signals across an audio output or a MIDI system.

18.1 How Timecode Works

Traditionally, Timecode is a data signal that runs parallel to image data in a video signal. Each picture is clearly labeled with Timecode data containing clear information of hours, minutes, seconds, and frames. The number of frames used in each specific Timecode is determined by the original video format with the sending and receiving ends set to the same frame rate to be effective for syncing. In modern usage, Timecode may be used independent of a video signal. There are a number of different Timecode frame rates available through QLab to fit any application.

The advantage of using Timecode is the creation of a reference point for playback of separate systems. One great example of this would be running audio from a QLab computer that needs to be synced with a video signal sent from a video server remote to the QLab system. Timecode will ensure that the video will be triggered to follow the audio exactly. This is especially important in instances of dialogue lip-syncing to a video. Likewise, it is beneficial to use Timecode to trigger a cue at a very specific point in the Timecode stream. Consider the use of Timecode to send cues to trigger lighting effects in perfect sync with an audio track. Effects like this are particularly useful in theme parks, museum displays, and dance concerts (all situations in which the cueing is particularly linear with a very rigid and inflexible timeline).

One important concept to understand regarding Timecode is drop frame. NTSC color video uses a frame rate of 29.97 frames per second (fps), which means that the frame rate is .03 seconds slower than the nearest whole number Timecode of 30 fps. In order to compensate for this, drop frame timing is used to drop Timecode numbers periodically to assure that the Timecode aligns with the true frame rate of the video. Drop frame timing is used relatively infrequently – only for NTSC video.

In terms of QLab, Timecode is typically used in one of two ways: as an incoming signal to trigger QLab cues or as a Timecode Cue that generates a Timecode signal to be sent to other computers or devices.

18.2 Timecode Settings

Timecode Settings are located in the Workspace Settings window under the "Timecode" heading. After selecting this button, a window will open to the right featuring two options. The first option is the selection of a default frame rate for new Timecode Cues. Choices are 24 fps, 25 fps, 30 fps non-drop, 30 fps drop, 23.976 fps, 24.975 fps, 29.97 fps non-drop, and 29.97 fps drop.

The second option is the selection of the default output type, either MIDI Timecode (MTC) or Linear Timecode (LTC). The LTC (sometimes referred to as SMPTE) is the aforementioned audio signal typically recorded to tape and decoded by a synchronizer originally used to synchronize audio and video equipment. With the proliferation of MIDI devices in the 1980s, a new method was required for syncing analog devices with computer MIDI sequencers. MTC was developed for this reason. For all practical purposes, MTC can be thought of as SMPTE in MIDI form. QLab 3 can generate both LTC and MTC.

18.3 Triggering Cues from Timecode

One of the strengths of QLab is its ability to allow cues to be triggered by incoming Timecode signals. There are a few steps necessary to enable this process. The first step is to enable the cue list to be triggered by Timecode. To do so, first click on the "Cue Lists and Active Cues" button in the lower right hand corner of the QLab screen. This will open up all available cue lists in the upper right hand corner of the screen. Click on the desired cue list and then select the "Sync" tab in the Inspector Panel. Click on the checkbox labeled "trigger cues in this list from incoming Timecode." This will enable cues within the cue list to be triggered by incoming Timecode.

In order to trigger an individual cue with Timecode, there is one remaining step. First, click on the desired cue and open the Basics tab in the Inspector Panel. The last row on the right side of the screen is a checkbox labeled "Timecode trigger." By clicking this checkbox, you can insert the appropriate Timecode signature at which point you want the cue to be triggered. Once a Timecode signal is present, QLab will listen for the appropriate time to trigger the cue. It is important to note that QLab does not "chase" Timecode. It only triggers cues from the start of the cue and does not try to compute a position mid-stream based on the Timecode stream.

18.4 Timecode Cues

To insert a Timecode Cue into your cue list, click on the Timecode Cue icon in the Toolbar or drag it into your workspace. Once the cue has been inserted, click on the Settings tab in the Inspector Panel. The Settings are relatively simple and straightforward. First, there is the Timecode type tool that allows you to select between MTC and LTC. After selecting the type, the next step is to select the destination, or output patch, for the Timecode signal. MTC is transmitted across a MIDI patch, whereas LTC is sent out through an audio patch.

Frame rate is the next variable for Timecode Cues. As discussed earlier, frame rate must match the frame rate of the receiving end's frame rate setting, otherwise nothing will happen.

Finally, the last variable for Timecode Cues is the start time of the Timecode. Insert into the window the desired start time of any Timecode to be outputted through the system.

Index

Note: **Boldface** page numbers refer to figures and tables.